Scheduling in Distributed Computing Systems

Analysis, Design & Models

(A Research Monograph)

T0143043

Scheduling in Distributed Computing Systems
Computing Systems
Analysis, Design & Models

(A Research Monograph)

by

Deo Prakash Vidyarthi
Jawaharlal Nehru University
New Delhi, India

Biplab Kumer Sarker
Primal Fusion Inc.
Waterloo, Canada

Anil Kumar Tripathi
Banaras Hindu University
Varanasi, India

Laurence Tianruo Yang
St. Francis Xavier University
Antigonish, Canada

 Springer

Authors:

Deo Prakash Vidyarthi
Jawaharlal Nehru University
School of Computer & Systems Sciences
New Mehrauli Road
New Delhi-110067
India
dpv@mail.jnu.ac.in

Biplab Kumer Sarker
Primal Fusion Inc.
Research and Development
7–258 King Street North
Waterloo, Ontario N2J 2Y9
Canada
biplab.sarker@gmail.com

Anil Kumar Tripathi
Banaras Hindu University
Institute of Technology
Department of Computer Engineering
Varanasi-221005
India
anilkt@bhu.ac.in

Laurence Tianruo Yang
St. Francis Xavier University
Dept. Computer Science
PO Box 5000
Antigonish NS B2G 2W5
Canada
ltyang@gmail.com

ISBN 978-1-4419-4503-7   e-ISBN 978-0-387-74483-4

Printed on acid-free paper

springer.com

ACKNOWLEDEGEMENT

We would like to acknowledge all individual and institution that helped in any form in the contribution of this book. It will not be out of place to pay sincere thanks to Prof. V.V.Menon, (Retired Professor, Department of Applied Mathematics, Institute of Technology, Banaras Hindu University, Varanasi, India) for his nice suggestions and accomplishments throughout our research activities. We would also like to acknowledge Prof. A.N.Mantri (Ex- Head, Department of Computer Science, Banaras Hindu University, Varanasi, India) for his sincere advice towards our research. Our students Mr. Alok Singh, Mr. Neeraj Asthana has provided technical support towards the completion of this book.

Our sincere thanks to Mr. Lutfi M. Omer Khanbary, a Ph.D. student, for typesetting the whole manuscript as per the specifications.

Finally, we would like to thank our family for their understanding and support while writing this book.

PREFACE

The rapid growth of network technologies, processor architecture and software development has facilitated meaningful attempts to exploit the capabilities of a collection of computers for speeding up computations and services. A distributed system consists of various servers integrated in such a manner so as to appear as one system, whereas a distributed computing system (DCS), also appearing as one system to the user, aims at distributing the parts of a task submitted to it, to various participating nodes of the system. Thus one may view a distributed computing system as one that tries to minimize the execution time of tasks submitted to it by exploiting as many computing nodes as possible and plausible. A distributed system may also have computing nodes that may be known as compute servers, and co-operatively execute various modules of tasks submitted; apart from the services that it runs e.g. print, mail, name etc. In this book, distributed system has been used quite frequently to refer to the distributed computing system, because the objective is scheduling of the computational load.

The distribution of a computation load across processing nodes, forming a DCS, has been a challenging task. Many researchers have contributed to study of this problem during the last two decades. The problem consists of allocation of task modules to various processing nodes so as to incur as minimum as possible inter-processor communication overhead and thereby obtaining good execution speed as opposed to a single processor execution. Many a times the inter-processor communication may be too substantive compared to the total execution time.

The approaches for task scheduling in operating system for a distributed computing system must consider the multiplicity of processing nodes with underlying interconnection network unlike the case of a single processor system. In the case of uniprocessor system, the objective is to make the processors busy executing jobs all the time by insuring that it does not idle and this serves the purpose.

In a distributed computing system, the scheduling of various modules on particular processing nodes may be preceded by appropriate allocation of modules of the different tasks to various processing nodes and then only the appropriate execution characteristic can be obtained. Thus task allocation becomes the important most and major activity in the task scheduling within the operating system of a DCS.

Various research papers have addressed this problem during the last two decades. As the problem is quite difficult, most of the solutions proposed had simplifying assumptions. The very first assumption has been: consideration of a single task only, second no consideration of the status of processing nodes in terms of the previously allocated modules of various tasks and third the capacity and capability of the processing nodes. The solutions reported in the beginning even assume that the precedence constraints amongst the modules of a task are non existent or negligible. Nevertheless many good algorithms were proposed for the purpose.

This book consists of various proposed algorithms for task allocation as part of scheduling in an operating system for DCS. It starts with analyzing the existing propositions, considering the precedence constraint and improving the known algorithms, proposing a solution for minimizing intermodule communication apart from the main and important contribution, made in this book, in the form of the allocation algorithms that aim at distribution of computational modules belonging to multiple tasks onto the various processing nodes considering there status in terms of previous allocations and capacity. As the problem is NP-Hard, the techniques of A*, GA etc. have been purposefully used to propose the algorithmic solutions.

The meaningful contributions have been organized in the chapters as given below:

Chapter 1 discusses the possible performance improvement in computing system. It also addresses how the distributed computing system has evolved over the years and the issues in DCS research.

Chapter 2 briefs about the distributed computing system. It discusses various architectural models of DCS. Transparency is one of the biggest issues in the design of a DCS that gives the DCS a single system image. Chapter 2 points out transparency issues of the DCS. Fault tolerance and synchronization in the DCS has also been briefed in chapter 2.

Chapter 3 defines the scheduling problem and identifies the characteristic parameter for a scheduler. It indicates the task allocation issues. Assumptions and notation, used in this book, have been kept together at one place in chapter 3.

Chapter 4 addresses the load balancing problem in a DCS. It defines load distribution, load balancing methodology, migration and also the conflict between load balancing and task allocation.

Chapter 5 briefs the earlier task allocation models. Propositions, which consider the precedence amongst the modules of the task and multiprogramming of the individual nodes, have been proposed in section 5.3 of chapter 5 using list schedule. In the same chapter an inter module communication reduction model is also proposed (sec. 5.4), which incurs a heavy penalty in total turnaround time of any task.

Chapter 6 proposes a few Load Balancing Task Allocation (LBTA) models. It discusses the LBTA strategy and its solution for single and multiple tasks.

Chapter 7 uses the important search technique of GA in proposing two allocation models, one, which incorporates problem specific knowledge for quick convergence and the other to maximize the reliability of the DCS with allocation.

Chapter 8 considers the important proposition of multiple tasks allocation and proposes a few models. In section 8.1, an allocation algorithm based on A* is proposed and in section 8.2 a new and novel idea of cluster based allocation is proposed. Cluster based allocation model avoids the priori requirement of execution time of modules of the task on the processing nodes and thus can be proved to be very useful model of task allocation. Sections 8.3 and 8.4 deal with the LBTA strategy using A* and GA respectively.

Chapter 9 proposes few other approaches for task allocation models. These are hybrid and object oriented models.

Computational Grid is an emerging form of distributed computing. Chapter 10 concentrates on Grid Computing systems and discusses the scheduling problem for a computational grid. "What are the various issues in Scheduling for Grid Computing systems?" finds place in chapter 10.

Finally concluding remarks are made in chapter 11. This chapter also discusses the structure and place of a scheduler in a DCS.

TABLE OF CONTENTS

CHAPTER 1

Introduction

A Distributed Computing System (DCS) falls in the category of disjoint memory multiple processor architecture with an underlying processor-to-processor interconnection network. Such a private memory-processor interconnection network is known to constitute a multi-computer system only if the programmers need to consider the multiplicity of the machines, in programming a solution to the problem. In case of a distributed computing system the entire system appears as a centralized system to the user submitting a task; meaning thereby that it is the responsibility of the system to distribute the computational modules of the given task to various processing nodes for their efficient execution unlike the case of multi-computer system as stated above.

With the proliferation of large-scale inter-networks, the idea of distributed computing system has been gaining importance. In a distributed computing system various computational and informational resources are dispersed over a wide geographical area with appropriate servers maintaining them at locations and providing services to clients hooked onto these systems. The idea is that a distributed computing system may receive a task that requires various named services from various servers and in this case the job of the operating system is to provide the appropriate connectivity and the service mechanism. In case of a computational task, consisting of various modules, the requirement is that of identification of appropriate computing nodes in the distributed computing system for scheduling the executable modules of the task so as to achieve a good turnaround for such a task and possibly an increase in the throughput of the computing system. This problem has been studied as task scheduling or task allocation problem in the literature [1-7]. This book deals with the problem of task scheduling/ allocation in a distributed computing system.

The following section 1.1 reviews the various ways of performance improvement in computing system including parallel computing with multiprocessors, multi-computers and distributed computing environment for the sake of completeness. Section 1.2 discusses the role of distributed computing system in high speed computing. Section 1.3 takes a view how the DCS has evolved, as a computing system, over the time. Section 1.4 deals with the research issues in distributed computing systems. Final section 1.5, describes the organization of the book.

1.1 Performance Improvement in Computing System

Parallel processing has emerged as a key enabling technology in modern computers, driven by the increasing demand for higher performance, lower cost and sustained productivity in real-life applications. Concurrent events are taking place

in today's high performance computers due to common practice of multiprogramming, multiprocessing and multi-computing. Modern computers are equipped
with powerful hardware facilities driven by extensive software packages [8].

Parallel processing and distributed processing are closely related. In some cases
certain distributed techniques are used to achieve parallelism. As the communication technology advances progressively, the distinction between parallel and distributed processing becomes smaller and smaller. In this extended sense, we may
view distributed processing as a form of parallel processing in a special environment [9].

It has long been recognized that the concept of computer architecture is no
longer restricted to the structure of the bare machine hardware. It is an integrated
system of machine hardware, system software, application programs and user in-
terfaces. Depending on the nature of the problems, the solutions may require different computing resources. The rapid progress made in hardware technology has
significantly increased the economic feasibility of building a new generation of
computers adopting parallel processing. Two categories of parallel computers are
architecturally modeled. These physical models are distinguished by having a
shared common memory and unshared distributed memories. Multiprocessors are
called tightly coupled systems due to the high degree of resource sharing (including memory). Symmetric multiprocessors are those in which all processors have
equal access to all peripheral devices. In such system, all the processors are
equally capable of running the executive programs, such as OS kernel and I/O ser-

vice routines etc. In contrast to this, in an asymmetric multiprocessor system only one or a subset of processors is of executive capable [8].

The distributed memory multi-computer consists of multiple computers, often called nodes, interconnected by a message-passing network. Each node is an autonomous computer consisting of a processor, local memory and sometimes attached disks or I/O peripherals.

Distributed computing system falls in the category of distributed memory parallel architecture and is characterized by resource multiplicity and system transparency. The advantage of the DCS is that they are capable of incremental growth[5] i.e. it is possible to gradually extend the power and functionality of a distributed computing system by simply adding additional resources (both hardware and software) to the system as and when the need arises. For example, additional processors can be easily added to the system to handle the increased workload of an organization that might have resulted from its expansion. With the rapidly increasing power and reduction in the price of microprocessors, DCS potentially have a much better price performance ratio than a single large centralized system. Moreover the existing microcomputers, minicomputers or even a workstation can be added to the DCS for its better utilization.

1.2 High Speed Computing and DCS

In practice, parallelism appears in various forms, such as look ahead, pipelining, vectorization, concurrency, simultaneity, data parallelism, partitioning, interleaving, overlapping, multiplicity, replication, time sharing, space sharing, multitasking, multiprogramming, multithreading and distributed computing at different processing levels. All forms can be attributed to levels of parallelism, computational granularity, time complexities, communication latencies, scheduling policies and load balancing [10]. DCSs are naturally attractive as existing interconnected computers can be used to assign them various parts of a computational task to achieve parallelism.

The definition of high speed computing has undergone many changes in recent years. Perhaps, the most notable development in the evolution from the industry, dominated by vector mainframe architectures, to one in which massively parallel computers have been the primary choice for solving computationally intensive problems. As an alternative to massively parallel computers, increasing interest has immerged in distributed computing in which networked collection of dedicated or general purpose workstations are treated as a parallel computer. Although this method has existed for many years, two developments have served as catalysts to the rapid growth in the use of such cluster-based computing. First, high performance workstations with microprocessors that challenge custom-made architectures are widely available at relatively low cost. Second, several software packages have been developed to assist the programmer in process management, inter-process communication and program monitoring/debugging in a distributed environment [11].

The researches in the area of parallel computing have been indicating the availability of immense computing power, for execution of properly distributed and
coordinated parts of jobs submitted to the system from time to time. The conflu-
ence of low-cost high performance processors and interconnection technologies
has spurred a great interest in the advancement of computer architectures. The of-
ten-cited advantages of these architectures include high performance, availability,
and extensibility at lower cost. As pointed out earlier, the computer architectures,
consisting of interconnected multiple processors are of two types:

(i)   Multiprocessors, known as tightly coupled systems, allow sharing of
        global memory by multiple processes running on their processors and
        communication amongst the processes is actuated by use of the shared
        variables. In such coupled systems, the number of processors that can be
        usefully deployed is usually small and limited by the bandwidth of shared
        memory.

(ii)   Multicomputers and DCSs consist of a number of independent processors
        with private memory units and the IPC is done by message passing mak-
        ing use of the processors interconnection.

1.3 Evolution of the DCS

The processors in a DCS may vary in the size and the functionality. They may include small microcomputers, workstations, minicomputers and large general purpose computer systems. For a particular processor its own resources are local, whereas the other processors and their resources are remote. Together, a processor and its resources are usually referred to as a node or site or machine of the distributed computing systems. Resource sharing, computational speedup, reliability and communication over distances are the main reasons for building the DCS [12].

DCSs have become more and more attractive in recent years due to the advancement of VLSI and computer networking technologies. DCS not only provide the facility for utilizing remote computer resources and data but also increase the throughput by providing facilities for multiprogramming and parallel processing [13]. Furthermore, modularity, flexibility and reliability of the DCS make them attractive for many types of application.

The advent of time-sharing systems was the first step towards building the DCS because it provides us with two important concepts used in DCS; the sharing of computer resources simultaneously by many users and the accessing of computers from the different places. The centralized time-sharing systems had a limitation that their terminals/workstations could not be placed very far from the main computer room/system (like in minicomputers) since ordinary cables were used to connect the terminals to the main computer. But the advancement of computer networking technologies LAN (Local Area Network) and WAN(Wide Area Network) allow hundreds, even thousand of computers to be connected (may be residing in different cities or countries or continents) in such a way that the small amounts of information can be transferred between computers in a fraction of second or so. Recently there has been another major advancement in networking technology, the ATM (Asynchronous Transfer Mode) technology, which makes very high speed networking possible in both LAN and WAN environments. The availability of such high bandwidth networks allows DCSs to support a completely new class of distributed applications called multimedia applications that deal with the handling of a mixture of information, including voice, video and ordinary data [14].

The operating systems commonly used for DCS can be broadly classified into two types- Network Operating System (NOS) and Distributed Operating System (DOS) [14].

In NOS, the users are aware of the multiplicity of the machine and can access the resources either by logging into the appropriate remote machine or transferring the data from the remote machine to their own machine. On the other hand, in DOS the users would not be aware of the multiplicity of machines. It provides a single system image to its users. Users access remote resources in the same manner as they access local resources. A DOS dynamically and automatically allocates tasks to the various machines of the system for its processing.

In NOS, each computer of the system has its own local operating system (the operating systems of different computers may be the same or different) that functions independently of the other machines meaning thereby that each one makes inde-

pendent decisions about the creation and termination of their own processes and

management of local resources. Due to the possibility of difference in local oper-

ating systems, the system calls for different machines of the same DCS may be

different in this case. On the other hand, in DOS which is a single system wide

operating system and each machine of the DCS runs a part of this global operating

system. There is a single set of globally valid system calls available on all com-

puters of the DCS.

The fault tolerance capability of a DCS is usually very high as compared to that of

a networked system. If some computers fail in NOS, then several users are unable

to continue with their work. On the other hand, in case of a DOS, most of the users

can continue their work normally with only some percentage of loss in perform-

ance of the DCS.

1.4 Issues in DCS Research

The hardware issues of building a distributed computing system were fairly well

understood, the major stumbling block is the availability of adequate software for

making these systems easy to use and exploit its power fully. Therefore, since

1970, a significant amount of research work was carried out in the area of distrib-

uted operating system. Designing a distributed operating system is more difficult

than a centralized one mainly because of the non-availability of complete information about the system environment [4-7, 12, 14]. There is no common clock and various resources are physically separated in DCS in contrast to a centralized system. Despite these, the users of the DCS are to be provided all the advantages of the system. To meet these challenges the researchers, in the DCS discipline, must deal with several important issues. Some of these key issues are identified and discussed below.

The distributed computing system is designed in such a way that the collection of various machines, connected by an interconnection network, appears as a virtual uniprocessor system. Achieving complete transparency is a difficult task and research is still continuing on this issue. Of the several transparency issues identified by the ISO Reference Model for Open Distributed Processing, location transparency, migration transparency and concurrency transparency are very important [6-7, 14].

The often-advocated advantage of the DCS, in comparison to the centralized system, is the reliability due to the existence of multiple resources. However, only the multiple instances of resources cannot increase the reliability of the DCS, rather the various processes of the distributed operating system (viz. memory manager, task scheduler etc.) must be designed properly to increase the reliability by extracting the characteristic features of the DCS.

Another important issue is flexibility. It is more required for open distributed system [4-5, 14].

Performance improvement of an application running on the DCS than that of single processor system is another desired feature. To achieve this though the various components of the distributed operating system are taken into account, but the most important role is that of a scheduler or task allocator. The turnaround and throughput are the two important characteristic measures for the performance improvement.

Another issue in DCS research is scalability that refers to the capability of the system to adapt to an increase in the service load. A distributed computing system should be designed to cope with the growth of the processing nodes and the users as well. How to design a system so that such growth should not cause any serious disruption of services is very important research issue in the DCS.

Growth, in the number and types, of processing nodes introduces another dimension that is inevitable to have dissimilar hardware or software. Many users often prefer heterogeneity because it provides the flexibility of different computer platforms for different applications. Designing heterogeneous system is far more difficult than a homogeneous one.

In order that the users can trust the system, the various resources must be protected against destruction and unauthorized access. Enforcing security in a DCS is another important research area and is much more difficult than in a centralized one.

The book discusses one of the research issues that of task scheduling/allocation thoroughly. The problem is as such an NP-Hard problem and thus various feasible solutions are possible. The authors present and discuss all those task scheduling models that have been proposed by the authors themselves.

1.5 Organization of the Book

The book is organized in ten chapters. The current chapter, which is the first one, is an introductory chapter. Second chapter defines the task scheduling problem of the DCS. Chapter 2 takes a cursory look over the distributed system. What is exactly expected out of scheduling and how it has been addressed in this work, is detailed in chapter 3. Load balancing is an important aspect of the scheduling problem and is pursued in the chapter 4. Some of the earlier task allocation models, their limitations and few proposed trivial models for task allocation have been discussed in chapter 5. A precedence constrained task allocation model, in which the emphasis is on the precedence of the modules [15] and that minimizes the turn-around time of the given task is discussed in sec 5.3 of chapter 5. The effect of already allocated modules of unrelated tasks, on the processing elements comprising the system, is considered (assuming round robin scheduling) in this model.

Communication amongst the modules adds to the cost of overall execution of the task, for the allocation being considered, if its modules are to execute onto the distant processing nodes of the DCS. An IMC cost reduction model (section 5.4), an aid in allocation algorithms, uses fuzzy logic to consider high and low communicating modules. The same fuzzy function is applied to determine near or distant nodes of the DCS. This IMC cost reduction model can be introduced in any task allocation algorithms at minimum cost [16].

Load balancing task allocation models find place in chapter 6. This chapter considers load balancing strategies and discusses the LBTA solutions for both the single and multiple task allocation.

As the task allocation problem is an NP-hard problem, Genetic Algorithms (GA) is found to be suitable to solve it. Two task allocation models, based on GA, have been proposed in chapter 7. First one aims at minimizing turn-around time of a task (sec. 7.1) and the second (sec. 7.2) gives an allocation that maximizes the reliability of the DCS as desired in some systems. The TA model proposed in section 7.1 [17], is based on a finding that the incorporation of some problem specific knowledge in construction of the GA, improves its performance and solution converges quickly [18]. This algorithm considers the inclusion of all possible constraints in the model, and as suggested in [19] will converge quickly.

Task allocation models for maximizing reliability of a DCS have appeared in the past [20-22]. We applied GA to maximize reliability of the DCS with task allocation and the same is discussed in section 7.2. The algorithm not only gets the advantage of GA for quick convergence but also produces better solutions in terms of allocation with improved reliability [23]. The result is compared with that of

Shatz [21] and it shown that the proposed model performs better. Many more in-

ferences are drawn.

The TA models, proposed by researchers in the past, have considered the mod-

ules of a single task and assume that processing nodes have enough memory to ac-

commodate unlimited modules. In a realistic situation multiple tasks arrive and at

any instance of time, the Processing Element (PE) has modules of earlier tasks al-

located and the memory occupied by it. In chapter 8, multiple tasks allocation in

DCS is deliberated. Multiple task allocation, using A*, appears in sec. 8.1 [24]. To

implement this, the concept of Global Table is introduced. Section 8.2 proposes a

new idea of cluster-based approach of load partitioning and allocation in DCS.

Cluster of the modules, based on communication requirement and cluster of PEs

based on interprocessor distance is formed. Allocation is decided from task cluster

to processor cluster. This model has the advantage that it does not require the pri-

ori knowledge of execution time of the modules of the tasks onto nodes of the

DCS. As the allocation algorithms, in this chapter, consider multiple tasks and

status of PEs due to previous allocations, these are not comparable with other

models proposed in the literature. Section 8.3 discusses the load balancing task al-

location for multiple tasks execution in DCS using A* and section 8.4 discusses

the same using GA.

Chapter 9 makes a comparative analysis of scheduling models based on A* and GA and proposes a hybrid model using both A* and GA. This chapter also discusses the object allocation as most of the system are going object oriented.

Grid Computing is another form of Parallel and Distributed Computing. Computational grid is an emerging computing system so chapter 10 is dedicated to the discussion on the scheduling in computational grid. This chapter details various research issues in Grid scheduling.

Chapter 11 is the concluding chapter that summarizes the whole book. Structure and place of scheduler in Distributed Operating System is briefed in sec. 11.2 of this chapter.

The abbreviations used in the book are listed at one place for quick reference.

Finally, we have listed few programs written to carry out the experiments in the appendix given is last.

BIBLIOGRAPHY

[1] V.Rajaraman, C.Siva Ram Murthy, *Parallel Computer: Architecture and Programming*, Prentice Hall of India Ltd, 2000.
[2] M. Sasikumar, Dinesh Shikhare, P. Ravi Prakash, *Introduction to Parallel Processing*, Prentice Hall of India Ltd, 2000.
[3] Sanjeev K. Setia, Mark S. Squillante, Satish K. Tripathi, "Analysis of Processor Allocation in Distributed –Memory Parallel Processing Systems", *IEEE Trans. on Parallel & Distributed Systems*, Vol. 5, No. 4, April 1994, pp. 401-420.
[4] A.S.Tanenbaum, *Distributed Operating Systems*, Prentice-Hall, Englewood Cliffs, NJ, 1995.
[5] A.S.Tanenbaum, R. Van Ressen, "Distributed Operating Systems," *ACM Computing Surveys*, Vol. 7, No.4, 1985, pp. 419-470.

[6]G.Colouris, J. Dollimore, T. Kindberg, *Distributed Systems: Concepts and Design*, Addison-Wesley Publishers Ltd., 1994.

[7]G.Nutt, Operating Systems: A Modern Perspective, Addison Wesley, 2000.

[8]Kai Hwang, *Parallel Computer Architecture*, Mc-Graw Hill International Edition, 1995.

[9]Kai Hwang, F.A.Briggs, *Computer Architecture and Parallel Processing*, McGraw Hill International Edition, 1995.

[10]Kai Hwang, Advanced Computer Architecture: Parallelism Scalability and Programmability, Mc-graw Hill, 1993.

[11]M.Hamdi and C.K.Lee, "Dynamic Load Balancing of Image Processing Applications on Clusters of Workstations," *Parallel Computing*, 22(1997), pp.1477-1492.

[12]A.Silberschatz and P.B. Galvin, *Operating Systems Concepts*, Addison- Wesley, 1998.

[13]C.C.Shen and W.H.Tsai , "A Graph Matching Approach to Optimal Task Assignment in Distributed Computing System Using a Minimax Criterion," *IEEE Trans. Computers*, Vol. c-34, no.3, March. 1985. pp. 197-203.

[14]P.K.Sinha, Distributed Operating Systems: Concepts and Design, Printice-Hall of India, 1997.

[15]D.P.Vidyarthi, A.K.Tripathi, "Precedence Constrained Task Allocation in Distributed Computing System", *Int. J. of High Speed Computing*, Vol. 8, No. 1, 1996, pp. 47-55.

[16]D.P.Vidyarthi, A.K.Tripathi, " A Fuzzy IMC Cost Reduction Model for Task Allocation in Distributed Computing Systems", *Proceedings of the Fifth International Symposium on Methods and Models in Automation and Robotics*, Vol. 2, Szczecin, Poland, August 1998, pp. 719-721.

[17]A.K.Tripathi, D.P.Vidyarthi, A.N.Mantri, "A Genetic Task Allocation Algorithm for Distributed Computing System Incorporating Problem Specific Knowledge", *International J. of High Speed Computing*, Vol.8, No.4, 1996, pp. 363-370.

[18]John J. Grefenstelle, "Incorporating Problem Specific Knowledge into Genetic Algorithm", *Genetic Algorithm and Simulated Annealing*, Morgan Kaufrman Publisher, California, 1987.

[19]K.Efe, "Heuristic Models of Task Assignment Scheduling in Distributed Systems", *IEEE Computer*, Vol. 15, June 1982, pp. 50-56.

[20]S.Kartik, C.S.Ram Murthy, "Task Allocation Algorithms for Maximizing Reliability of Distributed Computing Systems", *IEEE Trans. on Computers*, Vol.46, No.6, June1997, pp. 719-724.

[21]Sol.M.Shatz, Wang Goto, "Task Allocation for Maximizing Reliability of Distributed Computing Systems", *IEEE Trans. on Computers*, Vol.41, No.9, September 1992, pp. 1156-1168.

[22] Karthik, C. Siva Ram Murthy, " Improved Task Allocation Algorithms to Maximize Reliability of Redundant Distributed Systems", *IEEE Trans. on Reliability*, Vol. 44, No. 4, Dec. 1995, pp. 575-586.

[23]D.P.Vidyarthi, A.K.Tripathi, "Maximizing Reliability of Distributed Computing Systems with Task Allocation using Simple Genetic Algorithm", *J. of Systems Architecture*, Vol. 47, 2001, pp. 549-554.

[24]D.P.Vidyarthi, A.K.Tripathi, B.K.Sarker, "Multiple Task Management in Distributed Computing Systems", The *Journal of the CSI*, Vol. 31, No. 1 Sep. 2000, pp. 19-25.

CHAPTER 2

An Overview of a Distributed System

This chapter takes a cursory view of a distributed system. It discusses various architectural models of a distributed system and various types of transparencies involved. It also discusses fault tolerant, one of the very important property of a distributed system. A clock of the distributed system makes its computing nodes independent. How the system will be synchronized, in spite of the distribution of the clock, has been discussed in this chapter. The objective in this chapter is to introduce briefly the important properties of a distributed system to its readers, before moving to the scheduling aspect in a distributed computing system. The discussion, in general, is on a distributed system as the distributed computing system differs from the distributed system in its objective of handling the computational load as mentioned at other places as well.

2.1 DCS Architecture Models

Various models for the design of a distributed computing system have been proposed. We discuss here few models.

2.1.1 Workstation model

The workstation model is the simplest one and is consists of several workstations connected by a common communication network (Fig. 2.1). This is the most
popular model also as it uses the available legacy systems in designing a distributed computing system. It has been observed that not often all the workstation in
an organization are used all the time, whereas they are on and can be used for the
execution of the jobs belonging to the other user. Thus by connecting all the workstation of an organization, all the workstation can be utilized fully and this will result in parallel execution of the jobs reducing the overall completion time.

The issue may arise that what happens when a workstation was executing a
job of some other workstation. These issues have been addressed by Tanenbaum
[2].

A user logs onto his/her workstation and submits the job to be executed. This
job will be exploited for available parallelism and thus various concurrent modules of the job will be allocated onto any free workstation. This way the coopera-
tion amongst the workstation will result in the concurrent execution of the job.

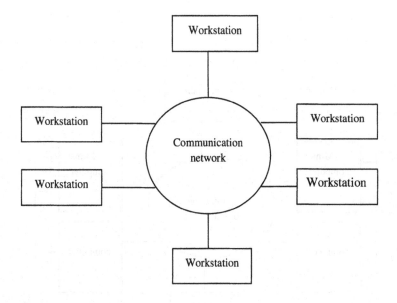

Fig. 2.1 Workstation Model

2.1.2 Minicomputer Model

This model comprised of the minicomputers, in place of the workstations, and is simple extension of the centralized timesharing system (Fig. 2.2). As usual, each minicomputer may have several terminals attached and a user can fire the job for execution from any of the terminals. The job can be executed on the minicomputer, from which it has been fired, or on any other minicomputer.

This type of model is very much useful when resource sharing with remote users is required. For example, sharing databases of different types, with each type of the databases located on a different minicomputer.

The early ARPAnet is an example of a distributed system based on the minicomputer model.

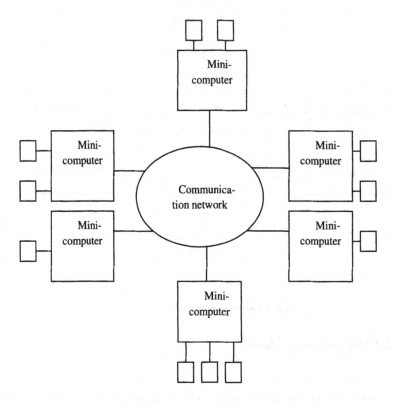

Fig. 2.2. Minicomputer Model

2.1.3 Client-Server Model

This model considers that the services of the system are concentrated over few dedicated machines and these services can be accessed from various remote nodes. These dedicated machines are referred as server and the machine accessing the services are called client (Fig. 2.3). Basically, the clients are minimal machine with less functionality. Servers are highly capable processors with one or more functionality. User can log onto any of the client machine and can fire the job. Normal computation can be performed on the client machine itself and the job re-

quiring specific services will be forwarded to the special server and will be executed there.

The client machine may be even the diskless workstations and the servers may
be the minicomputers equipped with large, fast disks.

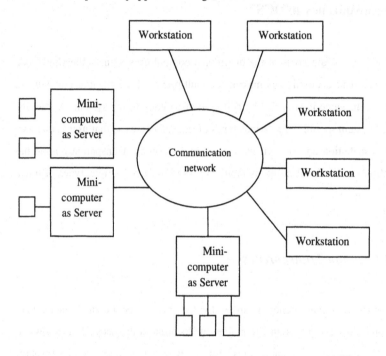

Fig. 2.3. Client-Server Model

2.1.4 Hybrid Models

In hybrid models all above models can be integrated into one. We may have
the nodes that can act as the server as well as the client as and when the need
arises. We can have the workstations, minicomputers, mainframe computers or
even the multiprocessor systems integrated into one to conceive a distributed

computing system. This type of model introduces heterogeneity in the design of the distributed system, but provides the possibility of integrating all types of computing nodes for maximum utilization.

2.2 Transparency in DCS

One of the main goals of the distributed computing system is the single system image. This is possible by making the multiplicity of the machines invisible to the user. The same is provided by adding transparency to the system. A true distributed system should have various types of transparencies so that user is unaware of the distribution and one views it as a single system. Transparency issue has been discussed in detail in the literature [1]. We brief here various types of transparencies in DCS.

2.2.1 Location Transparency

The location transparency is further divided in two. One, in which the name of a resource does not reveal anything about its location in the network, is known as Name transparency. The name transparency suggests that the name of a resource should be independent of the topology of the network. Further, the movable resources in the network are allowed to move across the network without any change in their names.

The other one is in which user is allowed to use the resources from any of the hosts without any change in the names of the resource. For example, a user can refer a file with the same name independent to the question where from the user's log in. This is referred as user mobility.

2.2.2 Replication Transparency

Redundancy is a technique by which the reliability of a system is increased. It is the property of a distributed system to introduce redundancy for reliability and better performance. Replicated resources and activity should be transparent to the user of a distributed system. The distributed system needs to handle the naming of replicas so that various copies of the same replica can be addressed by the same name. Replication control deals with how many of such replicas to be created, when it should be deleted etc.

2.2.3 Migration Transparency

Migration of the modules of a task is one of the important activities of the distributed system and has been addressed extensively in this book. The objective of the migration transparency is to allow the migration of the object in a user transparent manner. More discussion on the migration is in section 4.3 of chapter 4.

2.2.4 Access Transparency

Access transparency suggests that it is invisible to the user that whether a resource is remote or local. So a distributed system allows a user to access even remote resources in the same manner as the local ones.

2.2.5 Concurrency Transparency

As the distributed system consists of number of nodes it allows the execution of concurrent modules of a given task. The concurrency transparency suggests that these modules can be executed concurrently invisible to the user. However, concurrency control is an important issue, which must be addressed by the system designer.

The concurrency transparency also indicates that users can execute the concurrent modules of their tasks, in parallel, as and when the nodes can be allowed to execute so without the knowledge of the user.

2.2.6 Performance Transparency

This requires from the system to configure it dynamically, as and when required, to improve the performance of the system. We, in this book, have proposed a task allocation model in which the system is reconfigured to use it to the maximum possible extent (sec. 8.2 chapter 8).

2.2.7 Failure Transparency

This deals with allowing making the necessary changes in case of partial failure in the system. An often used term is graceful degradation that says to redistribute the load of a failed processor to all other processor in such a manner that is invisible to the user. Though, it is not possible to handle complete failure transparency, it is done to its maximum possible extent. Sometimes it is not possible to hide the failure of the processor, even if the load is shared by all other because the system will become slow and will be noticeable to the user. So a system having full failure transparency is not justified also.

2.2.8 Scaling Transparency

This says that system is allowed to scale up and down without affecting the users.

2.3 Introduction to Fault Tolerance

A fault is a mechanical or algorithmic defect that may generate error [1]. Failure is the repercussion of a fault. System failures have been characterized into two types. One, in which the system stops functioning after detecting a fault, is called as the fail-stop failure. The second one, in which system continues to function and produces wrong results even after detecting a fault, is referred as Byzantine failure. It is obvious that Byzantine failures are much more difficult to handle than the fail-stop failure.

Faults are handled by the methods of tolerance, avoidance and detection and recovery.

2.3.1 Fault Tolerance

Fault tolerant is the ability of a system to continue functioning even if the system fails partially. The term is referred as the "graceful degradation" in which the load of the failed node is given to the other nodes resulting in degraded performance. Fault tolerance is strongly related to dependable systems. Dependability requires the following [2]:

- Availability
- Reliability

- Safety
- Maintainability

Availability is defined as the probability that the system is available at any given moment to perform its function on behalf of its users. Highly available system is one that will most likely be working at any given instant of time.

Reliability is defined in terms of the time interval in contrast to an instance in time defined in availability. A highly reliable system is one that will continue working for a long period of time. If a system goes down for one millisecond every hour, it has more than 99 percent availability but is highly unreliable. Further, if a system never crashes but is shutdown for two weeks in one year has high reliability but only 96 percent availability.

Safety refers the situation in which the safety of the system is ensured so that it can perform properly. For example, if a control system that send people in space fails even for a brief moment, it could be disastrous. Safety of such systems is very much required.

Maintainability expresses how the system can be maintained for the future action i.e. if a system fails how easily and quickly the system can be repaired.

2.3.2 Fault Avoidance

This deals with the component design that tries to minimize the faults. The components whose failure rate is least are used to design a system and the system eventually minimizes the fault occurrences. Both the hardware and software components are taken care of this way.

2.3.3 Fault Detection and Recovery

This deals with mechanism of determining the occurrence of a failure and then to correct it in order to work the system properly. The failure is notified by the system and a corrective measure is taken to overcome the fault. Roll back is a mechanism that is often used for the corrective measures.

The detection method should be able to detect all types of faults, be it node failure, link failure or other software failure.

2.4 Synchronization

Synchronization is very important activity in a distributed system as the distributed system is not having a global central clock. It is desired that synchronization be done based on actual time. Many algorithms have been proposed in the literature that deals with synchronization of actual physical clocks [3-5].

It has been noted that sometimes only the relative ordering of the event is important than the ordering in absolute time. Logical clock synchronization deals with the ordering aspects of the events rather than the physical clock synchronization. We will discuss only the Lamport time stamping here that deals with logical ordering [6-7].

Physical clock synchronization deals with how the two nodes of a distributed system for which the time on physical clocks are different will be synchronized. It is important also otherwise it may become catastrophic. For example, in a distributed system a job is being executed that compiles all the files belonging to that job and then execute it. These files for the job may be located on different nodes of the system. Suppose the owner of the job changes a file on any of the node. Before execution of the job, it needs to check if any file has been modified and if so to compile it afresh. Whether a file has been modified or not will be indicated by the time of creation and execution only. Suppose the machine on which the file is being compiled gives more time than on which it has been modified, the modification will not be noticed and the job will execute only the old version of the object file. Thus there is a need to synchronize the physical clock. Christian algorithm is a famous one for physical clock synchronization [3].

For many purposes, it is sufficient that all machines agree on the same timings of their clocks. It is not necessary that their clocks should have the real time. This results in dealing with ordering of the events. This defines a logical clock. Lamport time stamping is very important move for the logical clocks.

2.4.1 Lamport Timestamps

Lamport defined a relation called "happens before". If all processes agree that an event x happened before y, the same can be represented as $x \rightarrow y$. This relation is a transitive relation. If two events happen in different processes that do not exchange messages, then this relation does not hold. These events then said to be concurrent [2].

A time value $T(x)$ is assigned to the events to the events with the agreement of all the processes. Thus, if $x \rightarrow y$ holds, then $T(x) < T(y)$ i.e. if event x occurs before event y within the same process then $T(x) < T(y)$. Similarly if x represent the sending of the message and y receiving of the message then $T(x) < T(y)$. Further, the time value T must always advance.

The processes running on different machines with their own clock on a distributed system must be synchronized. The clocks of the processors of the DCS may have its own speed. The events can be synchronized using Lamport algorithm. Lamport algorithm suggests that if a message has been delivered at time t on a machine A can not reach at time t-x on some other machine B. If it is observed so, then the time of the machine B will be advanced as t+1. This way the logical time stamping will be done.

For other synchronization mechanism the readers may refer [2].

BIBLIOGRAPHY

[1]Pradeep K. Sinha, Distributed Operating System: Concepts and Design, Prentice Hall of India, 1998.

[2]Andrew S. Tanenbaum, Marteen Van Steen, Distributed Systems: Principles and Paradigms, Pearson Education, 2002

[3]Christian F., Probabilistic Clock Synchronization, Distributed Computing, Vol.3, 1989, pp. 146-158

[4]Drummond R., Babaoglu O., Low cost Clock Synchronization, Distributed Computing, Vol. 6, 1993, pp. 193-203

[5]Kopetz H., Ochsenreiter W., Clock Synchronization in Distributed Real Time Systems, IEEE Trans. On Computers, Vol. C-87, No.8, Aug. 1987, pp. 933-940

[6]Lamport L., Time, Clocks and the Ordering of events in a distributed system, ACM Communications, Vol. 21, No. 7, July 1978, pp. 558-565

[7]Lamport L., Concurrent Reading and writing of Clocks, ACM Trans. On Computer Systems, Vol. 8, No. 4, Nov. 1990, pp. 305-310

CHAPTER 3

Scheduling Problem

The problem addressed in this book is concerned with the scheduling aspects of computations being submitted to a system that consists of distributed and properly networked collection of individual computing nodes. In other words, the main function of the scheduler of the operating system of such a computing infrastructure has to be allocation of different parts of a given task to various processing nodes of the computing system in such a way so as to be able to exploit efficiently the computing resources of the system and improve execution characteristic of any given task compared to its execution on a single processor system. This problem has been addressed in the literature during the last two decades but the assumptions made in those work simplify the problem extensively. For example, most of the models assume (i) only one task and their modules; (ii) ignore the capacity and status of processing elements etc.

The scheduling policies of a single processor system have been developed keeping in mind the fullest exploitation of the underlying CPU of the given machine. The idea there was to achieve the best execution of given computational task by making the CPU busy all the time. In case of a distributed computing system, multiple parts (modules) of a given task are allocated onto the various processing nodes so that they can execute in parallel (if possible) to produce better turn around time apart from utilizing the processing elements of the DCS. Hence the scheduling aspects of a DCS consists of two main functionalities: a) allocation of modules of any given task by selecting appropriate computing nodes of the DCS and b) the mechanism of execution of various modules of different tasks on a particular computing node of the DCS.

This chapter discusses about functioning of the DCS in section 3.1 and desirable characteristics of a scheduler in section 3.2. The job of the scheduling has been defined as the allocation of the tasks. Section 3.3 discusses scheduler as a task allocator. Issues in task allocation have been briefed in section 3.4. For the purpose of clarity the task allocation problem is discussed in section 3.5. The necessary assumptions, notation, and abbreviations used in the book, concludes the chapter.

3.1 On Functioning of a DCS

It will not be out of place to consider the functioning of a DCS, as the scheduling aspects are very much concerned with the way of functioning of these systems. Distributed computing system falls in the category of disjoint memory architecture. This type of system consists of multiple computing nodes that do not share memory and clock. The participating nodes have their own private memory. These nodes are connected in some fashion [1]. The nodes communicate with one another using communication links of the interconnection network. There has been a continuous research for improving the communication performance of the inter-connection networks [1-2].

As has been said earlier, a distributed system consists of multiple processing nodes that provide one or the other services to the users of the system. A user logs onto the system as one interconnected unit and multiplicity of the participating machines is hidden within the internals of the collection. When a substantive computation load is submitted to the distributed computing system, the scheduler must work out whether one or multiple number of computing nodes should be util-ized to execute the computational work. In case of the possibility of providing the service from the task-receiving-node itself, the work is simpler and the computa-tion is scheduled there itself. In the event of this computation being a request for some particular service, to be obtained from some other participating sites (nodes), the appropriate assignment will have to be carried out. The job of the scheduler becomes difficult if multiple computing nodes, for obtaining the best execution of the submission, must share the computational load.

The method of communication, architecture of interconnection network, the type of participating computing nodes, their capacities and the organization of ser-vices of the operating system of the DCS are some important issues related to the functionality of a DCS that affect the above said-the main and difficult most part of the scheduling of tasks on the DCS [3].

Next section describes the important characteristics of a scheduler of the DCS.

3.2 Desirable Characteristics of a Scheduler

A scheduler must coordinate the execution of a given task by utilizing the available computational resources for satisfying the execution characteristics expected. As detailed above, on receiving a task the scheduler must distinguish between the requirement of a general service (either from the receiving node or from some remote server) and the requirement of distribution of the computational load across multiple computing nodes of the system. It is a latter case of cooperative execution of multiple modules of a computational task on various participating nodes of the DCS that happens to be the main and difficult function of the scheduler in a distributed computing system. This function of the scheduler is known, in the literature, as task allocation or task mapping in multi-computer / distributed computing system [4-9]. It should be noted that multiple tasks from various users are submitted on any nodes of the DCS from time to time. The scheduler must also accommodate this multiplicity of the disjoint task. Three major aspects of scheduling that are characteristic parameters for any scheduler are known to be turn-around time, throughput and interactive response time. Turnaround time is a task-oriented characteristic that considers the time duration between submission and completion of a task. Obviously, it will be desirable to minimize this time. Similarly, the throughput of the system is a characteristic that measures the number of tasks successfully executed in unit time. This quantity must be maximized. The interactive response talks about the requirement of interactive users during the execution of the tasks. One or some modules of a task may continue to reside on the recipient node, whereas all other modules of a task that do not participate in the interactive communication may be allocated onto the multiple processing elements. Reliability, with allocation, is also a characteristic parameter often required for a real-time DCS though it is an added advantage for any DCS.

This way, a model of the scheduling activity must aim at maximization of throughput by considering the inter module communication of the given task and the interconnection pattern of the given DCS with appropriate task allocation methodology. The various aspects of task scheduling in a DCS are considered by making use of task graphs & processor graph to make appropriate allocation.

3.3 Scheduler as a Task Allocator

The concept of scheduling has been very extensively explored in the context of a single processor system, wherein the attention of the CPU is switched from one job to another. This insures appropriate implementation of certain policies that aim at providing fair share of CPU time to jobs. In a DCS, we have multiple processors and the idea of scheduling works on identification of CPUs for individual components of a job so that the effect of parallelism is obtainable. This obvious requirement considers the computational job in form of a task, consisting of number of modules that may execute concurrently and exchange messages as per requirements of the computational jobs. This understanding defines the scheduler whose main activity becomes allocation of various modules of individual tasks onto the processing nodes available in the DCS. Thus, in this book, the terms scheduler and allocator have been used interchangeably to carry the same meaning.

3.4 Task Allocation Issues in DCS

The following are certain pertinent points that need consideration, as these would affect the allocation activity:

- The criterion for allocation,

- Static vs. dynamic allocation,

- Single vs. multiple task allocation,

- Task migration, and

- Load balancing.

Given a task at hand, for allocation, the scheduler is to allocate it onto the processing nodes of the DCS. The job of the scheduler, as an allocator, can be divided in two phases. First, that exploits the concurrency presents in the program and divides the program into various concurrent modules. The second allocates these modules onto the processing nodes.

Further, there are two ways to exploit concurrency. The programming languages designed for the DCS can support concurrency by providing the parallel constructs in the programming languages of the DCS. Many available languages for DCS provide such constructs viz. FORK-JOIN, Cobegin-Coend, Parfor etc. These parallel constructs can be used to specify the parallel portion of the program

by writing it in the program. On the other hand, the allocator can explore the concurrency in the program by applying various methods (viz. Bernsteins conditions
etc.) [10].

Both the above said methods produce parallel executable modules of the program. For the task allocation problem, it is assumed that a task is given in form of
the executable modules. The allocator allocates these modules to achieve improvement in one or more characteristic parameters (sec. 2.2). Normally the task
allocation algorithms optimize the COST (completion time) parameter out of the
allocation. Cost is defined as the sum of the processing cost of all the modules of a
task and the communication among the modules. The other often-used parameter,
to be optimized, is the reliability of the system that is defined as the probability of
the successful execution of a task on the system. The reliability is very important
characteristic parameter for the Real Time DCS.

Choice is also made between static and dynamic scheduling. In static scheduling, the modules once allocated stick to the same node for their lifetime. This
seeks to optimize completion time of a finite set of tasks. To accomplish this goal,
the characteristics of all the tasks, including their sizes and service demands, must
be known in advance. Static scheduling is appropriate to a very specialized class
of systems including some real time systems in which this information is priori
available. Obviously, this limits the use of the DCS and consequently affects the
throughput of the system, but easier to implement as other unrelated tasks are not
going to affect the execution.

Dynamic scheduling assumes a continuous stochastic stream of incoming tasks. Very little parameters are known in advance for dynamic scheduling. Obviously, it is more complex than static scheduling for implementation, but achieves better throughput. Also it is the most desired because of the application demand.

Another concern is that of a single task versus multiple task allocation. As evident, single task allocator allocates only one task and concentrates only for its completion. Multiple task allocator considers and handles more than one task for execution. To maintain the track of the execution of the multiple tasks (with their modules) and status of nodes a corresponding data structure is required.

To achieve the load balancing in the system, often the modules of the task migrates from one node to the other from time to time. This activity is known as task migration[25]. In dynamic allocation, task migration comes into effect for proper load balancing. Several load balancing policies are suggested in the literature [7, 12-25].

3.5 The Task Allocation Problem

The task allocation problem involves the development of a task allocation model for the DCS. The model allocates the tasks among the processing nodes of a given DCS to achieve the following [26]:

1) Allow specification of a large number of constraints,

2)   Optimize the cost function,

3)   Balance the utilization of the processing nodes of the DCS.

The task allocation problem assumes a task consisting of computational modules mostly requires computation but in between these modules may communicate with each other. The computational modules do not require any specific processing node, in general, and may be allocated on any of the processing node. The objective of the allocation is to optimize some characteristic parameter as mentioned in sec. 2.2. The word task has been used to refer it to process, job and other similar entities, through out the book. Modules are further division of the task as mentioned earlier.

Thus the task allocation problem considers the task graph and a processor graph. The task allocation model maps the task graph to processor graph.

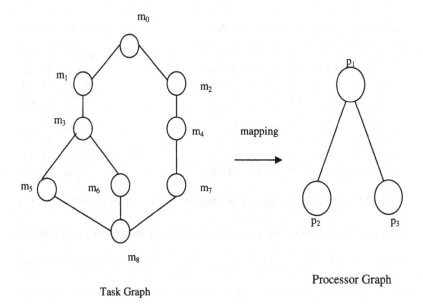

Fig. 3.1Mapping of Task Graph to Processor Graph

Figure 3.1 shows a task graph consisting of nine modules (m_0, m_1, m_2, m_3, m_4, m_5, m_6, m_7, m_8) and the processor graph of three nodes (p_1, p_2, p_3). The position of the modules shows its precedence. Generally two types of task graph are possible. One in which the edges between the modules shows the communication between them. This is called Task Interaction Graph. The other, in which the edges show the precedence between the modules, is known as Task Precedence Graph. We use the task precedence graph in most of the models discussed in this book and call it the task graph in general. Further, it is assumed that the communication among the modules is given in an inter module communication matrix. The execution time matrix shows the execution time of the modules of the task on the processing nodes of the DCS. Example IMC and Execution time matrices are shown below.

c_{ij}	m_0	m_1	m_2	m_3	m_4	m_5	m_6	m_7	m_8
m_0	0	20	0	40	15	10	0	15	20
m_1	20	0	5	30	10	0	15	20	10
m_2	0	5	0	35	0	30	20	10	15
m_3	40	70	35	0	10	35	20	10	12
m_4	35	15	20	25	0	20	25	10	15
m_5	20	25	0	20	15	0	10	35	12
m_6	10	35	15	25	20	10	0	15	10
m_7	20	30	25	0	15	20	10	0	0
m_8	0	25	30	35	20	10	15	20	0

e_{ik}	p_1	p_2	p_3
m_0	10	20	30
m_1	40	5	10
m_2	70	50	80
m_3	50	80	20
m_4	20	30	20
m_5	30	25	20
m_6	20	20	20
m_7	15	20	15
m_8	20	25	20

Inter Module Communication (IMC) Matrix   Execution Time Matrix

The IMC matrix shows the communication among the modules of a task viz. communication between the modules m_0 and m_1 is 20. Communication is measured in terms of data units transferred. Execution time matrix shows the execution time of the various modules of the task on the processing nodes of the DCS viz. m_0 takes 10 unit of time on p_1. Execution time can be considered in terms of msec.

There are number of constraints which are to be met out for the task allocation model. Precedence of the module of the task, memory limitation of the processing nodes etc. is among the few [26].

Completion time of the task is one of the well-known criterions for allocation and mostly the cost function considers the completion time of the job. Reliability of the system is another important criterion considered in some allocation models [27-31].

This book aims at the consideration of existing algorithms with their simplifying assumptions for proposing better algorithms that consider the realistic situations of a DCS such as

(i)   Precedence constraints,

(ii)   The fact that multiple tasks, each consisting of a number of modules are received by a DCS for execution,

(iii)   The processing nodes of the DCS have certain capacities and they may or may not be in a situation of accepting more work at any time OR assigning more work to such nodes may degrade execution characteristics of tasks.

The chapter hereafter contain our proposed algorithms that make use of known efficient search techniques like GA, A* etc. apart from the data structures required for tackling the situation.

3.6 Assumptions & Notation

As the task allocation problem remains to be NP-hard, various heuristic solutions have been proposed with one or other assumptions. This work also makes certain assumptions that are as follows.

1. Distributed Computing System imposes some limitations on the task allocation. One of them is the limitation of memory. To simplify our problem we are making the assumption that the memory of the processors in DCS is not limited in some of the models. Though this step can be easily incorporated, in the problem, at the cost of few more steps.

2. Tasks are disjoint and have no inter-task communication. Only the modules within a task have interdependencies and communication requirements.

3. Execution and communication matrices for the task graph are assumed to be given. Only one of the models proposed does not require the execution time (sec. 8.2).

4. The assumption of the availability of interconnection graph accommodates non-regular type of interconnection networks.

5. Processing node, processing element, computing node, processor have

    been used to refer to the same.

Few other assumptions, specific to particular TA models, are ascribed with the

corresponding models as depicted in the rest of the book.

Notation

T	task: set of modules to be executed
m	$|T|$: number of modules forming the task T
m_i	module i of task T
P	set of processing nodes in the DCS
n	$|P|$: number of processing nodes in P
P_k	Processing node k in P
e_{ik}	execution time for module m_i running on processor P_k during the execution
X	m×n binary matrix corresponding to a task assignment
x_{ik}	element of X; $$x_{ik} = \begin{cases} 1 & if \ \mod ule \ m_i \ is \ assigned \ to \ \Pr ocessor \ P_k \\ 0 & otherwise \end{cases}$$
c_{ij}	IMC cost between m_i and m_j during the execution
d_{kl}	distance between processing nodes P_k and P_l defined as the number of links
n_k	number of modules already allocated on P_k at some instance of time
q	time quantum of the processor for round robin scheduling
$Height(m_i)$	position of module m_i from the root
G(h)	set of modules of height h
M_i	amount of memory required by module m_i

S_k memory capacity of processing node P_k

$R(T,X)$ reliability of DCS when task T is allocated by the assignment X

$R_k(T,X)$ reliability of processing node P_k

$R_{pq}(T,X)$ reliability of link l_{pq}

l_{pq} link connecting node P_p and P_q

λ_k failure rate of node P_k

λ_{pq} failure rate of link l_{pq}

W_{pq} transmission rate of link l_{pq}

C_{ijh} communication between modules m_i and m_j of task T_h

e_{ihk} execution time of module m_i of task T_h on processing node P_k

x_{ihk} element of assignment matrix for multiple task allocation

$$x_{ihk} = \begin{cases} 1 & \textit{if module } m_i \textit{ of task } T_h \textit{ is assigned to Processor } P_k \\ 0 & \textit{otherwise} \end{cases}$$

M_{ij} memory requirement of module m_i of task T_j

L_{avg} Load Average

$L_{max}.$ Load Maximum

eff Effiency

eff_{min} Effiency Minimum

BIBLIOGRAPHY

[1]A.S. Tanenbaum, *Computer Networks*, Englewood cliff, NJ: Prentice-Hall, 1994.

[2]D.P.Bertsekas, J.H.Tsitsiklis, *Parallel and Distributed Computation*, Prentice Hall International, 1989.

[3]P. Krueger, T.H.Lai, V.A.Dixit-Radiya, "Job Scheduling is more Important than Processor Allocation in Hypercube Computer", *IEEE Trans. on Parallel & Distributed Systems*, Vol. 5, No.5, May 1994, pp. 488-497.

[4]V.Rajaraman, C.Siva Ram Murthy, *Parallel Computer: Architecture and Programming*, Prentice Hall of India Ltd, 2000.

[5]M. Sasikumar, Dinesh Shikhare, P. Ravi Prakash, *Introduction to Parallel Processing*, Prentice Hall of India Ltd, 2000.

[6]Sanjeev K. Setia, Mark S. Squillante, Satish K. Tripathi, "Analysis of Processor Allocation in Distributed –Memory Parallel Processing Systems", *IEEE Trans. on Parallel & Distributed Systems*, Vol. 5, No. 4, April 1994, pp. 401-420.

[7]Pradeep K. Sinha, *Distributed Operating System*, IEEE Press, Prentice Hall of India Ltd., 1998.

[8]G.Colouris, J. Dollimore, T. Kindberg, *Distributed Systems: Concepts and Design*, Addison-Wesley Publishers Ltd., 1994.

[9]G.Nutt, *Operating Systems: A Modern Perspective*, Addison Wesley, 2000.

[10]A.Silberschatz, P.B. Galvin, *Operating Systems Concepts*, Addison-Wesley, 1998.

[11]A.Corradi, L.Leonardi, F. Zambonelli, "Diffusive Load Balancing Policies for Dynamic Application", *IEEE Concurrency*, January-March 1999, pp.22-31.

[12]D.J.Evans, W.U.N.Butt, "Dynamic Load Balancing Using Task-Transfer Probabilities," *Parallel Computing*, Vol.19, No.8, Aug. 1993, pp.897-916.

[13]D.L.Eager, E.D.Lazowska, J.Zahorjan, "Adaptive Load Sharing in Homogeneous Distributed Systems," *IEEE Trans. On Software Engg.*, Vol.12, No.5, May 1986, pp.662-675.

[14]E. Horowitz, S. Sahni, S. Rajasekaran, *Computer Algorithms*, W.H.Freeman and Company, 1997.

[15]F.C.Lin, R.M.Keller, "The Gradient Model Load Balancing Method", *IEEE Trans. On Software Engg.* Vol. SE-13, No.1, Jan.1988, pp.32-38.

[16]F.Muniz, E.Zaluska, "Parallel Load-Balancing: An Extension to the Gradient Model", *Parallel Computing*, Vol.21, 1987, pp. 287-301.

[17]L.M.Ni, C.W.Xu, T.B.Gendreau, "A Distributed Drafting Algorithm for Load Balancing", *IEEE Trans. on Software Engineering*, Vol. SE-13, No.10, October 1985, pp.1153-1161.

[18]M.Hamdi, C.K.Lee, "Dynamic Load Balancing of Image Processing Applications on Clusters of Workstations", *Parallel Computing*, No. 22, 1997, pp.1477-1492.

[19]M.H.Willebeek-LeMair, A.Reeves, "Strategies for Dynamic Load Balancing on Highly Parallel Computers", *IEEE Trans. on Parallel and Distributed Systems*, Vol.4, 1993, pp.979-993.

[20]P.H.Enslow Jr., "What is a "Distributed" Data Processing System", *IEEE Computer*, Vol.11, No.1, January 1978, pp.13-21.

[21]S.H.Bokhai, "Dual Processor Scheduling with Dynamic Reassignment", *IEEE Trans. on Software Engg.*, Vol.SE-5, No.4, July 1979, pp.329-335.

[22]S.Zhou, "A Trace Driven Simulation Study of Dynamic Load Balancing", *IEEE Trans. On Software Engg.*, Vol.14, No.9, Sept.1988, pp.1327-1341.

[23]T.C.K. Chou, J.A.Abraham, "Load Balancing in Distributed Systems", *IEEE Trans. On Software Engg.*, Vol. SE-8, No.4, July 1982, pp.401-412.

[24]T.Kunz, "The Influence of Different Workload Descriptions on a Heuristic Load Balancing Scheme", *IEEE Trans. on Software Engg.*, Vol.17, July 1991, pp.725-730.

[25]T.T.Y.Suen, J.S.K.Wong, "Efficient Task Migration Algorithm for Distributed System", *IEEE Transaction on Parallel and Distributed System*, Vol.3, No.4, July 1992, pp.484-499.

[26]D.P.Vidyarthi, A.K.Tripathi, "Precedence Constrained Task Allocation in Distributed Computing System", *Int. J. of High Speed Computing*, Vol. 8, No. 1, 1996, pp. 47-55.

[27]S.Kartik, C.S.Ram Murthy, "Task Allocation Algorithms for Maximizing Reliability of Distributed Computing Systems", *IEEE Trans. on Computers*, Vol.46, No.6, June1997, pp. 719-724.

[28]Sol.M.Shatz, Wang Goto, "Task Allocation for Maximizing Reliability of Distributed Computing Systems", *IEEE Trans. on Computers*, Vol.41, No.9, September 1992, pp. 1156-1168.

[29]S. Karthik, C. Siva Ram Murthy, " Improved Task Allocation Algorithms to Maximize Reliability of Redundant Distributed Systems", *IEEE Trans. on Reliability*, Vol. 44, No. 4, Dec. 1995, pp. 575-586.

[30]A.K.Tripathi, D.P.Vidyarthi, A.N.Mantri, "A Genetic Task Allocation Algorithm for Distributed Computing System Incorporating Problem Specific Knowledge", *International J. of High Speed Computing*, Vol.8, No.4, 1996, pp. 363-370.

[31]D.P.Vidyarthi, A.K.Tripathi, "Maximizing Reliability of Distributed Computing Systems with Task Allocation using Simple Genetic Algorithm", *J. of Systems Architecture*, Vol. 47, 2001, pp. 549-554.

CHAPTER 4

Load Balancing in DCS

This chapter considers one very important proposition for the scheduling problem in distributed computing system. This is load balancing aspect.

4.1 Load Distribution in a DCS

Performance improvement is one of the most important issues in DCS. Obvious but expensive ways of achieving this goal are to increase the capacity of the nodes and to add more nodes to the system. Adding more nodes or increasing the capacity of some of the nodes may be required in the cases in which all of the nodes in the system are overloaded. However, in many situations poor performance is due to uneven load distribution throughout the system. Sometimes, the random arrival of tasks in such environment can cause some nodes to be heavily loaded while other nodes are idle or lightly loaded. Load distribution improves the performance by transferring tasks from heavily loaded nodes, where service is poor, to lightly loaded nodes where the tasks can take advantages of computing capacity that would otherwise go unused [1].

If workloads at some nodes are typically heavier than at others, or if some nodes execute tasks more slowly than others, the situation of lightly loaded/ heavily loaded/ moderately loaded nodes are likely to occur often. It is shown that even in such a homogeneous DCS, at least one machine is likely to be idle while other machines are heavily loaded because of the statistical fluctuations in the arrival of tasks to the system and task service time requirements. Therefore, even in a homogeneous DCS, system performance can be potentially improved by the appropriate transfer of the workload from heavily loaded nodes (senders) to idle or lightly loaded nodes (receivers). Meaning of performance here is the average response time of tasks. The response time of a task is the time elapsed between its initiation and its response. Minimizing the average response time is often the goal of load distribution. The performance of the system can often be improved to an acceptable level simply by redistributing the load among the nodes. Therefore, load redistribution is a cost-effective way for the improved performance. The problem of load redistribution in DCS is recognized as load balancing or load sharing [2].

Load indices that have been studied and used include the length of the CPU queue, the average CPU queue length over some period, the amount of available memory, the context-switch rate, the system call rate, and CPU utilization. Researchers have consistently found significant differences in the effectiveness of such load indices and these simple load indices are particularly effective. For example, in [3] it is found that the choice of a load index has considerable effect on performance. The most effective of the indices, we have mentioned, is the CPU queue length i.e. the number of tasks in a queue of a processor. Finally, no performance improvement is found over this simple measure when combinations of all these load indices were used.

The main goal of load balancing algorithms is to balance the workload across all the nodes of the system. A node's workload can be estimated on some measurable parameters [3-4] such as total number of processes on the node at the time of load estimation, resources demand of these processes, architecture and speed of the node's processor.

4.1.1 Load Sharing (LS) versus Load Balancing (LB)

Load sharing approach attempts to conserve the ability of the system to perform work by assuring that no node idles to which processes (tasks) wait for being processed [3]. On the other hand, load balancing approach in which all the processes submitted by the users are distributed among the nodes of the system so as to equalize the workload among the nodes. Some researchers differentiate load balancing from load sharing by their objective. The term load balancing is used if the goal is to equalize certain performance measures such as the percentage of server's idle time, marginal job response time etc [3]. On the other hand, if the objective is to improve some performance measure such as average job response time by redistributing the workload, it is called load sharing.

4.2 Load Balancing Methodology

The following is a brief account of the LB methodology wherein task migration happens to be an essential and important activity. The idea of the cost of Task migration (TM) appears here. The abstract goal of load balancing can be stated as follows [5]:

"Given a collection of tasks comprising a computation and a set of computers on which these tasks may be executed, find the mapping of tasks to computers that results in each node having an approximately equal amount of work."

A mapping that balances the workload of the processors will typically increase the overall efficiency of a computation. Increasing the overall efficiency will typically reduce the runtime of the computation. In considering the load balancing problem, it is important to distinguish between problem decomposition and task mapping. Problem decomposition involves the exploitation of concurrency in the control and data access of an algorithm. The result of the decomposition is the set of communicating tasks that solves the problem in parallel. These tasks, divided into suitable modules, are mapped to the computing nodes in the manner that best fits the problem. One concern in task mapping is that each node has a roughly equal workload. This is the load balancing problem as stated above. In some cases, computation time associated with a given task can be determined a priori. In such circumstances, one can perform the task mapping before beginning the computation; this is called static load balancing. For an important and increasingly common class of applications, the workload for a particular task may change over the course of computation and can not be estimated beforehand. For these applications, the mapping of tasks to computing nodes must change dynamically during the computation.

A practical approach to dynamic load balancing can be divided in five phases [5]: load evaluation, profitability determination, work transfer vector calculation, task selection and task migration.

4.2.1 Load Balance Initiation

For effective load balance one has to determine first when to balance the load. Doing so is comprised of two phases: first to detect that a load imbalance exists and secondly to determine if the cost of load balancing exceeds its possible benefits.

The load balance of a computation is the ratio of the average processors' load(L_{avg}) to the maximum processor load(L_{max}), i.e. Efficiency eff= L_{avg} / L_{max}. A load balancing framework might, therefore, consider initiating load balancing whenever the efficiency of a computation is below some user specified threshold eff_{min}. In applications where the total load is expected to remain fairly constant, load balancing would be undertaken only in those cases where the load of some nodes exceeds L_{avg} / eff_{min}, where Lavg is calculated initially or provided by the application [6-8].

Even if a load imbalance exists, it may be better not to do load balance, simply because the cost of load balancing would exceed the benefits of a better load distribution. The time required to load balance can be measured directly using available facilities. The expected reduction in run time due to load balancing can be estimated loosely by assuming that the efficiency will be increased to eff_{min} or, more precisely, by maintaining a history of the improvement in past load balancing steps. If the expected improvement exceeds the cost of load balancing, the next stage in the load balancing process should begin [9].

4.3 Task Migration

A DCS may receive the number of tasks with the numbers of modules at different times. Similarly various modules of a task and various tasks with all their modules may leave the DCS after completion or due to some other system policy decisions. It should be noticeable that due to this situation some processor may become lightly loaded from time to time whereas others may remain heavily loaded. In such a situation an activity known as task (process) migration is initiated to balance the load across the system.

A process (task) may be migrated either before it starts executing on its source node or during the course of its execution. A process migration can be expressed by the following steps [3, 10]:

1. Selection of a process that should be migrated

2. Selection of the destination node to which the selected process should be migrated

3. Actual transfer of the selected process to the destination node.

A process migration in DCS dynamically relocates running tasks (processes) among the component machines. Such relocation can help cope with dynamic fluctuations in loads and service needs, meet real time scheduling deadlines, bring a process to a special device, or improve the system's fault tolerance. Even successful migration facilities are not common in DCS, due to largely the inherent complexity of such facilities and the potential execution penalty if the migration policy and mechanism are not tuned correctly. Not surprisingly, some DCS terminate remote processes rather than rescue them by migration [11].

There are several reasons why migration is hard to design and implement. The mechanism for moving tasks must reliably and efficiently detach a migrant process from its source environment, transfer it with its context, and attach it to a new environment on the destination machine. Migration may fail in case of nodes and communication failures, but it should do so completely in that, the effect should be as if the process were never migrated at all or, at worst, as if the process had terminated due to machine failure [11].

4.3.1 Migration Overhead

Migration overhead is a very important factor when process migration usually takes place. Sometimes it can incur an overhead, which can adversely affect the throughput of the system. For the following issues migration overhead should be kept in mind while moving the tasks from one node to another:

- Data about the modules residing on particular nodes i.e. module name, size, IPC request, number of threads,

- Threshold of processors in terms of modules and memory that it can support,

- The type of processor i.e. includes migrating a job to a node having a faster CPU or to a node, at which it has minimum turnaround time,

- From processor to processor i.e. to migrate the tasks of a job to the different nodes that consist of different processors of the system,

- Various kinds of processes need various I/O resources like printers, disk drivers etc.

- Various software resources like databases, files etc.

- Copy or replication of critical processes to another node due to system reliability, and

- Mixing I/0 and CPU bound processes on a global basis for increasing the throughput of the system.

4.4 Threads

Modern programming languages and operating systems encourage the use of threads to exploit concurrency and simplify program structure. A process consists of an address space and one or more threads of control. Each thread of a process has its own program counter, its own register states, and its own stack. Threads are referred to as lightweight processes and traditional processes are referred to as heavyweight processes. Threads can be used to improve application performance through parallelism. Threads can also be used to minimize context switching time, allowing the CPU to switch from one unit of computation to another unit of computation with minimal overhead.

In this book, the thread can be treated as part of a module and the size of a module can be considered to be as follows:

Size of a module = (Expected no. of threads in the modules ×

Average size of thread)

Here, it is assumed that each module consists of at least one thread.

4.5 Conflicts between TA and LB

The main purpose of a single task allocation in a DCS is to reduce job turn-around time. It is done by maximizing the utilization of resources while minimizing any communication between processing nodes. The benefits of task allocation can make distributed processing desirable but several problems must be solved before they can be realized. For example, when the number of processors in a system increases beyond a certain level, then throughput decreases. This is known as saturation effect [12]. In reality, however, a lower processing speed results, caused by such factors as control overheads, communication between processors, unbalanced loading, queuing delays, and precedence order of the parts of task assigned to separate processors. In order to eliminate or minimize saturation, these inhibiting factors must also be eliminated. Dynamic allocation algorithm and proper load distribution must be provided for a system as a means of balancing and minimizing both IPC, queuing delays and control overhead problem.

So a DCS has conflicting requirements [12]:

1) While minimizing IPC tends to assign the whole of a task to a single processor, load balancing tries to distribute the task evenly among the processing nodes.

2) While a real-time constraint uses as many processors as maximize parallel execution, the precedence relations limit parallel execution.

3) The saturation effect suggests the use of fewer processors since inefficiency increases with the number of processors.

Obviously, it is not possible to satisfy all these requirements simultaneously; therefore a compromise must be made to find the optimal allocation policy with load balancing for the tasks. We should attempt to achieve maximization of throughput.

The algorithms, described as earlier work, in sec.5.1 are moderately well to perform load balancing on network of workstations which are in most cases homogeneous DCS. In these algorithms some of the simplifying assumptions have been taken into considerations including constant time or even free inter-task communication, processors with the same instruction sets, uniformity of available files and devices and existence of plentiful primary and secondary memory, which are not always realistic.

The algorithms [12-17] also consider allocation of the modules of only a single task to various processing nodes, whereas the number of tasks, for execution, is usually substantive. In reality, a DCS facilitates concurrent execution of modules belonging to various unrelated tasks. The modules of a particular task, having IMC, do co-operatively execute and do not depend on the modules of the other tasks. *This leads us to conclude that a processing node may be assigned modules belonging to various unrelated tasks i.e. multiple tasks.*

The algorithms [3, 18-22] consider task migration but that always incur overhead, which is not always meaningful in doing load balancing, and affects the throughput of the system.

So, the major factors that affect while allocating tasks in a heterogeneous DCS with load balancing are speeds of processors, processor architecture, memory, different file spaces, and characteristics of operating systems and application software. So the future support mechanisms will have to make this information available for allocation algorithms to fully utilize a large, heterogeneous DCS.

Consideration of all the above factors, in the following chapters, leads to development of a model of "Load balancing Task Allocation (LBTA)" strategy in this book. The model aims at minimization of turnaround time of tasks and promises possible better throughput. The results presented in the subsequent chapter shows that by attempting to minimize the turnaround time of all the tasks up to the possible extent within the constraints of the system in terms of the load already being shared by the processing nodes due to previous allocation of modules of tasks, better throughput is achievable, as compared to existing task allocation algorithms which can play a vital role as a task allocator in a DCS of heterogeneous nature by considering the multiple tasks with their corresponding modules. A concept of Global Table (GT) has been considered to keep track of allocation of multiple tasks.

In this book and as in literature a) the terms 'task' and 'process', b) the terms 'processing node', 'processor', 'machine', 'computer' c) the term 'allocation' and 'assignment' have been used interchangeably.

BIBLIOGRAPHY

[1]T. T. Y. Suen and J. S. K. Wong, "Efficient Task Migration Algorithm for Distributed System," *IEEE Transaction on Parallel and Distributed System*, Vol.3, No.4, July 1992, pp.484-499.

[2]H. C. Lin and C.S. Raghavendra, "A Dynamic Load Balancing Policy with Central Job Dispatcher (LBC)," *IEEE Trans. On Software Engg.* , Vol.18, No.2, Feb. 1992, pp.148-158.

[3]P. K. Sinha, *Distributed Operating Systems: Concepts and Design*, Printice-Hall of India, 1997.

[4]M. Hamdi and C. K. Lee, "Dynamic Load Balancing of Image Processing Applications on Clusters of Workstations," *Parallel Computing*, 22(1997), pp.1477-1492.

[5]J. Watts and S. Taylor, "A Practical Approach to Dynamic Load Balancing", *IEEE Trans. on Parallel and Distributed Systems*, Vol. 9, No.2, March 1998, pp. 235-248.

[6]F. C. Lin and R. M. Keller, "The Gradient Model Load Balancing Method," *IEEE Trans. On Software Engg*. Vol. SE-13, No.1, Jan. 1988, pp.32-38.

[7]F. Muniz and E. Zaluska, "Parallel Load-Balancing: An Extension to the Gradient Model", *Parallel Computing*, Vol.21, 1987, pp. 287-301.

[8]J. Ousterhout, D. Scelza, and P. Sindhu, "Medusa: An Experiment in Distributed Operating System Structure", *Communication. of ACM*, Vol.23, No.2, Feb. 1980, pp. 92-105.

[9]M. H. Willebeek-LeMair and A. Reeves, "Strategies for Dynamic Load Balancing on Highly Parallel Computers", *IEEE Trans. Parallel and Distributed Systems*, Vol.4, 1993, pp.979-993.

[10]A. S. Tanenbaum, *Distributed Operating Systems*, Prentice-Hall, Englewood Cliffs, NJ, 1995.

[11]Y. Artsy and R. Finkel, "Designing a Process Migration Facility, The Charlotte Experience", *IEEE Computer*, Vol. 22, No.9, September 1989, pp.47-56.

[12]K. Efe, "Heuristic Models of Task Assignment Scheduling in Distributed Systems", *IEEE Computer*, Vol. 15, 1982, pp.50-56.

[13]A. K. Tripathi, D. P. Vidyarthi and A. N. Mantri, "A Genetic Task Allocation Algorithm for Distributed Computing Systems Incorporating Problem Specific Knowledge," *International Journal of High Speed Computing*, Vol.8, No.4, 1996, pp.363-370.

[14]C. C. Shen and W. H. Tsai, "A Graph Matching Approach to Optimal Task Assignment in Distributed Computing System Using a Minimax Criterion", *IEEE Trans. Computers*, Vol. C-34, No.3, March, 1985. pp. 197-203.

[15]D. P. Vidyarthi and A.K.Tripathi, "Precedence Constrained Task Allocation in Distributed Computer Systems," *International Journal of High Speed Computing*, Vol.8, No.1, 1996, pp.47-55.

[16]P.Y.R.Richard Ma, E.Y.S.Lee and J. Tsuchiya, "A Task Allocation Model for Distributed Computing Systems," *IEEE Trans. Computer*, Vol. C-31, No.1, Jan.1982, pp. 41-47.

[17]W.W.Chu and M.T.Lan, "Task Allocation and Precedence Relations for Distributed Real-Time Systems," *IEEE Trans. Computer*, Vol.C-36, No.6, June 1987, pp. 667-679.

[18]A.B.Tucker, Jr., *The Computer Science and Engineering Handbook*, CRC Press, 1997.

[19]Edwind S.H. Hou, N. Ansari and H.Ren, "A Genetic Algorithm for Multiprocessor Scheduling", *IEEE Trans. Parallel and Distributed Systems*, Vol.5, 1994, pp.113.

[20]F.C.Lin and R.M.Keller, "The Gradient Model Load Balancing Method," *IEEE Trans. on Software Engg*. Vol. SE-13, No.1, Jan. 1988, pp.32-38.

[21]L.M.Ni, C.W.Xu and T.B.Gendreau, "A Distributed Drafting Algorithm for Load Balancing," *IEEE Trans. on Software Engg.*, Vol.SE-13, No.10, Oct. 1985, pp.1153-1161.

[22]T.C.K. Chou and J.A.Abraham, "Load Balancing in Distributed Systems," *IEEE Trans. Software Engg.*, Vol. SE-8, No.4, July 1982, pp.401-412.

CHAPTER 5

Known Task Allocation Models

This chapter contains some representative Task Allocation (TA) algorithms in section 5.1 that have appeared in literature [1-5]. These algorithms had certain assumptions that simplify the realistic DCS, such as the tasks have no or little precedence etc. We proposed a TA algorithm in sec. 5.3 that gets rid of this assumption and considers precedence constraint, as most of the tasks received by any DCS shall have precedence constraint depicted in their task graphs [6].

Furthermore, a good task partitioning is a prerequisite for any TA method. Though in this book we are concentrating only on the TA algorithms, nevertheless in section 5.4 an IMC cost reduction model is proposed [7].

The researchers of the discipline have proposed various task allocation algorithms for the distributed computing systems. These algorithms seek to assign the modules of a task on the nodes of the DCS to achieve one or more characteristics. Most of the models, proposed, minimize the turnaround time of the given task. Often advocated advantage of a Parallel/Distributed System is the fast work and that can be achieved only by the minimization of the turnaround time of the task. This turnaround time includes the communication time also which occurs between two processes/modules situated on the different nodes. This is known as InterProcess Communication (IPC)/InterModule Communication (IMC). Some of the algorithms concentrate only on the minimization of IPC/IMC as it may result in heavy turnaround. Few proposed models consider the reliability of the system with task allocation. Whatsoever is the parameter of allocation, goal is to achieve high degree of parallelism with proper load balancing of the system [8].

These goals may conflict with each other. For example, minimization of IMC cost tends to assign all the modules of a task onto the same nodes of the DCS, as the modules on the same node will incur zero IMC. Thus a proper load balancing on the PEs of the DCS is also desired.

5.1 Early Models

The task allocation model imposes various constraints. Precedence of the modules of the task is very important constraint and an allocation algorithm is almost useless if this constraint is ignored in the model. Precedence is the priority of the execution of modules of a task. Some modules may depend on the result of the other module and thus the dependent module has less precedence over the module from which it has to get some computed result.

A memory limitation of the processing nodes of the DCS is another constraint. All the processing nodes have some fixed amount of the memory and thus can accommodate a certain number of modules. This constraint is also to be given due consideration while allocating the task.

Some modules of the task may demand some specific service that is available only on some specific processing node. Thus all the processing nodes cannot be treated equal for all the modules. This is the functionality of the processors and is to be considered while allocation.

The property of the interconnection network of the DCS plays a significant role in allocation [9]. Two modules, which require heavy communication, are to be allocated on to the same or the neighboring nodes.

Earlier proposed models consider very few constraints, listed above, in their models. Some of the representative models are briefed below.

5.1.1 Heuristic Task Allocation Models for DCS

Richard, Lee and Tsuchiya [1] have presented a task allocation model that allocates task, among processors in a DCS, satisfying

1) Minimum InterProcess Communication cost

2) Balanced utilization of each processor and

3) All engineering application requirements

A cost function is formulated to measure the IPC and processing cost. In their model, memory limitation constraint is imposed by limiting the memory at the processing nodes of the DCS. Other allocation constraints, considered in their model, are

a. Task Preference: a task is preferred to be allocated to a certain processor,

b. Task Exclusion: certain pair of tasks must not be assigned to the same processor, and

c. Task Redundancy: certain tasks must be assigned to two or more processors

Cost function is formulated as the sum of the IPC cost and the processing cost. IPC cost is a function of both task coupling factors and interprocessor distances. Coupling factor c_{ij} is the number of data units transferred from task i to task j. Interprocessor distance d_{kl} is certain distance related communication cost associated with one unit of data transferred from processor k to l.

Processing cost q_{ik} represents the cost to process task i on processor k. The assignment variable is defined as

$$X_{ik} = \begin{cases} 1 & \text{if task } i \text{ is assigned to Pr} ocessor \ k \\ 0 & otherwise \end{cases}$$

The total cost for processing the task is stated as

$$\sum_{l}\sum_{k}(wq_{ik}X_{ik} + \sum_{l}\sum_{j}(c_{ij}d_{kl})X_{ik}X_{jl})$$

The normalization constant w is used to scale the processing cost and the IPC cost to account for any difference in measuring units.

The task allocation algorithm was derived from a Branch and Bound (BB) method. To employ the BB technique, the allocation problem is represented by a search tree. The allocation decision represents a branching at the node corresponding to the given task. The algorithm was implemented for an Air Defense application.

Chu and Lan [2] proposed an algorithm that considers Precedence Relationship(PR), Inter Module Communication(IMC) and Accumulative Execution Time(AET) to search for minimum bottleneck assignment. In their model, the AET of a module running on a processor is the total execution time incurred by this module running on that processor during the mission i.e. the product of the number of times this module executes during the mission and the average time units for each execution on that processor. The Inter Module Communication between two modules is the product of the number of times they communicate and the average number of words exchanged, each time they communicate. They proposed the model of task allocation for Real Time Systems. The processor with the heaviest load, in a distributed system, is the one that causes the bottleneck. The processor load consists of the loads due to program module execution and Inter Module Communication. Therefore, both AET and IMC play important roles in module assignment and influence task response time. In their model, the algorithm consists of two phases. Phase I reduces J modules to G groups (G<J) which corresponds to a much smaller assignment tree for phase II. Each group generated at the end of phase I is a set of modules, which will be assigned as a single unit to a

processor. In phase II these groups are assigned to the processors such that the bottleneck (in the most heavily utilized processor) is minimized.

Ramakrisnan et al.[10] presented a refinement of the A* algorithm that can be used either to find optimal mappings or the final approximate mappings. The algorithm uses several heuristics based on the sum of communication costs for a task, the task's estimated mean processing cost, a combination of communication cost and the difference between the minimum and maximum processing costs for a task.

Price and Salama [11] describe heuristic for assigning precedence-constrained tasks to a network of identical processors with the first heuristic; the tasks are sorted in increasing order of communication and are interactively assigned so as to minimize total communication time. The second heuristic creates pairs of tasks that communicate, sorts the pairs in decreasing order of communication, and then groups the pairs into clusters. In third method, simulated annealing starts with a mapping and uses probability based functions to move towards an optimal mapping.

5.1.2 Graph Matching Approach to Allocation

Shen and Tsai [4] proposed a graph matching approach to solve the task allocation problem of a DCS. A cost function is proposed for evaluating the effectiveness of allocation. A new optimization criterion, called the minimax criterion, is also proposed based on which both minimization of IPC and balance of processor loading is achieved. Graphs are used to represent the module relationship of a given task and the processor structure of a distributed computing system. Module assignment to system processors is transferred into a type of graph matching, called weak homomorphism. The search of optimal task assignment is formulated as a state space search problem. It is then solved by the well-known A* algorithm, with proper heuristic information for speeding up the search.

The cost function is total turnaround time that is the sum of execution time and the communication time.

Although some constraints are included in the model, but some important constraints are ignored. DCS is assumed to be heterogeneous. The most important precedence relationship among the modules does not figure in their model.

5.1.3 Reliability Oriented Task Allocation

Reliability oriented task allocation model in redundant distributed system is proposed by Shatz and Wang [5]. Reliability oriented DCS are often desired for Real Time DCS, though reliability is an added advantage for any type of DCS. Hardware redundancy is a common technique to achieve reliability. Redundancy of different levels for both processors and links is considered in their model.

A Redundant Distributed System (RDS) of redundant level r can be thought of as being obtained from a non-redundant distributed system in the following manner. At every processing node "r" identical processors, processing the same job simultaneously, replace the single processor; and every link is replaced by "r" identical links.

Each module of a task executes on one of the processing nodes (therefore, executes on every one of the r processors at that node) and communicates with other modules of the task. The task allocation problem for an RDS can be stated as follows. Given a task consisting of m modules and an RDS with n processing nodes, allocate each of the m modules to one of the n processing nodes such that an appropriate objective function is optimized subject to constraints imposed by the environment.

Reliability of the DCS is defined as the probability that the task T can run successfully on the RDS during the mission under task assignment X.

The reliability expression of processing node P_k is derived as below.

$$R_k(T, X) = \exp(-\lambda_k \sum_{i=1}^{m} x_{ik} e_{ik}) \ldots\ldots\ldots \ldots\ldots ..(5.1)$$

λ_k is failure rate of node P_k

x_{ik} is value of assignment matrix X

e_{ik} is the Accumulative Execution Time (AET) of module mi on node P_k

Similarly the reliability of link l_{pq} is

$$r_{pq}(T, X) = \exp(-\lambda'_{pq} \sum_{j=1}^{m-1} \sum_{i=j+1}^{m} c(i,j,p,q) / w_{pq}) \dots \dots \dots (5.2)$$

λ'_{pq} is failure rate of link l_{pq}

$c(i,j,p,q)$ is a measure of IPC.

w_{pq} is transmission rate of link l_{pq}.

Thus the system reliability is

$$R^r(T, X) = \prod_{k=1}^{n} b \inf(r-1; R_k(T, X), r) \prod_{lpq} b \inf(r-1; r_{pq}(T, X), r) \dots \dots \dots (5.3)$$

binf( ) is the binomial function. The reliability function (5.3) is optimized in the model.

The RDS is heterogeneous, but other constraints such as memory, precedence are overlooked.

5.1.4 Load Balancing Task Allocation

Aloson and Cova [12] proposed a double-threshold policy called the 'high - low policy' for load balancing. The high -low policy uses two threshold values called 'high mark' and 'low mark', which divide the space of possible load states of a node into the three regions: over-loaded above the high-mark and low-mark values; normal-above the low-mark value and below the high-mark value and un-der loaded-below both values. The high-low policy guarantees a predefined level of performance to the node owners. It accounts for the overhead that the load balancing algorithm may incur in transferring and receiving a remote process. A process will not be transferred to another node unless it is worthwhile, and a remote process will not be accepted unless there is enough excess capacity to handle it.

Gao et. al. [13] proposed a class of load balancing algorithms for systems consisting of identical processors. It assumes that each processor periodically informs all other processors of its load. Based on this load estimate, the job dispatcher on each processor may decide for migration of some tasks to other processors. Gao's algorithm balances either the average arrival rate or the amount of unfinished work on each host. This scheme has a high overhead because the load estimation step requires extensive mathematical calculations and the precise numerical load of each processor has to be sent to every other processor in the network.

Ni .et al. [14] proposed a drafting algorithm for task migration. It is observed that the processors do not need to communicate precise numerical load measurements for a dynamic load balancing scheme to be effective. Therefore, a 3-level (heavy, normal and light) system is used. A processor communicates only with a group of processors called the candidate processors. A lightly loaded processor requests a heavily loaded candidate processor to send a bid for task migration. A task is migrated from the heavily loaded processor after the lightly loaded processor has sent a select message to it. Since broadcasting the load at every change in load level may create too much communication traffic (and hence a longer response time), piggybacking is recommended to reduce the number of messages. However, unless a processor has every other processor in the system as its candidate processor, a lightly loaded processor may not notice the existence of some heavily loaded processor. Therefore, this scheme guarantees that every possible task migration will be carried out only when all load messages are broadcasted to every other processor in the system.

Lin and Keller [15] proposed a gradient model for load balancing algorithm for a class of large diameter multiprocessor systems. Task migration from heavily loaded processors is governed by a pressure gradient indirectly established by requests from nearby idle processors. Global balance is achieved by successive migration of tasks to underutilized processors. However, a task may be migrated many times without making progress as the load of the processors in the system changes.

Bryant and Finkel [12] proposed the method pairing policy for load balancing to reduce the variance of loads only between pairs of nodes of the system. In this method, two nodes that differ greatly in load are temporarily paired with each other and the load balancing operation is carried out between the nodes belonging to the same pair by migrating one or more processes from the more heavily loaded node to the other node. Several node pairs may exist simultaneously in the system. A node only tries to find a partner if it has at least two processes, otherwise migration from this node is never reasonable. This kind of algorithm makes great migration delay and IPC costs.

Woldspurger et al [16] proposed policy for load balancing by bidding process where each node in the network is responsible for two roles: the manager and the contractor. The manager represents a node having a process in need of a location to execute, and the contractor represents a node that is able to accept remote processes. Here a single node takes on both these roles and no nodes are strictly managers or contractors alone. To select a node for its process, the manager broadcasts a request-for-bids message to all other nodes in the system. Upon receiving this message, the contractor nodes return bids to the manager node. The main two drawbacks of bidding algorithms are that they create a great deal of communication overhead and it is very difficult to decide a good pricing policy. Both factors call for a proper choice of the amount and type of information exchanged during bidding.

The paper [17] indicates that the goal of solution is to balance the load among the processors in the system in some way. The solution actually fits into the static, optimal and queuing theoretic class. It minimizes the execution of the entire program to maximize performance and the algorithm is derived from results in Markov decision theory.

5.2 Limitations of Earlier Models

Many other models in the literature are more or less of the same nature as discussed above. These models suffer due to one or more realistic limitations that do not allow these models to be implemented in the design of the Distributed Operating System. The model presented in the section 5.1.1, considers the memory limitations at each processing node. It considers other application specific constraints viz. task preference, task exclusion and task redundancy. These models lack some very important constraints e.g. precedence of the modules, maximum no. of modules that can be assigned to each processing nodes etc.

Model quoted in section 5.1.2 incorporates some realistic assumptions, though it assumes no precedence relationship among the modules of the task to avoid processor idleness. They have used the graph matching approach to map the task graph onto the processor graph. A heuristic is used to find a weak homomorphism from task graph to processor graph. Their lower bound estimate h(n) has chances of further improvement[19].

Reliability oriented task allocation, as stated in section 5.1.3, is advocated for such distributed computing system where reliability is of prime concern. Such systems are often required in missile projection or other real time systems. Though the model presented does not consider the real time distributed computing systems, yet it incorporates some realistic constraints. It includes constraints of memory, processing capacity and bounds for completion time, but the precedence is overlooked again. It takes AET (Accumulative Execution Time) in their model, which is just difficult to estimate. Their cost function is based on reliability computation, which is an easy expression to compute.

A number of load balancing task allocation models, discussed in sec. 5.1.4, do suffer with one or more limitations. In fact, it is very difficult to consider all the constraints to furnish a realistic model of task allocation. Thus the task allocation problem has to simplify the assumptions and is to find an optimal solution in presence of all the constraints.

We have developed some realistic models, considering the existing models and their simplifying assumptions, which take up the realistic constraints into consideration for the purpose of the task allocation in this book.

5.3 Precedence Constrained Task Allocation

The following proposition considers the precedence, an important characteristic of time relationship among the modules of a task, apart from round-robin scheduling on the individual processing nodes [6].

The task allocation policies for the DCS aim mostly at minimizing the turnaround time of a task. The following parameters impose constraints under which the algorithms have to work. First of all, the participating nodes of the DCS must be evenly loaded during the course of execution of the tasks. The modules of a task may require different amount of memory and demand varying execution time, and hence the time quantum chosen for round robin scheduling of processes are important candidate for consideration. The interconnection topology of the DCS also plays an important role as communicating modules must reside on the nodes that are connected and at the same time communication distance of these nodes must not be large because of the obvious reasons. In case of heterogeneous DCS the functional limitations of the nodes need also to be considered.

The precedence relationship among the modules of the task can be analyzed to identify such modules that may coexist on one and the same node as the sequential execution of concurrent module sets may allow this [2].

The model proposed here considers the precedence relationship along with the round robin scheduling of individual processors, and provides a solution for allocation as shown by some examples.

5.3.1 The Allocation Model

To prepare a mathematical model, the following parameters are relevant

i) The cost function,

ii) The constraints, and

iii) An algorithm that looks for an optimal cost allocation

The cost function is in terms of time unit and is the sum of the module execution time and InterModule Communication time (IMC). Processing cost e_{ij} represent the execution time to execute module m_i on processor p_j. The Inter Module Communication at the node p_k can be calculated as

$$\sum_l \sum_j (c_{ij} * d_{kl}) x_{ik} x_{jl} \ .... \ .... \ ...(5.4)$$

Where c_{ij} is the total communication between module m_i and m_j, X_{ik} is the assignment matrix and x_{ik} (element of X_{ik}) is defined as

$$x_{ik} = \begin{cases} 1 & if \ module \ m_i \ is \ assigned \ to \ node \ p_k \ , \\ 0 & otherwise; \end{cases}$$

d_{kl} is the distance between the processing nodes p_k and p_l Obviously if $p_k = p_l$ then $d_{kl} = 0$ and IMC cost becomes zero.

The total cost for processing a task on a DCS will become

$$\sum_i \sum_k (w * e_{ik} * x_{ik} + \sum_l \sum_j (c_{ij} * d_{kl}) x_{ik} x_{jl}) \dots\dots\dots\dots\dots\dots(5.5)$$

The normalization constant w is used to scale processing cost and the IPC cost to adjust the difference in measuring units. The abovesaid formula has been mentioned by Richard, Lee & Tsuchilya [1].

We have modified the formulae considering the individual processing node scheduling and have incorporated it in the cost function. It assumes that the processors of the DCS are scheduled in a round-robin fashion of time quantum q. For an incoming module mi on processor p_k at any time the turnaround will be

$$n_k \times q + e_{ik}$$

Where n_k is the number of modules already allocated on processor p_k.

Thus the total allocation cost of a module m_i on processor p_k will become

$$n_k * q + w * e_{ik} * x_{ik} + \sum_l \sum_j (c_{ij} * d_{kl}) x_{ik} x_{jl} \dots\dots\dots\dots\dots\dots(5.6)$$

While allocating a module on processing nodes this cost function will be considered.

5.3.2 Constraints

The constraint introduced in this model is memory limitation of the processing

nodes. The other constraint, precedence is being considered in the beginning itself

and it limits the allocation.

If M_i is the amount of memory required by module mi and S_k represents the

memory capacity of processor p_k then allocation of any new module must satisfy

the following constraint.

$$\sum_{i=1}^{n+1} M_i x_{ik} \le S_k$$

n modules are already allocated on P_k

5.3.3 The Algorithm Derivation

Some crucial issues in deriving the algorithm are the priority of the modules

and their (module's) arrangement.

Priority

The modules will have the priority of their execution according to their prece-

dence. Root node of the task graph will have the highest priority. The priority of

other nodes in the graph will be calculated according to their level in the graph.

Ties have to be resolved for the nodes of the same level. Murthy, Murthy &

Sreenivas suggested that the node with the highest value of MAX (incident edges) should get the highest priority [20].

Modules Arrangement

The modules of the task graph are arranged in a list according to their priority. The highest priority module (i.e. root node of the task graph) will be at the front of the list. This scheduling is known as list scheduling and has been discussed in [21]. The updation of the list will take place during the allocation. In beginning the list will be of maximum length, subsequently will be reduced and finally be empty. The empty list indicates the complete task allocation.

Each processing node needs to maintain a process table (job table), which is to be referred to obtain the earlier allocation. After the allocation, the process table is to be modified (updated). Maintenance of process table is very important for the purpose of execution as per allocation.

5.3.4 Algorithm

1. Compute priority of the modules.

2. Order modules in a list with the highest priority module in front.

3. While (list is not empty) do

   begin

get a module mi from front of the list

   for each processor p_k do

      Calculate cost of assignment of mi on pk and arrange it in a list

      COST with   processor index.

   Sort the list COST in descending order.

CHECK: The front of COST is min(COST) allocation.

   If it satisfies memory requirement of module on the processor

   then

            assign it;

   otherwise

      begin

            remove it from COST;

            go to CHECK;

      end;

   Modify the Status table of processors.

   Remove the module from the list.

end.

5.3.5 Examples

Number of examples for the different network topologies has been illustrated, using above algorithm. These examples give the view of allocation and load balancing. The time quantum of round robin scheduling, of the processing nodes, is assumed to be unity.

Example1

In our first example, we have taken 4 modules of a task and three processing nodes. The processor graph and task graph are given in fig. 5.1.

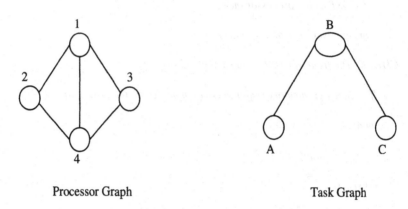

Processor Graph   Task Graph

Fig. 5.1. Task and Processor Graphs

The IMC and execution time matrices are as follows.

c_{ij}	1	2	3	4
1	0	20	0	40
2	20	0	5	70
3	0	5	0	35
4	40	70	35	0

e_{ik}	A	B	C
1	10	20	30
2	40	5	10
3	70	50	80
4	50	80	20

After executing the algorithm the assignment is as follows

$$1 \rightarrow A$$
$$2 \rightarrow C$$
$$3 \rightarrow B$$
$$4 \rightarrow C$$

Turn-around time comes to be 95 time unit, whereas on sequential machine the average turn-around time is 152.

Example 2

For the same task graph (same IMC) but different processor graph with execution time matrix

e_{ik}	A	B	C	D
1	0	20	30	25
2	40	5	10	15
3	50	10	75	20
4	30	40	25	40

and topology

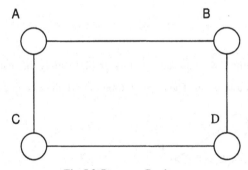

Fig. 5.2. Processor Graph

The assignment is

$$1 \to A$$
$$2 \to B$$
$$3 \to B$$
$$4 \to B$$

The turn-around time in this case is 80 time unit. On sequential machine the
average turn-around time is 109.

Example 3

In another example we have changed the topology to be STAR but with the same IMC and execution time matrix, the assignment remains the same (the turn-around also remains the same).

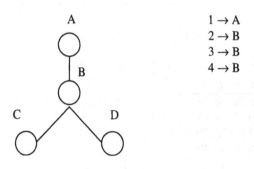

$1 \rightarrow A$
$2 \rightarrow B$
$3 \rightarrow B$
$4 \rightarrow B$

Fig.5.3. Processor Graph

Example 4

In the last example we expanded the task graph to study the real impact of our algorithm on task allocation. The network topology for the example is SQUARE.

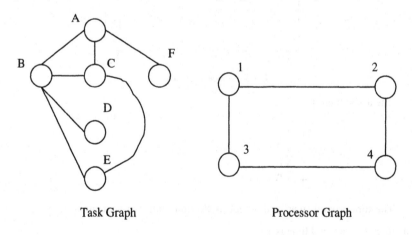

Task Graph   Processor Graph

Fig. 5.4. Processor Graph

To keep the allocation simple, we assumed the execution time of each module on each processor as well the communication among the module to be the same.

$$e_{ik} = 5, \quad c_{ij} = 5, \quad i \neq j.$$

The allocation that took place is

$$A, B, C \rightarrow 1$$
$$F \qquad \rightarrow 2$$
$$D, E \quad \rightarrow 3$$

It is evident that a dense task graph (i.e. consisting of more number of modules with precedence) utilizes all the processors and allocation appears to be more meaningful.

Given a set of task graphs for allocation, by this algorithm, a good utilization of all the nodes of a DCS can be made as multiprogramming of the processors has also been considered.

5.4 IMC Cost Reduction using Fuzzy Logic

All the reported TA algorithms assume that a meaningful and proper partitioning of the task has created the modules of a given task [7]. The following proposition shows a method of meaningful partitioning of a given task into modules having as its objective the reduction of IMC, as IMC is the main contributor to the time taken by a task when executed on a system.

Inter Module Communication in distributed computing systems is performed by the communication links directly or through intermediate nodes. A sizeable fraction of the total time is experienced in intermodule communication. Communication penalty (CP), experienced by the network, is defined as the ratio [22]

$$CP = T_{total} / T_{comp}$$

Where T_{total} is the time required by the algorithm to solve the given problem and T_{comp} is the time attributed to computation. If T_{comn} is the time involved in communication among different modules of the task, then

$$T_{total} = T_{comp} + T_{comn}$$

As obvious, less communication will reduce the communication penalty.

The model proposed below discusses the reduction in communication cost using fuzzy logic.

5.4.1 The Fuzzy Approach

Fuzzy approach is based on the premise that the key elements in human thinking are not numbers but can be approximated to tables of fuzzy sets, in which the transition from membership to nonmembership is gradual rather than abrupt. Much of the logic behind human reasoning is not the traditional two valued or even multivalued logic but logic with fuzzy rules of inference.

Fuzzy set introduces vagueness by eliminating the sharp boundary dividing members of the class from nonmembers. A fuzzy set can be defined mathematically by assigning to each possible individual in the universe of discourse a value representing its grade of membership in the fuzzy set. This grade corresponds to the degree to which that individual is similar to or compatible with the concept represented by the fuzzy set. These membership grades are represented by real values ranging in the closed interval between 0 and 1 [23].

5.4.2 The Cost Reduction Model

Communication between the modules of the task that are allocated on the distant nodes will increase the communication cost. Obviously, the modules that are allocated on the same node will incur zero communication cost. This requirement may allocate all the modules of the task on the same node to reduce overall communication cost, which will result in load imbalance. The object is to only allocate highly communicating module on the same or neighbor nodes. To determine high communicating and low communicating modules, fuzzy concept is explored.

A set of samples whose membership values are known may be used to test the function in question. This set may constitute the ideal element or the prototype. The proposed model considers that there is a prototype or an ideal element for a class, and the degree of membership of each element is directly related to the similarity of the element to the ideal.

Let $d(X,C)$ be the distance of an element with feature vector $X=[x1,x2,...xN]$ from the prototype vector $C=[c1,c2,...cN]$ of a class, where $d(X,C) \geq 0$.

Two simple forms of membership functions are [24]

$$\mu = \frac{1}{1 + d(X,C)} \dots\dots\dots(5.7)$$

$$\mu = \frac{1}{\exp(d(X,C))} \dots\dots\dots(5.8)$$

The communication cost for the task allocation in DCS is $c_{ij}*d_{kl}$, where c_{ij} is the communication between modules m_i and m_j and d_{kl} is the distance between processors p_k and p_l. The cost is effective if m_i and m_j are allocated on p_k and p_l respectively.

The fuzzyfication can be applied on both c_{ij} and d_{kl} by considering how large c_{ij} and how long d_{kl} is. The prototype for c_{ij} is the largest possible communication between any two modules. Diameter of the network is the prototype for applying the membership function on d_{kl}.

For our model, the maximum communication C, between any two modules, is the ideal element. Membership function for the communication is

$$\mu(c_{ij}) = \frac{1}{1 + diff(c_{ij},C)} \dots\dots(5.9)$$

Where diff $(c_{ij},C) = |\ c_{ij}-C\ |$

Similarly D, the diameter of the network, is the ideal element for the nodal distance. The membership function for the distance is

$$\mu(d_{kl}) = \frac{1}{1 + diff(d_{kl}, D)} \ldots\ldots(5.10)$$

Where diff $(d_{kl}, D) = |d_{kl} - D|$

The other membership fuzzy equations (5.8) can also be applied in (5.9) and (5.10).

Thus, this chapter discusses some representative models and their limitations in sec. 5.1 and 5.2 respectively. A precedence constrained task allocation model is proposed in sec. 5.3. Precedence is an essential requirement of a task and is to be given due consideration, that has been ignored in earlier models (sec. 5.1).

Furthermore an IMC cost reduction model is proposed in section 5.4. This is a prerequisite for any TA models and can be incorporated easily in any model.

BIBLIOGRAPHY

[1] Pereng-yi RICHARD MA, Edward Y.S.LEE, Masahiro TSUCHIYA, "A Task Allocation Model for Distributed Computing Systems", *IEEE Trans. on Computer*, Vol.C-31, No. 1, January 1982, pp. 41-47.
[2] W.W.Chu, M.T.Lan, "Task Allocation and Precedence Relations for Distributed Real-Time Systems", *IEEE Trans. on Computer*, Vol. C-36, No.6, June 1987, pp. 667-679.
[3] C.C.Price, S. Krishnaprasad, "Software Allocation Model for Distributed Computing Systems", *Proceedings of 4th Int. Conference Distributed Computing Systems*, May 1984, pp.40-48.
[4] Chien-Chung Shen, Wen-Hsiang Tsai, "A Graph Matching Approach to Optimal Task Assignment in Distributed Computing Systems using a Minimax Criterion", *IEEE Trans. on Computers*, Vol. C-34, No.3, March 1985, pp. 197-203.

[5]Sol. M. Shatz, Jia-Ping Wang, "Models & Algorithm for Reliability-Oriented Task allocation in Redundant Distributed Computer Systems", *IEEE Trans. on Parallel and Distributed
Systems*, Vol.38, No. 1, April 1989, pp. 16-27.

[6]D.P.Vidyarthi, A.K.Tripathi, "Precedence Constrained Task Allocation in Distributed Computing System", *Int. J. of High Speed Computing*, Vol. 8, No. 1, 1996, pp. 47-55.

[7]D.P.Vidyarthi, A.K.Tripathi, " A Fuzzy IMC Cost Reduction Model for Task Allocation in
Distributed Computing Systems", *Proceedings of the Fifth International Symposium on
Methods and Models in Automation and Robotics*, Vol. 2, Szczecin, Poland, August 1998, pp.
719-721.

[8]T.C.K. Chou, J.A.Abraham, "Load Balancing in Distributed Systems", *IEEE Trans. on Software Engg.*, Vol. SE-8, No.4, July 1982, pp.401-412.

[9]A.S. Tanenbaum, *Computer Networks*, Englewood cliff, NJ: Prentice-Hall, 1994.

[10]S.Ramakrishnan, I.H.Cho and L.Dunning, "A Close Look at Task Assignment in Distributed
Systems", *INFOCOM'91, IEEE*, April 1991, pp.806-812.

[11]C.C.Price and M.A.Salama, "Scheduling of Precedence-constrained Tasks on multiprocessors", *The Computer Journal*, Vol. 33, March 1990, pp. 219-229.

[12]R.Aloson and L.L.Cova, "Sharing Jobs among Independently owned Processors", *Proceedings of the 8th International Conference Systems, IEEE*, New York, June 1988, pp.282-288.

[13]C.Gao, J.W.S.Liu and M.Railey, "Load Balancing Algorithms in Homogeneous Distributed
Systems", *Proceedings of the 1984 International Conference on Parallel Processing*, CRC
Press, Bocaraton, Fl, August 1984, pp.302-306.

[14]L.M.Ni, C.W.Xu and T.B.Gendreau, "A Distributed Drafting Algorithm for Load Balancing," *IEEE Trans. on Software Engg.*, Vol.SE-13, No.10, October1985, pp.1153-1161.

[15]F.C.Lin and R.M.Keller, "The Gradient Model Load Balancing Method", *IEEE Trans. on
Software Engg.* Vol. SE-13, No.1, Jan. 1988, pp.32-38.

[16]R.M.Bryant and R.A. Finkel, "A Stable distributed Scheduling Algorithm", *Proceedings of
the 2nd International Conference on Distributed Computing Systems, IEEE*, New York, April
1981, pp.314-323.

[17]C.A.Waldspurger, T.Hogg, A.B.Huberman, J.O.Kephart and W.S.Stonetta, "Spawn: A Distributed Computational Economy", *IEEE Trans. on Software Engg.*, Vol.18, No.2, Feb.1992,
pp.103-117.

[18]T.C.K. Chou and J.A.Abraham, "Load Balancing in Distributed Systems", *IEEE Trans. on
Software Engg.*, Vol. SE-8, no.4, July 1982, pp.401-412.

[19]E. Horowitz, S. Sahni, S. Rajasekaran, *Computer Algorithms*, W.H.Freeman and Company,
1997.

[20]C. Siva Ram Murthy, K.N.Balsubramaniya Murthy, A.Sreenivas, "Scheduling of Precedence-Constrained Parallel Program Tasks on Multiprocessors", *Microprocessing and
Microprogramming*, Vol. 36, 1992/93, pp. 93-104.

[21]C.Siva Ram Murthy, V. Rajaraman, "Task Assignment in Multiprocessor Systems", *Microprocessing and Microprogramming*, Vol.26, 1989, pp. 63-71.

[22]D.P.Bertsekas, J.H.Tsitsiklis, *Parallel and Distributed Computation*, Prentice Hall International, 1989.

[23]G.J.Klir, T.A.Folger, *Fuzzy sets: Uncertainty and Information*, Prentice Hall International,
1997.

[24]Sankar K. Pal, Dwijesh K. Dutta Majumdar, *Fuzzy Mathematical Approach to Pattern Recognition*, Wiley Eastern Limited, 1986.

CHAPTER 6

Load Balancing Task Allocation (LBTA)

This Chapter discusses briefly the various existing load balancing strategies and proposes the model of Load Balancing Task Allocation (LBTA) strategy. The LBTA strategy, incurs little communication and no migration overhead in nature. Issues in considering and designing of LBTA strategy for a single task have been presented. The "load" of a processing node for a single task has been presented. Issues considering multiple tasks and their implications for a DCS have been identified. The "load" of each processing node for LBTA strategy, considering multiple tasks for a DCS has been formulated and discussed in this chapter. A data structure called Global Table (GT) is used for the multiple tasks to keep track of allocation and load on each processing node. Some known load balancing strategies have been presented in sec.6.1. Researchers have studied "Load Balancing" and "Task Allocation" problem separately. We have considered here a combined approach with a new strategy namely "Load balancing Task allocation (LBTA)". This strategy ensures better performance characteristics of a DCS like maximization of throughput. The model of the LBTA strategy has been elaborated from Sec. 6.2 onwards.

6.1 Known Load Balancing Strategies

Load balancing strategies in DCS fall into two categories: static and dynamic. Static load balancing computes information such as execution time, execution cost etc. from the task before load distribution. Dynamic load balancing uses little or almost nil priori task information and must satisfy changing requirements by making task distribution decisions during runtime. For certain tasks, dynamic load balancing is preferable because then the problem's variable behavior matches more closely with available heterogeneous computational resources. But dynamic load balancing incurs communication and migration overhead because of its heterogeneous topology dependent architecture [1]. Researchers have proposed several load balancing strategies. We present a brief description of the strategies in the following section. Our "Load Balancing (Task Allocation)" strategy follows this discussion.

1) The Gradient model

In this strategy each processing node interacts only with its immediate neighbors. A lightly loaded processor informs of its state to other processors in the DCS. The overloaded nodes respond by sending a portion of their load to the nearest lightly loaded processor in the system. In DCS when execution begins, every processor computes its total load. This strategy uses double threshold policy with three regions; lightly, heavily or moderately loaded. A processing node having a total load below the low water mark is considered lightly loaded. One that exceeds the high water mark is heavily and one where the total load is in between is moderately loaded [2].

2) The Sender-Initiated (SI) Strategy

Here, an overloaded processing node (sender) trying to send a task to an under-loaded processing node called receiver to initiate load distribution. In [1], there are three fully distributed sender-initiated strategies discussed. The difference in these strategies is the policy used in locating the processing nodes to transfer or receive tasks. In the first strategy, the network simply transfers a task to a randomly selected processor without any information exchange between the processors aiding the decision. The second strategy is similar but with the introduction of a threshold value to prevent tasks from being transferred to an overloaded processor. In the third strategy, the network polls a number of randomly selected processing nodes and compare their load sizes. The network then transfers the task to a processor with the smallest load.

3) The Receiver Initiated (RI) Strategy

The RI strategy is like the converse of the SI strategy. Here, receiver initiates the load balancing rather than sender in SI. An under-loaded (receiver) node tries to get tasks from an overloaded node (sender). In this strategy, the network identifies, as the receiver, a node whose load size falls below the threshold value. Then it either broadcasts a message indicating its willingness to receive processes for executing or randomly probes the other nodes one by one to find a heavily loaded node that can send one or more of its tasks to it. A node is able to transfer one of its tasks only if it does not reduce its load below the threshold value. In the broadcast method, a suitable node is found as soon as the receiver node receives reply message from the other nodes. Otherwise a random probing continues until either a node is found from which a tasks can be obtained or the number of probes continues up to a limit [1].

4) The Central Task Dispatcher Strategy

In this strategy, a processing node acts as a central job dispatcher, which makes load balancing decisions based on global state information. The strategies discussed above which use local state information are different from this strategy. The dispatcher keeps all the information containing the number of waiting tasks in each processor. The central task dispatcher keeps the information whenever a task arrives or departs from a node. Each node notifies the task dispatcher whenever its state changes, rather than the job dispatcher collecting such information periodically [3]. According to this information the most heavily loaded processor are requested to transfer loads for the requesting lightly loaded nodes. The amount of overhead depends on the way the global information is collected.

5) The Prediction Based Strategy

This strategy uses some predicted process requirements for achieving load balancing. In the prediction based strategy proposed in [4], some predictions have been demonstrated like prediction of CPUs, memory and I/O requirements of a process, before its execution. Statistical pattern–recognition method has been used for this purpose. However, even though the predicted values are close to the actual ones, this strategy incurs significant computation overheads. Other researchers have proposed a strategy that uses task transfer probabilities to predict a processor's load requirements [4]. Here the network can estimate a processor's load at any time without querying that node.

We have proposed the following strategy for load balancing.

6.2 Issues of LBTA Strategy

The main goal of this strategy is to assign tasks to different nodes so that it is almost evenly distributed amongst the node. Tasks are partitioned into modules and the modules of different multiple tasks can be allocated to the different nodes of the given DCS by minimizing the turn around time of the task. This LBTA strategy incurs a little communication and no migration overhead.

In a DCS, the nodes may share some specified load according to their memory capacity constraints considering the arrival of multiple tasks. Most of the algorithms proposed in the literature considered task allocation and load balancing as a separate issue. But, in this strategy, we have considered both (multiple task allocation that keeps balancing the load across the processing nodes) together. An arrival of tasks (multiple disjoint tasks) with their modules can be accepted by individual nodes of the DCS with their memory capacities. Factually the task allocation problem must consider the load balancing as its own essential feature. A body of literature [2, 5-9] has been proposed that discusses the load balancing problem separately.

Another related area is the task migration that actuates movements of tasks across the processing nodes to achieve balance of the load. An alternative solution may provide task allocation taking into consideration the existing allocation and as and when the modules of tasks finish off and leave the DCS, the load balancing activity may be initiated by the system. But it may cause unnecessarily migration overhead, which may impact adversely in maximizing throughput of a DCS.

The LBTA problem in a DCS is defined as the mapping of the task graph to the processor graph so as to optimize some characteristic parameters. A real LBTA strategy has to consider various issues while mapping task graph to processor graph. The issues are:

a)   Precedence constraints among the modules of the task,

b)   Communication among the modules,

c)   Functionality of the processing nodes of DCS,

d)   Interconnection networks of DCS,

e)   Entry and exit of the tasks in a dynamic fashion,

f)   Balancing the load of the processors while allocating the tasks, and

g)   Use the concept of a Global Table (GT) to keep track the updated information of allocation.

6.3   The LBTA Solution

A task consists of number of modules and is represented by a Task Graph (TG). The TG depicts the precedence and communication requirements amongst the modules. The interconnection of nodes in a DCS is represented by another graph known as Processor Graph (PG). The problem of allocation is to map TG onto PG [10].

A task submitted into a DCS is partitioned into the suitable modules and then these modules are allocated to the processors [10]. Each task can be represented by a Task Graph $TG=(V_t, E_t)$, where (1) V_t is a set of vertices, each of which represents a module of the task $\{\ m_1,\ m_2,.....m_n\ \}$ and (2) $E_t \subseteq V_t \times V_t$ is a set of edges each of which represents the IMC between the two modules at the end of the edge. We can also represent the network of processors $\{\ p_1,\ p_2,\ ......\ p_n\ \}$ in a DCS as a Processor Graph $PG=(V_p, E_p)$; where vertices represent the processors and the edges represent the communication links between processors.

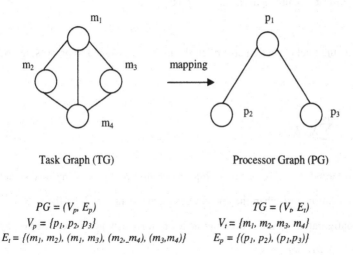

Task Graph (TG)   Processor Graph (PG)

$$PG = (V_p, E_p)$$
$$V_p = \{p_1, p_2, p_3\}$$
$$E_t = \{(m_1, m_2), (m_1, m_3), (m_2, m_4), (m_3, m_4)\}$$

$$TG = (V_t, E_t)$$
$$V_t = \{m_1, m_2, m_3, m_4\}$$
$$E_p = \{(p_1, p_2), (p_1, p_3)\}$$

Fig. 6.1. Mapping of TG to PG

The goal is to allocate task graph (TG) to a network of processors in a DCS (i.e. to PG) to achieve the minimum turn-around time of a task. This problem can be considered as mapping problem [10] using relaxed assumptions -such that as arbitrary computation and task-graph communication requirements and a network of heterogeneous processors connected by an arbitrary topology.

If there are m modules, $1 \leq i \leq m$ in a task and n processing nodes $1 \leq p \leq n$, in a DCS, a n by m matrix M which is called assignment matrix, can be used to represent the mapping, where

$$Mip = \begin{cases} 1 & \text{if module } m_i \text{ is assigned to processing node } p, \\ 0 & \text{otherwise}. \end{cases}$$

We can execute a module m_i of the task from the set V_t on any one of the processing nodes. Each module has an associated execution cost, where X_{ip} is the execution cost of module m_i of the task on processor p.

Thus, the total execution cost of all the modules assigned to processing node p is

$$\sum_{i=1}^{m} X_{ip}.M_{ip} \qquad\qquad 6.1$$

Two modules, m_i and m_j, executing on two different processing nodes, incur a communication cost when they need to exchange data. Let L be the interconnection configuration of the processing nodes in a DCS which is represented by an n×n link matrix, where

$$L_{pq} = \begin{cases} 1 & \text{if processing node } p \text{ and } q \text{ are directly connected}, \\ 0 & \text{otherwise}. \end{cases}$$

Task mapping will assign two communicating modules to the same processors or to two different connected processors. A matrix represents communication among concurrent modules of a task, if they reside on two different processing nodes. Let C_{ij} be an m by m matrix representing the IMC cost of modules of a task.

Thus, the total communication cost for all the modules of a task in processing node p is [11]

$$\sum_{\substack{q=1 \\ q \neq p}}^{n} \sum_{i=1}^{m} \sum_{\substack{j=1 \\ j \neq i}}^{m} \left(C_{ij}.M_{ip}.M_{jp}.L_{pq}\right) \qquad 6.2$$

Here, in the above equation, M_{jq} indicates that whether module m_j is assigned to processing node q.

6.4   Loads in LBTA for Single Task

A processor's load comprises of all the execution and communication costs associated with its assigned modules [11]. The LBTA problem must find a mapping of the set of m modules of a task to n processors that will minimize the turn around time of a task.

The following equation then gives the 'load' on processor p for a single task:

$$\sum_{i=1}^{m} X_{ip}.M_{ip} + \sum_{\substack{q=1 \\ q \neq p}}^{n} \sum_{i=1}^{m} \sum_{\substack{j=1 \\ j \neq i}}^{m} \left(C_{ij}.M_{ip}.M_{jq}.L_{pq}\right) \qquad 6.3$$

The first part of the equation is the total execution cost of the modules allocated to p_i. The second part is the communication overhead on p. M_{ip} and M_{jq} indicate that module m_i and m_j are assigned to two different processors (p and q), and L_{pq} indicates the connectivity of the processors p and q.

To allocate the modules optimally so that no processor becomes overloaded, we need to compute the load on each of the n processing nodes. Here we assume that the matrix C & X are for a task and for every task these matrices will be different.

Several task allocation algorithms for DCSs have been reported in the literature [10-17]. These algorithms consider the execution time of different modules of a single task, executing on different processing nodes. The assignment problem must actually try to maximize the throughput of the system by allocating modules onto processing nodes so as to minimize the time taken, considering the IPC overhead. The assumptions of fixed execution time of a module on a particular processor can be valid if only one module is assigned to a particular processing node. The number of tasks is usually substantive, but these algorithms consider assignment of the modules of a single task to various processing nodes. In reality, a DCS facilitates concurrent execution of modules belonging to various unrelated tasks. The modules of any particular task, having IMC, do cooperatively execute and do not depend on the modules of the other tasks. This leads to the situation wherein a processing node may be assigned modules belonging to different tasks. It is to mention that the real issue of task allocation must not ignore the possibility of multiple module assignment of various tasks to the processing nodes in a dynamic fashion. So the task allocation problem must be reformulated. It is very much essential to do so because finally these task allocation algorithms are to be integrated to become a part of the distributed operating system.

6.5 Loads in LBTA for Multiple Tasks

It is to mention that the real model of LBTA must not ignore the possibility of module assignment of multiple tasks to the processing nodes of a DCS, in a dynamic fashion. We hereby wish to assert that the problem, solved by the methods proposed in the literature, must be reformulated to accommodate certain real issues as discussed above. It may be true that consideration of all the issues, in their entirety, may not be feasible. The newer models may include one or two important issues to begin with. It is very much essential to do so because finally these task allocation algorithms have to get integrated to become a part of the distributed computing systems.

We have modified the equation 6.3 for the multiple tasks. The LBTA problem must find a mapping of the set of m modules of k tasks to n processors that will minimize turn around time of all the tasks taken together.

Let, there be a set of n processing nodes in a DCS i.e. $P=\{ p_1, p_2,.....,p_n \}$,
a set of k tasks $T=\{ T_1, T_2,.....,T_k \}$,
every task T_i has a set of modules $m_i=\{m_1,m_2,.....,m\mid_{mi}\mid\}$
where, $\mid_{mi}\mid$ is the number of elements in the set m_i.
and the total number of modules of all the k tasks be

$$ m = \sum_{i=1}^{k} \mid m_i \mid $$

where, $\mid m_i \mid$ is the number of modules of ith task.

Task mapping, or assignment to processors, is given by a matrix M, where

$$Milp = \begin{cases} 1 & \text{if module } mi \text{ of task } l \text{ is assigned to processing node } p \\ 0 & \text{otherwise} \end{cases}$$

The following equation then gives the 'load' on processor p for multiple tasks:

$$\sum_{l=1}^{k}\sum_{i=1}^{m_i} X_{ilp}.M_{ilp} + \sum_{\substack{q=1 \\ q \neq p}}^{n} \sum_{l=1}^{k}\sum_{i=1}^{m_i}\sum_{\substack{j=1 \\ j \neq i}}^{m} C_{ijl}.M_{ilp}.M_{jlq}.L_{pq} \qquad 6.4$$

The first part of the equation 3.4 is the total execution cost of the modules of task l allocated to p. The second part is the communication overhead on p. M_{ilp} and M_{jlq} indicate that modules m_i and m_j of task l are assigned to two different processors (p and q), and L_{pq} indicates the connectivity of the processors p and q.

To allocate the modules optimally so that no processor becomes overloaded, the load on each of the n processing nodes needs to be computed. By finding the processor with heaviest load, the optimal assignment out of all possible assignments will allot the minimum load to the heaviest loaded processor. Here, it is assumed that the matrix C & X are for task l and for every task these matrices may be different.

A DCS receives a number of tasks, each consisting of various modules, from time to time. Similarly various modules of a task or the whole task itself with all their modules, may quit the DCS after successful completion or due to various other system policy decisions. It should be noticeable that due to these frequent ins and outs some nodes may become lightly loaded whereas others may remain heavily loaded. Thus a fundamental problem of DCS is the effective allocation of tasks onto nodes in order to achieve a balanced performance. Load balancing addresses this problem directly, providing a self-scheduling mechanism, by which the DCS can allocate a large number of tasks onto multiple nodes automatically

and efficiently. The purpose of load balancing is to promote better processor utili-

zation, greater throughput and faster response times [18].

BIBLIOGRAPHY

[1]P.K.K.Loh, W.J.Hsu, C Wentong and N. Sriskanthan, "How Network Topology Affects Dynamic Load Balancing," *IEEE Parallel and Distributed Technology*, Fall 1996, pp. 25-35.
[2]F.C.Lin and R.M.Keller, "The Gradient Model Load Balancing Method," *IEEE Trans. Software Engg.* Vol. SE-13, No.1, Jan. 1988, pp.32-38.
[3]H.C.Lin and C.S. Raghavendra, "A Dynamic Load Balancing Policy with Central Job   Dispatcher (LBC)," *IEEE Trans. Software Engg.* , Vol.18, No.2, February 1992, pp.148-158.
[4]K.K.Goswami, M.Devarakonda, and R.K.Iyer, "Prediction Based Dynamic Load Sharing
   Heuristics ," *IEEE Trans. Parallel and Distributed Systems*, Vol.4, No.6, June 1993, pp. 638-
   648.
[5]A.B.Tucker, Jr., *The Computer Science and Engineering Handbook*, CRC Press, 1997.
[6]Edwind S.H. Hou, N. Ansari and H.Ren, "A Genetic Algorithm for Multiprocessor Scheduling," *IEEE Trans. Parallel and Distributed Systems*, Vol.5, 1994, pp.113.
[7]L.M.Ni, C.W.Xu and T.B.Gendreau, "A Distributed Drafting Algorithm for Load Balancing,"
   IEEE Trans. on Software Engg., Vol.SE-13, No.10, October1985, pp.1153-1161.
[8]P.K.Sinha, *Distributed Operating Systems: Concepts and Design*, Printice-Hall of India,
   1997.
[9]T.C.K. Chou and J.A.Abraham, "Load Balancing in Distributed Systems," *IEEE Trans. Software Engg.*, Vol. SE-8, No.4, July 1982, pp.401-412.
[10]C.C.Shen and W.H.Tsai , "A Graph Matching Approach to Optimal Task Assignment
   in Distributed Computing System Using a Minimax Criterion," *IEEE Trans. Computers*,
   Vol. c-34, No.3, Mar. 1985. pp. 197-203.
[11]M.Kafil and I.Ahmed, "Optimal Task Assignment in Heterogeneous Distributed   Computing System," *IEEE Concurrency*, July - September 1998, pp. 42-51.
[12]A.K.Tripathi, D.P.Vidyarthi and A.N.Mantri, "A Genetic Task Allocation Algorithm for
   Distributed Computing Systems Incorporating Problem Specific Knowledge," *International
   Journal of High Speed Computing*, Vol.8, No.4, 1996, pp.363-370.
[13]D.P.Vidyarthi and A.K.Tripathi, "Precedence Constrained Task Allocation in Distributed
   Computer Systems," International Journal of High Speed Computing, Vol.8, No.1,1996,
   pp.47-55.
[14]Kai Hwang, *Advanced Computer Architecture: Parallelism Scalability and Programmability*, Mc-graw Hill, 1993.
[15]P.Y.R.Richard Ma, E.Y.S.Lee and J. Tsuchiya, "A Task Allocation Model for Distributed
   Computing Systems," *IEEE Trans. Computer*, Vol. C-31, No.1, pp. 41-47, Jan.1982.
[16]S.M.Shatz, J.P.Wang and M.Goto, "Task Allocation for Maximizing Reliability of Distributed Computer Systems," *IEEE Trans. on Computer*, Vol. 41, No. 9,1992, pp. 1156.
[17]W.W.Chu, M.T.Lan, "Task Allocation and Precedence Relations for Distributed Real-Time
   Systems," *IEEE Trans. Computer*, Vol.c-36, No.6, June 1987, pp. 667-679.
[18]B.K.Sarker, A.K.Tripathi and N.Kumar, "Some Observations on Load   Balancing in Distributed Computing Systems," *Proceedings of National Seminar on Applied Systems Engg.
   and Soft Computing*, Agra, 4-5 March, 2000, pp. 167-171.

CHAPTER 7

GA Based Task Allocation Models

The task allocation (TA) problem, as quoted earlier, is an NP-Hard problem and various heuristics are applied to solve this problem [1]. Genetic Algorithm (GA) has been proved to be useful for the optimization problems [2]. We have explored the GA and have used it to solve task allocation problem of the DCS. In this chapter, two propositions of task allocation algorithms are proposed. In section 7.1, a GA based TA model is proposed in which some problem specific knowledge is incorporated [3]. This is aimed to minimize the turn-around time of a task and is based on a finding that the incorporation of problem specific knowledge in GA, converge the solution quickly. Section 7.2 discusses GA based TA model to maximize reliability of the DCS. This algorithm not only gets the advantage of GA for quick convergence but also produces better solutions in terms of allocation with improved reliability [4].

Genetic Algorithms are stochastic algorithms whose search methods model some natural phenomena: genetic inheritance and Darwinian strife for survival. The idea behind genetic algorithms is to do what nature does [2]. The interest in heuristic search algorithms with underpinning in natural and physical processes began as early as the 1970s, when Holland first proposed GA. Kirkpatric, Gelatt and Vecchi's simulated annealing technique rekindled this interest in 1983. Simulated Annealing is based on the thermodynamic considerations, with annealing interpreted as an optimization procedure [5].

In nature, individuals best suited to competition for scanty resources survive. Adapting to a changing environment is essential for the survival of individuals of each species. Competition among individuals for scant resources such as food and space and for mates results in the fittest individuals dominating over weaker ones. Only the fittest individuals survive and reproduce, with a natural phenomenon called "the survival of the fittest". Hence, the genes of the fittest survive, while the genes of weaker individuals die out. The reproduction process generates diversity in the gene pool. The exchange of genetic material (chromosomes) is called crossover. Repeated selection and crossover cause the continuous evolution of the gene pool and the generation of the individuals [6].

Essential to the GAs working is a population of binary strings. Each string of 0s and 1s is the encoded version of a solution to the optimization problem. Using genetic operators, crossover and mutation, the algorithm creates the subsequent generation from the strings of the current population. This generational cycle is repeated until a desired termination criterion is reached. The simple structure of the GA is as below.

GA ( )

{   Initialize population;

Evaluate population;

While termination criterion not reached

{   select solutions for next population;

perform crossover & mutation;

evaluate population;   }

}

The above GA shows the following components:

- A population of binary strings

- Control parameters

- A Fitness function

- Genetic operators (crossover and mutation)

- A selection mechanism

- A mechanism to encode the solutions as binary strings

We have applied Genetic Algorithm on the task scheduling problem of the DCS.

7.1 Task Allocation using Genetic Algorithm

Genetic Algorithm has successfully been used to solve various optimization problems [6]. GA is parallel in nature and so, it suits better to the task allocation problem of the DCS [7]. The various phases of the GA can be performed on the various processing nodes of the DCS in parallel [8]. So the GA based scheduling model is well suited for its natural parallel execution in DCS.

A GA based task allocation model for multiprocessors has been proposed by Hou, Ansari & Ren[9]. We present a Genetic Task Allocation Algorithm for DCS, wherein we have considered the underlying interconnection networks of the processors, communication requirements among modules of the tasks apart from the precedence relation of the task graph that has been considered in [9] also. Multiprogramming at every processing node with related characteristic values has also been considered. We have, purposefully, made use of the finding [10] that the incorporation of the problem specific knowledge in construction of GA improves the initial population structures. The model and algorithm proposed [11] is sufficiently simple and adequately usable for the purpose of simulation experiments and its possible incorporation in future operating systems of the DCS. Incorporating problem specific knowledge into GA improves its performance, though it should be done carefully as GA is notoriously opportunistic and may converge quickly to a local optimum [10]. It is easy to formulate a good initial structure by incorporating some knowledge in the task allocation problem of DCS.

7.1.1 The Problem

The task in our problem is a group of number of modules, communicating with each other. The problem is to assign these modules to processing nodes of the DCS so that the precedence relations are maintained at the minimum cost. Cost includes execution time of the modules as well as intermodule communication, if any.

The task graph TG = (V, E)   where V, vertices, is the set of modules and E the set of edges connecting the modules.

Further any module mi is a predecessor of m_j and m_j is successor of m_i if e_{ij} εE.

We define two sets of modules:

PRED (m_i) - the set of predecessors of mj, and SUCC (m_i) - the set of successors of m_j.

The height function conveys the precedence of the modules, as shown in Fig. 7.1.

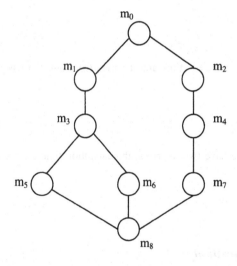

Fig. 7.1. Task Graph

Height of the various modules of the task graph on Fig.7.1 is as below.

Height(m_0) = 0,

Height(m_1) = Height(m_2) = 1,

Height(m_3) = Height(m_4) = 2,

Height(m_5) = Height(m_6) = Height(m_7) = 3,

Height(m_8) = 4,

Each module has execution time e_{ij} i.e. execution time of module m_i on processor p_j. The communication matrix c_{ij} gives the amount of communication between modules m_i and m_j.

The processor graph P = (V, E),

where V = set of processing nodes (processors) & E = set of edges connecting the nodes.

Each module has some execution time and it varies from one processor to another.

Thus in this problem we have two matrices; the execution time matrix and the communication matrix.

7.1.2 GA for Task Allocation

Genetic algorithms are available, as solutions, to the number of problems for which little prior knowledge is available. Grefenstelle[11] has discussed GA for TSP in which he has incorporated problem specific knowledge in GA. He is successfully able to infer that incorporating problem specific knowledge in initialization of strings not only produces good strings but also enables quick convergence, though it is to be done carefully to avoid premature convergence.

We made use of the findings of [10] and incorporated some problem specific knowledge in the initialization as well as in the crossover operations for the problem of task allocation in DCS [11]. The various phases of GA for TA are as follows.

Initial Population

Genetic Algorithm uses the notion of survival of the fittest by passing "good" genes to the next generation of strings and combining different strings to explore new search points. At the cost of few steps, some problem specific knowledge is introduced in generating the initial population. Thus the good initial structure is generated and the algorithm converges quickly. The steps involved in initialization are as follows.

INITIALIZE( )

(1) Compute height for every modules in TG and set I=0.

(2) Partition the modules into different sets G(h) according to their height h.

(3) Allocate the modules of G(I) [modules of height 0] onto different processor randomly.

(4) Repeat step (5) & (6) for all G(h).

(5) If IMC of allocated modules with modules in group G(I+1) is large enough, allocate it on the same processor otherwise allocate it on any different processor. Do it for all the modules of G(I+1).

(6) Set I=I+1.

Fitness Function

The fitness function of the string, in this problem, is the total cost that is the sum of IMC cost and the execution cost. The communication cost, c_{ij}, is the number of data units exchanged between module m_i to m_j and d_{kl} is the inter processor distance, as earlier. If the module m_i is assigned to the processor p_k and the module m_j is assigned to p_l then communication cost is $c_{ij}*d_{kl}$. If k=l then $d_{kl}=0$ and IMC cost reduces to zero i.e. the modules have been assigned onto the same processor. We have considered that the individual processors in DCS are multiprogrammed and the total cost of allocation of task is[9]

$$n_k \times q + e_{ik}x_{ik} + \sum_l \sum_j (c_{ij} \times d_{kl})x_{ik}x_{jl} \qquad (7.1)$$

The elements of the assignment matrix

$$x_{ik} = \begin{cases} 1 & \text{if } mod\,ule\ m_i\ \text{is assigned to processor}\ p_k, \\ 0 & \text{otherwise}; \end{cases}$$

Crossover Operation

The major consideration while performing the crossover is that, the strings generated after the crossover should be legal. Hou, Ansari, and Ren[9] have proved that if the crossover site is selected such as

(a) The height of the modules next to the crossover sites are different, and

(b) The height of all the modules immediately in front of the crossover sites are the same then the new strings generated will always be legal.

Grefenstelle showed that incorporating problem specific knowledge in crossover operator improves the strings generated [10]. Crossover for TA is as follows.

CROSSOVER( )

1. {Selection of crossover sites}

   Do for all the processors

   (a) Pick some crossover sites in both the strings such that the modules following and preceding the site have different height and height of the preceding module is same for all the processors.

   (b) Define a communication distribution over these sites.

   (c) Select one site based on the above distribution for all the strings.

   (If both following and preceding modules are having much of communication then it is not a good crossover site)

2. Using the crossover sites exchange the bottom halves of strings A and B for each processors.

Steps 1(b) and 1(c) are introduced to reduce IMC as highly communicating modules should be on the same processor.

Mutation

Genetic algorithms are not well suited for fine tuning structures which are very close to optimal solutions [10]. The mutation operator is applied to avoid the danger of getting caught in local minima. The probability of applying mutation is often very less. The routine for mutation has been summarized as below.

MUTATION ( )

For each of the strings perform the following:

(1) Randomly pick a module mi.

(2) Search the string for a module mj of the same height.

(3) Generate a new string by exchanging mi and mj.

Complete GA for Task Allocation

All above routines have been grouped to complete the GA for DCS.

(1) Call INITIALIZE( ) n times and store the strings in InitPop.

(calling n times to get n strings for crossover)

(2) Repeat steps (3) to (5) until algorithm converges.

(3) Compute the fitness value of strings in InitPop. BestString is the string with low fitness value. (Object is to minimize cost).

(4) Perform CROSSOVER( ). Put the new strings in NewPop.

(Probability of crossover is 1).

(5) For each of the string in NewPop, perform MUTATION( ) with the probability ProbMute. Put again the new strings in InitPop.

(6) Best String is the string with lowest fitness value.

Termination criterion can be chosen if the fitness value does not change after few iterations. The above TA model is based on a finding that the incorporation of problem specific knowledge in construction of GA improves its performance and solution converges quickly.

7.2 Maximizing Reliability of DCS with Task Allocation using GA

Reliability is one of the very important characteristic of the distributed computing system (DCS) and articles on task allocation to maximize reliability of DCS have appeared in the past [4, 12-15]. We have studied the effect of various parameters on reliability with allocation of a DCS [13]. Here, a TA model is proposed in which a simple genetic algorithm is used to optimize reliability of a DCS with task allocation. The various phases of the algorithm are summarized in the following sections.

7.2.1 Reliability Expression

The reliability of a DCS of n processing nodes (which is always better than a uniprocessor system as failure of some processors does not bring the system to a grinding halt) during the mission when a task (of m modules) is allocated, by the assignment X, can be expressed as [13]:

$$R(T, X) = \prod_{k=1}^{n} R_k(T, X) \prod_{lpq} R_{pq}(T, X) \qquad (7.2)$$

Where R_k (T, X) is the reliability of the processing node P_k and $R_{pq}(T,X)$ is the reliability of the link l_{pq}(connecting node P_p and P_q). This is the probability that unit P_k and l_{pq} is operational for time T under assignment X.

$$R_k(T, X) = \exp(-\lambda_k \sum_{i=1}^{m} x_{ik} e_{ik}) \qquad (7.3)$$

$$R_{pq}(T, X) = \exp(-\lambda_{pq} \sum_{j=1}^{m} \sum_{i \neq j}^{m} c_{ij} x_{ip} x_{jq} / W_{pq} \qquad (7.4)$$

Where λ_k and λ_{pq} is failure rates of the processing node P_k and link l_{pq} respectively, e_{ik} is the execution time of module m_i on node P_k, c_{ij} is the communication(in bytes transferred) between m_i and m_j, W_{pq} is transmission rate of link l_{pq} and x_{ik} is the element of the assignment matrix X i.e.

$$x_{ik} = \begin{cases} 1 & \text{if module } m_i \text{ is assigned to } P_k, \\ 0 & \text{otherwise;} \end{cases}$$

7.2.2 The Proposed Algorithm

A genetic algorithm makes use of some fitness function to identify candidate solutions of the next generation. In the proposed algorithm eqn. 7.2, as given above, is used as the fitness function. The following are the various parts of the GA based Task Allocation Algorithm.

Initial Schedule ( )

{

Compute height for each module in the task graph.

Keep modules of the same height (h) in the same group G (h).

Assign the modules of the same height from the same group G (h) onto the different processors. If some modules are unassigned again assign it from the first processors in the same order. The assignment is to satisfy the system constraints.

Assign the modules of the G (h+1) in the same order of the Processors as in 3.

}

A number of populations are generated by applying the *Initial_Schedule()* and changing the order of the processors.

Crossover ( )

{

Two modules of different height are chosen for crossover site in a generated population, and the portion of the strings is swapped.

}   // Length of strings should not change

Mutation ( )

{ Randomly alter 0 to 1 and 1 to 0 by keeping no. of 0 and 1 same }

// The probability of mutation is very less as it is an escape for premature convergence.

Reproduction ( )

    {

Use the fitness function of eqn. 7.2. Choose the few best strings (with good fitness value)

    }

Apply *Crossover ( )*, *Mutation ( )* and *Reproduction ( )* repeatedly, unless the solution converges.

7.2.3 Experimental Results

The algorithm, implemented in 'C' language, was applied on some representative cases that demonstrate the desirable allocations. Some results are as below [4].

7.2.3.1 Algorithm is executed for the same task (consisting of four modules) and the processor graph (shown in Fig. 7.2) as that of Shatz [13]. Node failure rate are shown in figure and the link failure rate are .0003 between P1 and P2, .0001 between P2 and P3 and .0002 between P2 and P4.

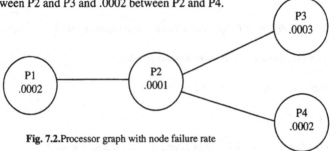

Fig. 7.2. Processor graph with node failure rate

The table for execution time and intermodule communication are shown in table 7.1 and 7.2 respectively

Table 7.1. Execution time matrix

	P1	**P2**	**P3**	**P4**
M1	5	3	∞	4
M2	3	4	5	6
M3	4	∞	2	5
M4	3	4	5	2

Table 7.2.IMC Matrix

	M1	**M2**	**M3**	**M4**
M1	-	12	5	6
M2	12	-	8	0
M3	5	8	-	3
M4	6	0	3	-

The result for both the models are shown as below.

Reliability in Shatz Algorithm = 0.9953

Allocation in Shatz Algorithm = P1←Nil,

P2←M1, M2,

P3←M3, M4,

P4←Nil

Reliability in Proposed Algorithm = 0.996705

Allocation in Proposed Algorithm = P1←Nil,

$$\text{P2←M1, M2, M3,}$$

$$\text{P3←M4,}$$

$$\text{P4←Nil}$$

7.2.3.2 Further a random task graph and processor graph is generated. Various

parameters, generated randomly, for the experiment are as below.

Link failure rates are in the range of 0.00010-0.00085

Node failure rates are in the range of 0.00010-0.00045

IMC are in the range of 0-15

AET are in the range of 1-11

The results obtained from the experiment are:

No. of iterations = 4

Reliability = 0.953448

Allocation   P1←M5, P2←Nil, P3←M1, M3, M4, P4←M2, M6, M7

The experiment is further conducted for same task graph and processor graph

but limiting the no. of modules on each processing node to two. This is to observe

that how load balancing is achieved. The results are as below.

Reliability = 0.995311

Allocation   P1←Nil, P2←M1, M2, P3←M3, M4, P4←Nil

7.2.3.3 Effect of load balancing is observed also by keeping the failure rate of a particular link (l24 in the PG and TG of Fig. 7.3) minimum to 0.0001. The parameters are listed below.

Link failure rate in the range of 0.00040-0.00090

Node failure rate in the range of 0.00010-0.00045

IMC in the range of 1-15

AET in the range of 1-10

The output observed is:

No. of iterations = 5

Reliability = 0.973945

Allocation P1←Nil, P2←M3, M5, M6, M7, P3←Nil, P4←M1,M2,M4,M8

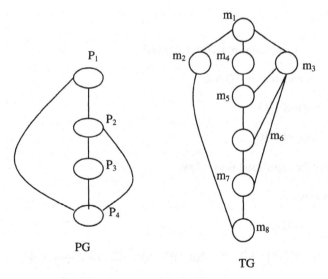

Fig. 7.3.Processor and Task Graphs

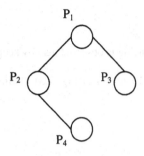

P_1

P_2 P_3

P_4

Fig. 7.4. Processor Graph

7.2.3.4 Further experiment observes the result by limiting the number of modules on the processor and making the failure rate of a processor minimum. We
kept the maximum number of modules on the processing node to 3 and the failure
rate of the processing node P3 minimum (0.0001) in the TG of Fig. 7.3 and PG of
Fig. 7.4. The input parameters are:

Link failure rate in the range of 0.00011-0.00065

Node failure rate uniformly 0.00040

IMC in the range of 1-15

AET in the range of 1-10

The output of the experiment is as below.

No. of iterations = 6

Reliability = 0.959887

Allocation P1←M2, M4, M7 P3←Nil   P2←M1, M5, M8 P4←M3,M6

7.2.4 Conclusion

In the experiment 7.2.3.1 it is observed that the proposed algorithm performs better than of Shatz because not only the reliability is increased but better load balance is also achieved.

Result of the experiment 7.2.3.2 shows balanced load with better reliability. As the processing nodes have their own capacity to carry modules, we confined the maximum number of modules in this experiment. Result seems to be very good.

To observe how the modules will concentrate towards some node if some link are more reliable. Experiment 7.2.3.3 shows that most of the modules are concentrated on P2 and P4 as the failure rate of the link connecting these two nodes are minimum.

Experiment 7.2.3.4 does both i.e. limits the number of modules and considers the failure rate of a processor to minimum. Conspicuous is that though P3 has low failure rate still modules are not allocated on it. The reason observed is may be it is because P3 is not well connected with other processing nodes.

The above results show that GA based TA model to maximize reliability of a DCS are well suited for this problem as it provides better reliability and balanced allocation.

This chapter discusses two GA based models. In sec. 7.1 finding of [10] is used which says that incorporation of some problem specific knowledge in GA improves its performance and leads to quick convergence. In sec. 7.2, GA is used in TA model to maximize the reliability of a DCS with allocation. The fitness function used in sec. 7.2 is the reliability expression. Result is compared with that of one earlier proposed model for the same [13] and it shows an improvement in reliability.

BIBLIOGRAPHY

[1] K.Efe, "Heuristic Models of Task Assignment Scheduling in Distributed Systems", *IEEE Computer*, Vol. 15, June 1982, pp. 50-56.

[2] Zbigniew Michalewicz, *Genetic Algorithms + Data Structures = Evolution Programs*, Springer-Verlag, Berlin, 1992.

[3] A.K.Tripathi, D.P.Vidyarthi, A.N.Mantri, "A Genetic Task Allocation Algorithm for Distributed Computing System Incorporating Problem Specific Knowledge", *International J. of High Speed Computing*, Vol.8, No.4, 1996, pp. 363-370.

[4] D.P.Vidyarthi, A.K.Tripathi, "Maximizing Reliability of Distributed Computing Systems with Task Allocation using Simple Genetic Algorithm", *J. of Systems Architecture*, Vol. 47, 2001, pp. 549-554.

[5] M. Srinivas, L.M.Patnaik, "Genetic Algorithms: A survey", *IEEE Computer*, June 1994, pp. 17-26.

[6] J.L.R.Filho, P.C.Treleaven, C.Alippi, "Genetic Algorithm Programming Environments", *IEEE Computer*, June 1994, pp. 29-42.

[7] Albert Y. Zomaya, Chris Word, Ben Macey, "Genetic Scheduling for Parallel Processor Systems: Comparative studies and Performance Issues", *IEEE Trans. on Parallel & Distributed Systems*, Vol. 10, No. 8, Aug. 1999, pp. 795-811.

[8] D.P.Vidyarthi, A.K.Tripathi, "Exploiting Parallelism in Genetic Task Allocation Algorithm", *Int. J. of Information and Computing Science*, Vol. 4 No. 1, June 2002, pp. 22-26

[9] Edwin S.H.Hou, Nirwan Ansari, Hong Ren, "A Genetic Algorithm for Multiprocessor Scheduling", *IEEE Trans. on Parallel and Distributed Systems*, Vol. 5, No. 2, Feb 1994, pp. 113-120.

[10] John J. Grefenstelle, "Incorporating Problem Specific Knowledge into Genetic Algorithm", *Genetic Algorithm and Simulated Annealing*, Morgan Kaufrman Publisher, California, 1987.

[11] A.K.Tripathi, D.P.Vidyarthi, A.N.Mantri, "A Genetic Task Allocation Algorithm for Distributed Computing System Incorporating Problem Specific Knowledge", *International J. of High Speed Computing*, Vol.8, No.4, 1996, pp. 363-370.

[12] S.Kartik, C.S.Ram Murthy, "Task Allocation Algorithms for Maximizing Reliability of Distributed Computing Systems", *IEEE Trans. on Computers*, Vol.46, No.6, June1997, pp. 719-724.

[13] Sol.M.Shatz, Wang Goto, "Task Allocation for Maximizing Reliability of Distributed Computing Systems", *IEEE Trans. on Computers*, Vol.41, No.9, September 1992, pp. 1156-1168.

[14]S. Karthik, C. Siva Ram Murthy, " Improved Task Allocation Algorithms to Maximize Reliability of Redundant Distributed Systems", *IEEE Trans. on Reliability*, Vol. 44, No. 4, Dec. 1995, pp. 575-586.

[15]D.P.Vidyarthi, A.K.Tripathi, "Studies on Reliability with Task Allocation of Redundant Distributed Systems", *IETE J. of Research*, Vol. 44, No. 6, Nov-Dec. 1998, pp. 279-285.

CHAPTER 8

Allocation of Multiple Tasks in DCS

This chapter consists of four propositions of TA algorithms: first of these addresses the realistic consideration of multiple tasks in a DCS whereas earlier proposed algorithms (Sec. 5.3 and 7.1) consider only one task at a time; the second proposition, a cluster based algorithm, does not require the priori knowledge of execution time of modules of a given task, as it is difficult to estimate the same, for allocation purposes. These propositions appear in sections 8.1 and 8.2 respectively. Section 8.3 and 8.4 deals with the LBTA strategies for multiple tasks using A* and using GA respectively.

The task allocation models & algorithms, discussed in previous chapters, concentrated on improvement of execution characteristics of an individual task, consisting of a number of modules, submitted to the DCS. A DCS, in fact, keeps on receiving multiple tasks from time to time. This calls for consideration of all the tasks for allocation, simultaneously, to the processing nodes of the DCS. Such an allocation would be able to aim at a good throughput of the system apart from improvement in the turn around time of the individual task. The idea of multiple task allocation is elaborated in section 8.1.

The major problem of the allocation techniques is the assumption that the execution time of the modules of the task on the PEs of the DCS and the communication among them are available priori. The execution time on the PEs of a DCS, prior to its execution, is just difficult to estimate. The allocation method that may work with other parameters, without prior knowledge of execution time, is desirable. The allocation model proposed in section 8.2 considers the inter module communication for grouping modules into the clusters and at the same time clustering of PEs are done based on the inter-processor distances. This cluster-based algorithm for the task allocation can make assignments by consideration of similar clustering of processing nodes for matching and mapping of module clusters onto these node clusters. Section 8.3 and 8.4 concentrates on LBTA strategy, as discussed in chapter 4, for multiple task allocation.

8.1 Multiple Task Allocation

Several task allocation algorithms for distributed computing systems have been reported in the literature [1-13]. These algorithms consider the execution time of the different modules, of a single task, executing on different processing nodes. The assignment problem, in these, optimizes some characteristic parameter by allocating modules onto the processing nodes, considering the Inter Module Communication (IMC) overhead. The number of tasks for execution is usually substantive, but these algorithms consider assignment of the modules of a single task to various processing nodes. In reality, a DCS facilitates concurrent execution of modules belonging to various unrelated tasks [15]. The modules of any particular

task, having IMC, do cooperatively execute and do not depend on the modules of

the other tasks. This leads to the situation wherein, a processing node may be as-

signed modules belonging to the different tasks. It is to mention that the real issue

of task allocation must not ignore the possibility of multiple module assignment of

various tasks to the processing nodes in a dynamic fashion.

Some assessments for multiple task allocation in a Distributed Computing Sys-

tems has been pointed out in section 8.1.1 [15].

8.1.1 Issues of Multiple Tasks Allocation (MTA)

Some important issues of MTA are as follows:

a) A DCS must consider execution of modules of different unrelated tasks.
    The modules of a particular task do cooperatively execute and do not de-
    pend on the modules of the other tasks.

b) The execution time of a particular module on a particular node will de-
    pend on the number of modules already executing on that particular node
    as per some chosen scheduling policy (Round Robin etc.).

c) While assigning modules of multiple tasks onto the processing nodes,
    IMC plays vital role in terms of speed and capability of the processing
    node besides memory constraints.

d) The task allocation models must consider the load on channels while con-
    sidering IMC. It is because of the queuing up of multiple modules on the
    processing node ends to make use of the channel.

e) The existing task allocation algorithms may cause either deadlock or starvation because of remote possibility of certain events at the time of allocation of the modules to the processing nodes that are already heavily loaded.

Considering these real issues the task allocation problem, proposed in the literature so far, needs to be reformulated. It is very much essential to do so because ultimately these task allocation algorithms are to be integrated as a part of the distributed operating system. Four models for multiple tasks assignment in a DCS have been presented in this chapter. A cost function, which considers effect of multiple tasks, is also presented.

8.1.2 Global Table

We propose a data structure, called Global Table, to manage the multiple tasks execution in a DCS. It is a table having many columns (as shown in Table 8.1) taking care of whole allocation. The memory capacity of the processing node determines if a module is to be accommodated onto the node or not. So, in the table, a column indicates the available memory of the processors. Modules of the processor will be represented by m_{ijk} i.e. module m_i of task T_j allocated on processor P_k.

While partitioning the task into modules, we assume that the memory requirements of the modules are also calculated by M_{ij} (memory requirement of module m_i of task T_j). After the allocation of this module onto the processing node, the memory of the node will reduce to

$M = M - M_{ij}$, if M be the available memory of the processing

node

While allocating the next module of any task on this node, the memory M will

be compared with the required memory. The 2-D Global Table (G) will be like

Table 8.1. Global Table

Processor	Memory Capacity	Modules Assigned				Remaining Memory
P_1	M	m_{1j1}	m_{3j1}		$\ldots$	$M- (M_{1i}+M_{3i})$
P_2	M	m_{2j2}	m_{1i2}	m_{2j2}	$\ldots$	$M- (M_{2i}+M_{1i}+M_{2i})$
P_3	M	m_{3i3}	$\ldots$		$\ldots$	$M- M_{3i}$
.	.	.	.	.		.
.	.	.	.	.		.
P_n	M	$\ldots$	$\ldots$		$\ldots$	M

This is a dynamic table, which keeps the information of remaining memory of

nodes and the modules allocated on the nodes. Whenever a new task arrives, this

table (G) is to be consulted and to be modified. The implementation of G will in-

cur an overhead in the algorithm but this is essential to maintain the track of mul-

tiple tasks execution in DCS [15].

8.1.3 Cost Function of MTA in DCS

To exploit effective parallelism in a DCS, tasks must be properly allocated to

the processing nodes. A task allocation algorithm seeks an assignment that opti-

mizes a certain cost-function, e.g. maximum throughput or minimum turnaround

time. However, most of the reported algorithms yield sub-optimal solutions. In

general, optimal solutions can be found through an exhaustive search, but as there is n^m ways in which m modules can be assigned to n processing nodes, an exhaustive search is often not possible. Thus, optimal solution algorithms exist only for restricted cases or very small problems. The other possibility is to use an informed search to reduce the state space [7].

The cost function of task allocation is formulated as the sum of the IMC cost and the execution cost [12]. IMC cost is a function of communication cost between two modules of task T_h and Inter-Processor distances onto which these two modules are assigned. Communication cost c_{ijh} represents the communication, in terms of bytes transferred, between the module m_i and m_j of the task T_h. The distance between processing node P_k to processing node P_l is denoted by d_{kl}. If modules m_i and m_j are assigned to processing nodes P_k and P_l respectively, the IMC cost is $(c_{ijh} \times d_{kl})$. If modules are assigned to the same processing node then $d_{kl}=0$ and effectively IMC cost becomes zero.

Execution cost e_{ihk} represents the cost to execute a module m_i of task T_h on processing node P_k. The assignment is given by,

$$X_{ihk} = \begin{cases} 1, & \text{if modules } m_i \text{ of task } T_h \text{ is assigned to processor } P_k \\ 0, & \text{otherwise} \end{cases}$$

The cost function for processing the task T_h, which consists of n modules, on the DCS is

$$\sum_{i=1}^{n} \left(e_{ihk} . X_{ihk} + \sum_{i=1}^{n} \sum_{j=i+1}^{n} (c_{ijh} . d_{kl}) X_{ihk} . X_{jhl} \right) \tag{8.1}$$

The execution of a module m_i of the other unrelated task T_m on the processing node P_k may affect the assignment of task T_h on the same processing node P_k. The various modules, allocated on the processing node P_k, may be allowed to execute as per some chosen scheduling policy (Round robin).

So, the cost function to assign a module m_i of task T_h on processing node P_k is

$$e_{ihk}.x_{ihk} + \sum_{i=1}^{n} \sum_{j=i+1}^{n} (c_{ijh}.d_{kl})x_{ihk}.x_{jhl} + \sum_{\substack{i \\ m \neq h}} e_{imk}.x_{imk} \qquad (8.2)$$

The third term in the equation signifies the effect of the other tasks T_m on the task T_h.

So, the total cost for assigning the task T_h is stated as

$$\sum_{i=1}^{n} \left(e_{ihk}.x_{ihk} + \sum_{i=1}^{n} \sum_{j=i+1}^{n} (c_{ijh}.d_{kl})x_{ihk}.x_{jhl} + \sum_{\substack{i \\ m \neq h}} e_{imk}.x_{imk} \right) \qquad (8.3)$$

The total cost of allocation on the DCS of k nodes is

$$\sum_{k} \left[\sum_{i=1}^{n} \left(e_{ihk}.x_{ihk} + \sum_{i=1}^{n} \sum_{j=i+1}^{n} (c_{ijh}.d_{kl})x_{ihk}.x_{jhl} + \sum_{\substack{i \\ m \neq h}} e_{imk}.x_{imk} \right) \right] \qquad (8.4)$$

8.1.4 Task Allocation Algorithms

The work assumes that the Task Precedence Graph (TPG) and the processor graph of a DCS are given. For Task Interaction Graph (TIG), a communication matrix is given. The execution times of all the modules of the task are given in Execution Matrix.

A heuristic approach is applied to solve multiple tasks allocation problem. The famous A* of Artificial Intelligence and the Uniform Cost Search algorithm have been used for multiple tasks allocation problem [16].

The A*

A* is a best-first search algorithm, which has been used extensively in artificial intelligence problem solving [16]. Programmers can use this algorithm to search a tree or graph. For a tree search, it starts from the root, called the start node (usually a null solution of the problem). Intermediate tree nodes represent the partial solutions, and leaf nodes represent the complete solution or goal. A cost function f computes each node's associated cost. The value of f for a node n, which is the estimated cost of the cheapest solution through n, is computed as in equation 8.5.

$$f(n) = g(n) + h(n) \qquad (8.5)$$

where $g(n)$ is the search-path cost from the start node to the current node and $h(n)$ is a lower-bound estimate of the path cost from current node to the goal node(solution), using any heuristic information available. The $g(n)$ is equal to the cost of assigning the module according to equation 8.2. The $h(n)$, in this case, is the communication cost of all the unassigned modules communicating with the assigned module, i.e.

$$h(n) = \sum_{\substack{for\ all\ unassigned\ modules}} cij \times xik \qquad (8.6)$$

To expand a node means to generate all of its successors or children and to compute the f value for each of them. The nodes are ordered for search according to the cost; that is the algorithm first selects the node with the minimum expansion cost. The algorithm maintains a sorted list, called OPEN, of nodes (according to their f values) and always selects a node with the best expansion cost. Because the algorithm always selects the best-cost node, it guarantees an optimal solution.

For the task allocation problem under consideration for a single task

- The search space is a tree;

- The initial node (the root) is a null-assignment node, i.e. no modules are assigned yet;

- Intermediate nodes are partial-assignment nodes, i.e. only some modules are assigned;

- A solution (goal) node is a complete-assignment node i.e. all the modules of the task are assigned.

The Uniform Cost Search

The heuristic function $h(n)$ in the above equation can be defined by several different approaches. The simplest way is to set $h(n)=0$ for all n and the resulting search is a uniform-cost search [17].

Uniform Cost Search Algorithm for Task Allocation

(1) *Calculate the status of the Global Table (G) for each processor in terms of available memory (M) and the modules that are assigned to it.*

(2) *Order a list T_j of all modules of incoming tasks according to their precedence.*

//from the Task Precedence Graph(TPG)

(3) *repeat (for all the modules of T_j in order)*

(4) *for the first module(m_{ij}) of T_j*

        do

      select the node P_k with the smallest f value

                // f value is the cost function of eqn.. (8.5)

(5) *if memory (M_{ij}) > M_k*   *// M_k is available memory of P_k, M_{ij} is memory*

        then   *requirement of module m_i of task T_j*

      choose next smaller f value;   *// memory requirement of the module*

        goto (5)   *exceeds the available memory of the node*

(6) *Update G by adding the assigned module and update memory by $M_k = M_k - M_{ij}$*

(7) *Until (T_j is empty)*   *// goal node is reached*

A* Algorithm for Task Allocation

(1) *Calculate the status of the Global Table (G) for each processing node in terms*

of the available memory (M) and the modules that are assigned to it.

(2) *Order a list T_j of all modules of incoming task according to their precedence.*

// from the Task Precedence Graph(TPG)

(3) *Put the initial node k=0 on a list called OPEN, and set f(k)=0 where f is a cost*

function given in equation 8.5.

(4) *Remove from OPEN the node n with a smallest f value and put it on a list*

called CLOSED.

(5) *If n satisfies the goal state, report the solution. Modify the Global Table G by*

adding the assigned module, update memory by $M_k = M_k$-M_{ij} and Stop.

Otherwise continue.

(6) *Expand node n and compute the value f(n) = g(n') + h(n') as explained earlier.*

// n' is the successors of n

g(n) is calculated as in eqn. (8.2)

h(n) is calculated as in eqn. (8.5)

Put all the successors of n on OPEN.

(7) *Go to step (4).*

It is assumed that the outgoing module will inform the allocator process to modify the Global Table (G) accordingly i.e. the number of modules belonging to the outgoing tasks and the memory occupied by the modules of this task will be freed in global table. This algorithm has been proposed considering multiple tasks allocation in a DCS. It is observed that the tasks arrive, for the execution, in a dynamic fashion. A task, will invoke the algorithm. The status of the Global Table is dynamic and the algorithm will include the modification in the table (G) with reference to a particular task. To ensure proper working, the code of allocator that modifies the Global Table is to be treated as critical section.

8.1.5 Illustrated Examples

Two simple examples have been illustrated below using the above A* algorithm for the task allocation problem and the cost function 8.2 [18].

EXAMPLE 1

We Consider four tasks (and their modules), that arrive for the execution, in a DCS consisting of four processing nodes as shown in fig. 8.1. The Execution Time Matrix and the Communication Matrices are assumed to be given as below in matrices. The memory requirement of the modules is also given.

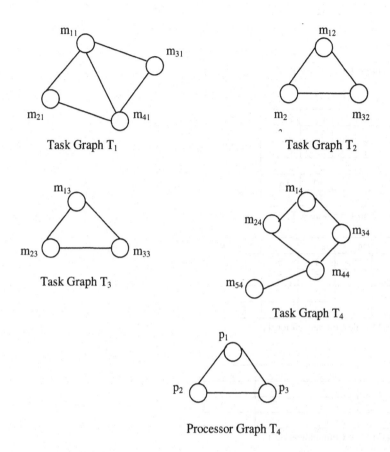

Fig. 8.1.Task Graph and Processor Graph

	P_1	P_2	P_3
m_{11}	7	8	9
m_{21}	4	5	6
m_{31}	1	2	3
m_{41}	7	5	2

Execution Time Matrix T_1

	P_1	P_2	P_3
m_{12}	4	5	6
m_{22}	1	2	3
m_{32}	9	6	3

Execution Time Matrix T_2

Scheduling in Distributed Computing Systems

	P_1	P_2	P_3
m_{13}	6	5	2
m_{23}	4	7	1
m_{33}	7	8	9

Execution Time Matrix T_3

	P_1	P_2	P_3
m_{14}	15	11	9
m_{24}	14	12	8
m_{34}	16	13	6
m_{44}	05	04	03
m_{54}	10	09	07

Execution Time Matrix T_4

	m_{11}	m_{21}	m_{31}	m_{41}
m_{11}	0	4	5	6
m_{21}	4	0	0	2
m_{31}	5	0	0	3
m_{41}	6	2	3	0

InterModule Communication T_1

	m_{12}	m_{22}	m_{32}
m_{12}	0	7	8
m_{22}	7	0	9
m_{32}	8	9	0

InterModule Communication T_2

	m_{13}	m_{23}	m_{33}
m_{13}	0	7	8
m_{23}	7	0	9
m_{33}	8	9	0

InterModule Communication T_3

	m_{14}	m_{24}	m_{34}	m_{44}	m_{54}
m_{14}	0	8	0	0	7
m_{24}	8	0	6	0	0
m_{34}	0	6	0	5	4
m_{44}	0	0	5	0	0
m_{54}	7	0	4	0	0

InterModule Communication T_4

m_{11}	m_{12}	m_{13}	m_{14}	m_{12}	m_{22}	m_{32}	m_{13}	m_{23}	m_{33}
1	2	3	1	1	1	1	2	1	1
m_{14}	m_{24}	m_{34}	m_{44}	m_{54}					
2	1	1	2	1					

Memory requirements of the modules (in MB)

The algorithm is applied for these tasks. Below are the tables showing modules assigned to the various processing nodes and the remaining memory of the nodes.

Task T_1 has been allocated as

Processor	Memory Capacity in M.B.	Modules Assigned	Remaining Memory
P_1	8	m_{41}	7 M.B.
P_2	8	m_{21}	6 M.B.
P_3	8	m_{11} , m_{31}	4 M.B.

Task T_2 has been allocated as

Processor	Memory Capacity in M.B.	Modules Assigned	Remaining Memory
P_1	8	m_{41} , m_{32}	6 M.B.
P_2	8	m_{21}	6 M.B.
P_3	8	m_{11} ,m_{31}, m_{12} , m_{22}	2 M.B.

Task T_3 is allocated as

Processor	Memory Capacity in M.B.	Modules Assigned	Remaining Memory
P_1	8	m_{41}, m_{32} , m_{33}	5 M.B.
P_2	8	m_{21} , m_{13} , m_{23}	3 M.B.
P_3	8	m_{11} ,m_{31}, m_{12} , m_{22}	2 M.B.

Task T_4 has been allocated as

Proc-essor	Memory Ca-pacity in M.B.	Modules As-signed	Remaining Mem-ory
P_1	8	m_{41} , m_{32} , m_{33} , m_{34}, m_{44} , m_{54}	1M.B.
P_2	8	m_{21} , m_{13} , m_{23} , m_{14}	1 M.B.
P_3	8	m_{11} , m_{31} , m_{12} , m_{22} , m_{24}	1 M.B.

The above table also shows the final status of the allocation.

EXAMPLE 2

In this five tasks are considered for allocation as shown below in fig 8.2. The relevant data follows the figures.

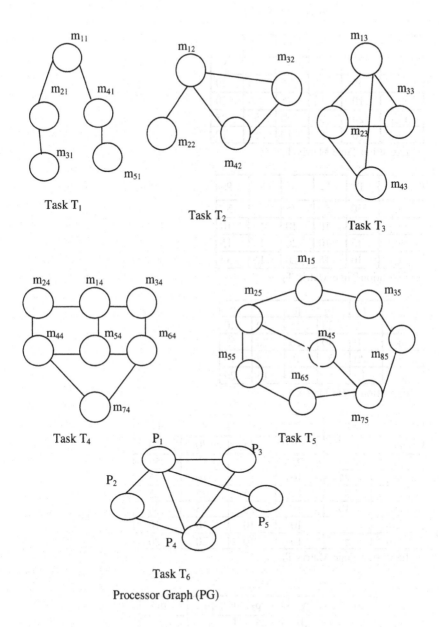

Task T_1

Task T_2

Task T_3

Task T_4

Task T_5

Task T_6

Processor Graph (PG)

Fig. 8.2. Task Graphs and Processor Graphs

The Different Matrices are as follows:

	p_1	p_2	p_3	p_4	p_5
m_{11}	10	20	5	25	5
m_{21}	35	10	15	15	10
m_{31}	10	15	25	10	20
m_{41}	20	35	20	5	25
m_{51}	10	5	10	5	10

Execution Time Matrix T_1

	p_1	p_2	p_3	p_4	p_5
m_{12}	20	5	35	10	5
m_{22}	10	10	10	10	10
m_{32}	15	10	20	15	15
m_{42}	10	15	20	15	30

Execution Time Matrix T_2

	p_1	p_2	p_3	p_4	p_5
m_{13}	15	25	15	10	10
m_{23}	30	40	25	20	5
m_{33}	20	5	10	15	10
m_{43}	10	5	5	15	20

Execution Time Matrix T_3

	p_1	p_2	p_3	p_4	p_5
m_{14}	5	10	25	20	30
m_{24}	10	25	5	5	5
m_{34}	25	10	5	10	25
m_{44}	5	10	15	25	25
m_{54}	10	15	20	25	30
m_{64}	5	10	10	10	10
m_{74}	5	10	10	20	20

Execution Time Matrix T_4

	p_1	p_2	p_3	p_4	p_5
m_{15}	5	10	6	3	2
m_{25}	7	8	10	3	1
m_{35}	6	5	15	10	20
m_{45}	8	10	12	14	16
m_{55}	11	10	12	5	6

m_{65}	5	10	12	8	6
m_{75}	6	8	10	11	12
m_{85}	8	9	2	3	1

Execution Time Matrix T_5

	m_{11}	m_{21}	m_{31}	m_{41}	m_{51}
m_{11}	0	10	20	20	5
m_{21}	10	0	10	0	20
m_{31}	20	10	0	0	10
m_{41}	20	0	0	0	20
m_{51}	5	20	10	20	0

InterModule Communication T_1

	m_{12}	m_{22}	m_{32}	m_{42}
m_{12}	0	5	10	10
m_{22}	5	0	0	0
m_{32}	10	0	0	5
m_{42}	10	0	5	0

InterModule Communication T_2

	m_{13}	m_{23}	m_{33}	m_{43}
m_{13}	0	5	15	10
m_{23}	5	0	10	5
m_{33}	15	10	0	0
m_{43}	10	5	0	0

InterModule Communication T_3

	m_{14}	m_{24}	m_{34}	m_{44}	m_{54}	m_{64}	m_{74}
m_{14}	0	5	10	15	15	15	20
m_{24}	5	0	0	10	0	0	15
m_{34}	10	0	0	0	0	5	10
m_{44}	15	10	0	0	10	15	5
m_{54}	15	0	0	10	0	5	5
m_{64}	15	0	5	15	5	0	5
m_{74}	20	15	10	5	5	5	0

InterModule Communication T_4

	m_{15}	m_{25}	m_{35}	m_{45}	m_{55}	m_{65}	m_{75}	m_{85}
m_{15}	0	5	10	10	15	20	40	45
m_{25}	5	0	0	5	10	15	35	40
m_{35}	10	0	0	0	0	0	0	10
m_{45}	10	5	0	0	0	0	10	15
m_{55}	15	10	0	0	0	5	25	30
m_{65}	20	15	0	0	5	0	20	25
m_{75}	40	35	0	10	25	20	0	5
m_{85}	45	40	10	15	30	25	5	0

InterModule Communication T_5

m_{11}	m_{21}	m_{31}	m_{41}	m_{51}	m_{12}	m_{22}	m_{32}	m_{42}	m_{13}	m_{23}	m_{33}	m_{43}	m_{14}
1	1	1	1	2	1	1	1	2	1	1	1	1	2

m_{24}	m_{34}	m_{44}	m_{54}	m_{64}	m_{74}	m_{15}	m_{25}	m_{35}	m_{45}	m_{55}	m_{65}	m_{75}	m_{85}
1	1	1	2	1	1	1	2	1	1	1	1	1	1

Memory requirement of the modules in MB

Again using the proposed algorithm the result is as follows

Task T_1 has been allocated as

Processor	Memory Capacity in M.B.	Modules Assigned	Remaining Memory
P_1	8		8 M.B.
P_2	8	m_{31} , m_{41}	5 M.B.
P_3	8	m_{11} , m_{51}	6 M.B.
P_4	8		8 M.B.
P_5	8	m_{21}	7 M.B.

Task T_2 has been allocated as

Processor	Memory Capacity in M.B.	Modules Assigned	Remaining Memory
P_1	8	m_{42}	6 M.B.
P_2	8	m_{31} , m_{41} ,m_{12}, m_{22}	3 M.B.
P_3	8	m_{11} , m_{51}	6 M.B.
P_4	8		8 M.B.
P_5	8	m_{21} , m_{32}	6 M.B.

Task T_3 has been allocated as

Processor	Memory Capacity in M.B.	Modules Assigned	Remaining Memory
P_1	8	m_{42} , m_{43}	5 M.B.
P_2	8	m_{31} , m_{41} , m_{12} , m_{22} , m_{33}	2 M.B.
P_3	8	m_{11}, m_{51}, m_{13} , m_{23}	4 M.B.
P_4	8		8 M.B.
P_5	8	m_{21} , m_{32}	6 M.B.

Task T_4 has been allocated as

Processor	Memory Capacity in M.B.	Modules Assigned	Remaining Memory
P_1	8	$m_{42}, m_{43}, m_{64}, m_{74}$	3 M.B.
P_2	8	m_{31} , m_{41} , m_{12} , m_{22} , m_{33}	2 M.B.
P_3	8	m_{11} , m_{51} , m_{13} , m_{23} , m_{14}	1 M.B.
P_4	8	m_{34}	7 M.B.
P_5	8	m_{21} , m_{32} , m_{24} , m_{44} , m_{54}	2 M.B.

Task T_5 has been allocated as (Final Table)

Processor	Memory Capacity in M.B.	Modules Assigned	Remaining Memory
P_1	8	m_{42} , m_{43}, m_{64} , m_{74} , m_{85}	2 M.B.
P_2	8	m_{31} , m_{41} , m_{12}, m_{22} , m_{33} , m_{55}	1 M.B.
P_3	8	m_{11} , m_{51} , m_{13} , m_{23} , m_{14} ,	1 M.B.
P_4	8	m_{34} , m_{25} , m_{35}, m_{45} , m_{65} , m_{75}	1 M.B.
P_5	8	m_{21} , m_{32} , m_{24}, m_{44} , m_{54} , m_{15}	2 M.B.

The final table shows that all the processors are being utilized for the purpose of execution. Further the tables show that the load of the DCS is well balanced. The resultant allocation infers that the modules of a particular task are also distributed among the processing nodes of the DCS. To observe the turn around time of tasks, this is to be implemented on a real DCS platform. The implementation of G will incur an overhead but this is inevitable for the management of the multiple tasks execution.

This work considers the realistic approach of multiple tasks, coming for the execution in DCS, dynamically. The proposed work can be a significant move towards the processor scheduling aspects of the Operating System of DCS.

8.2 Cluster-Based Load Partitioning and Allocation in DCS

A new workload partitioning and assignment algorithm is proposed for the tasks in large heterogeneous DCS, which attempts to find an assignment of task to processors that result in a feasible schedule. The aim of the contributions lies in:

1. its scalability to very large systems by taking advantage of dynamic cluster-ing,

2. its ability of handling arbitrary-topology heterogeneous systems and,

3. its use of a fuzzy based clustering heuristics which tends to increase feasible processor utilization bounds.

To overcome the scalability limitations, heuristic approaches[19-21] have been proposed for larger instances of the problem. Based on their performance measures, these approaches can be classified as schedulability-based[20, 21] or com-

munication based[22, 23]. One common way to reduce the allocation search space

is to cluster tasks into larger units of allocation, then allocating the resulting mod-

ule clusters, not individual modules, to available processors. Different flavor of

these are proposed in [22, 23]. In general, clustering heuristics, such as those in

[22], typically require the knowledge of module execution times and inter module

communication overhead. Computing these values, which depend on processor

speed and link bandwidth, requires a priori knowledge of task to processor as-

signment. Since the assignment is not known in advance, these heuristics are usu-

ally applicable only to homogeneous systems. For large distributed applications,

parts of which may span several heterogeneous platforms, this is a serious limita-

tion [24]. The approach here differs from other clustering approaches in three re-

spects. First, while in existing approaches, clustering is done only once, followed

by the allocation stage; we use a more scalable dynamic approach, which itera-

tively refines the solution. Second, the clustering algorithm can handle heteroge-

neous systems efficiently. And finally, we use the clustering, which is solely based

on the communication aspects of the task and the system. This avoids the priori

knowledge of task execution on the processors of the DCS.

8.2.1 Problem Formulation

We assume that the workload is composed of a set of tasks T_i, each of which is

characterized by a set of modules $m_i \in T_i$. Each module m_i has a worst case com-

putation requirement e_j measured in processor cycles (or in terms of other units) independent of processor speed. A module m_i may exchange messages with an-other module m_j of the same task. The hardware platform on which the application is to be executed is an arbitrary-topology distributed computing system, possibly composed of several dedicated and shared links. Links may be dedicated (point-to-point) or multiple access (e.g. an FDDI ring). A processor may have access to more than one link. The processors of distributed systems are on the same LAN or many LANs are connected through routers and gateways.

The modules of a single task are related and their relation is depicted by the task graph. The task graph considers the precedence and the Inter Module Com-munication among the modules (IMC matrix). A task that enters into the DCS is equipped with the following information

a)   IMC between m_i and m_j of task $T(c_{ij})$.

b)   Precedence among the modules of the task graph.

With these given parameters our object is to find an assignment of modules to processors, in a distributed computing system, for which feasible schedule is likely to be found by finding a suitable clustering and assignment.

8.2.2 Cluster Based Task Allocation

In a DCS, a sizable fraction of the total time is experienced in the inter-module communication. Communication penalty experienced by the system is defined as [25].

$$CP = \frac{T_{total}}{T_{comp}}$$

Where T_{total} is the time required by the algorithm to solve the given problem and T_{comp} is the time attributed to computation. If T_{comn} is the time involved in communication among different modules of the task, then

$$T_{total} = T_{comp} + T_{comn}$$

As obvious less communication overhead will reduce the communication penalty.

Factors that affect the communication in the system are as follows:

1) Bandwidth: It is defined as the number of bytes transferred in unit time.

2) Distance: It is inter processor distance in terms of links.

3) Connection: direct or through intermediate nodes.

4) Links: Time-shared or dedicated.

5) Communication devices: Gateways, routers etc.

The aim in the formation of the clusters (both task and processor) is to consider the above aspect of the communication and clusters are to be formed so as to reduce the communication penalty.

Cluster based task allocation involves the following steps

1) Divide the DCS (processor graph) into clusters of processors.

2) Divide the tasks into clusters of modules.

3) Map the clusters of modules onto the clusters of processors.

4) Dynamically reconfigure the cluster of processors as and when required.

8.2.3 Dynamic Formation of Clusters

The DCS can be partitioned into different subsystems, known as clusters. The formation of the cluster uses a heuristic. There are different possibilities of the cluster formation that depends on the network organization of the DCS. Some of the cluster formations have been depicted in figs. 8.3 and 8.4.

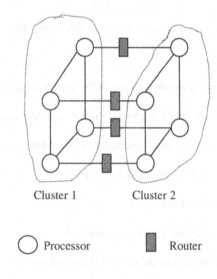

Cluster 1   Cluster 2

⭕ Processor   ▪ Router

Fig. 8.3. Hypercube structure

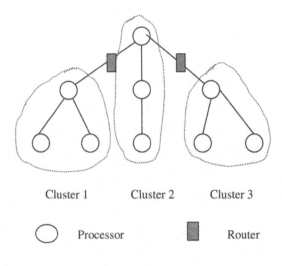

Cluster 1   Cluster 2   Cluster 3

◯   Processor   ▮   Router

Fig. 8.4. Tree structure

We need to consider two points while forming the cluster of processors. First, the connection among the processors (i.e. if the processors are directly connected, it is better to keep them in the same cluster) and second the placement of communication devices (routers and gateways). These devices delay the communication and so it is better to separate them out in the formation of the clusters.

There are two types of the processor cluster formation. One, in which once the cluster formed will be fixed during its operation. This is called static cluster formation. As the different clusters (group of processors) are connected with each other there are possibilities in which the structure of the cluster may change according to the need and availability of the processors. This is dynamic cluster formation. The examples given in Fig. 8.5 and 8.6 elaborate the dynamic cluster formation.

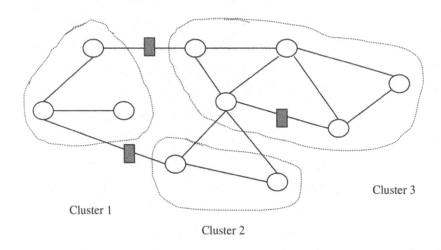

Cluster 1

Cluster 2

Cluster 3

Fig. 8.5. Dynamic cluster formation at time T for nonregular network of nodes

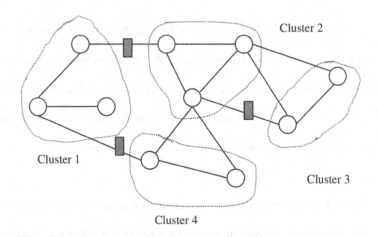

Cluster 2

Cluster 1

Cluster 3

Cluster 4

Fig. 8.6. Dynamic cluster formation at time T+ t for nonregular network of nodes

Similarly clusters of modules of a task can be formed. Usually these clusters

will be fixed throughout their execution.

Processor Clustering

Processor clustering attempts to identify group of processors, which can be treated as a single unit. These groups of processors are clustered together. In the present work, the attempt is to form cluster of processors based on the architecture of DCS and the application demand. The clusters may change dynamically depending on application. Usually number of processor clusters should be equal to the number of module clusters so that one to one mapping may result. Though it is not always possible as the different applications may demand different number of clusters.

The aim, to have the clustering of processors, is to reduce the communication overhead to its maximum possible extent. Thus while forming the clusters, the I/O speed of the processors and the bandwidth of the connecting links are to be considered. Abdelzer and shin[24] have defined the attraction force (B_{ij} / $\mu_i + \mu_j$) for the clustering of the processors. Here B_{ij} is the bandwidth of the link connecting two processors P_i and P_j of μ_i and μ_j speed respectively.

This work considers another aspect for the formation of the processor cluster. The communication between two processors, which are not directly connected, incurs more overhead than the communication between two directly connected processors. The more the distance the larger is the communication overhead.

A fuzzy logic is applied to define the membership of the processors and is sub-

sequently used to form the clusters of the processors. The fuzzy function will try

to keep those processors in the same cluster that are directly connected or at little

distance. Membership function is defined as follows:

Using the above membership function each processor of the DCS will get a

$$\mu(d_{kl}) = \frac{1}{1 + diff(d_{kl}, D)} \tag{8.7}$$

$$where \ \ diff(d_{kl}, D) = | \ d_{kl} - D \ |$$

$$d_{kl} = \text{the distance between processors } P_k \text{ and } P_l$$

$$D = \text{the diameter of the network}$$

membership value, which lies between 0 and 1. This membership value will help

in the formation of the processor clusters.

Processors on different LANs are interconnected via routers gateways etc.

These devices delay the communication. Thus as far as possible these devices

should be excluded in cluster formation.

Module Clustering

Modules of the tasks are clustered based on their communication requirement.

Highly communicating modules are clustered together to reduce communication

delays. We have applied the same fuzzy function to grade the high and low com-

municating modules.

Thus each module of the task will receive a membership value, which will help

$$\mu(c_{ij}) = \frac{1}{1 + diff(c_{ij}, C)} \tag{8.8}$$

$$where \ \ diff(c_{ij}, C) = | \ c_{ij} - C \ |$$

$$c_{ij} = \text{the communicat ion between th e modules } m_i \text{ and } m_j$$

$$C = \text{the maximum possible communicat ion between any two modules}$$

in the module cluster formation.

8.2.4 Cluster Allocation

Cluster allocation takes place after the clustering phase. Tasks clusters fit to the processor clusters according to four scheduling policies described below

a) **Best Fit**: Module cluster is placed in a processor cluster in which it fits almost exactly i.e. it tries to map one to one onto between module cluster and processor cluster as far as possible.

b) **First Fit:** Module cluster is placed in any available processor cluster, which can accommodate it.

c) **Worst Fit:** Module cluster is placed in the processor cluster, which leaves the maximum number of unused processor in the processor cluster.

d) **Reverse Fit:** This mapping is unlike to above three. Here, the number of modules in the module cluster is more than the number of processors in the processor cluster.

Obviously worst fit is of no use. Choice is to be made among the Best fit, First fit or Reverse fit as required.

Two more techniques are to be discussed in connection with the dynamic cluster formation of the processors.

i) **Merge:** If the no. of modules in the module cluster, exceeds the number of processors in a processor cluster, merging of the neighbor processor clusters may take place depending on the availability of the processors in the neighboring cluster.

ii) **Split:** Similarly the processor cluster may be split if the no. of processors in a processor cluster (P) is more than the number of modules in a module cluster (T_m) assigned. The whole cluster can be split into two parts with the unused processor in one cluster and the rest in the other. Obviously, these excluded processors may eventually merge with the other neighboring processors.

8.2.5 The Allocation Algorithm

The mapping of the module clusters to processor cluster takes place according to the following algorithm.

1)   *MODULE_CLUSTER( );*   *// form the clusters of modules of a task*
2)   *PROCESSOR_CLUSTER( );*   *// form the clusters of processors of the DCS*
3)   *Map the module clusters to the processor clusters using the scheduling policies:*

          BEST FIT
      or FIRST FIT
      or REVERSE FIT
4) *if*

BEST FIT

   then EXECUTE( )

  else if

      FIRST FIT

        then SPLIT( );

  else if

      REVERSE FIT

        then MERGE( );

Different functions used in the algorithm are as below.

MODULE_CLUSTER( )

{

a) *Estimate the fuzzy membership value for all the modules of the task in re-spect of IMC starting with the first module.*

b) *Cluster those modules which lie in the same membership value. Do it for all remaining modules. If any qualifying module is already clustered, ex-clude that module in the current cluster.*

}

PROCESSOR_CLUSTER ( )

{

a) *Estimate the fuzzy membership value for all the processors with other processors starting with the first processor*

b) *Cluster those processors, which lie in the same membership value.*

    c) *If there is a communicating device in between two processors, exclude the next processor from the cluster.*

    d) *Do step b) and c) for all the remaining processors and if any qualifying processor is already clustered, exclude that processor in the current cluster.*

}

SPLIT( )

{

    Exclude $(P-T_m)$ processors from the processor cluster;

    EXECUTE( );

}

MERGE( )

{

    Look for close to (T_m-P) free neighbor processors;

    Join these processors in the same processor cluster;

    EXECUTE( );

    if *none free (T_m-P) neighbor processors*

    then *allocate (T_m-P) modules on the same processors of the cluster*

    EXECUTE( );

}

EXECUTE( )

{

Execute all the modules of the clusters and quit the DCS;

}

8.2.6 An Example

An example is given to illustrate the algorithm. The task graph and processor graph are chosen at random and is given in fig. 8.7 and 8.9. The Inter Module Communication matrix is also assumed to be given. The relevant data is available below.

	m_1	m_2	m_3	m_4	m_5	m_6	m_7	m_8	m_9	m_{10}
m_1	0	1	1	1	1	2	2	2	4	4
m_2	1	0	1	2	3	1	2	3	3	4
m_3	1	1	0	1	2	2	1	2	2	3
m_4	1	2	1	0	1	3	2	1	3	2
m_5	1	3	2	1	0	3	2	1	3	2
m_6	2	1	2	3	3	0	1	2	2	3
m_7	2	2	1	2	2	1	0	1	1	2
m_8	2	3	2	1	1	2	1	0	2	1
m_9	4	3	2	3	3	2	1	2	0	3
m_{10}	4	4	3	2	2	3	2	1	3	0

IMC requirements of the modules

	m_1	m_2	m_3	m_4	m_5	m_6	m_7	m_8	m_9	m_{10}
m_1	0.2	0.25	0.25	0.25	0.25	0.33	0.33	0.33	1	1
m_2	0.25	0.2	0.25	0.33	0.5	0.25	0.33	0.5	0.5	1
m_3	0.25	0.25	0.2	0.25	0.33	0.33	0.25	0.33	0.33	0.5
m_4	0.25	0.33	0.25	0.2	0.25	0.5	0.33	0.25	0.5	0.33
m_5	0.25	0.5	0.33	0.5	0.2	0.5	0.33	0.25	0.5	0.33
m_6	0.33	0.25	0.33	0.5	0.5	0.2	0.25	0.33	0.33	0.5
m_7	0.33	0.33	0.25	0.33	0.33	0.25	0.2	0.25	0.25	0.33
m_8	0.33	0.5	0.5	0.25	0.25	0.33	0.25	0.2	0.33	0.25

m_9	1	0.5	0.33	0.5	0.5	0.33	0.25	0.33	0.2	0.5
m_{10}	1	1	0.5	0.33	0.33	0.5	0.33	0.25	0.5	0.2

Corresponding membership values of the modules

	P_1	P_2	P_3	P_4	P_5	P_6	P_7	P_8
P_1	0.25	0.33	0.33	0.33	0.5	0.5	0.5	0.5
P_2	0.33	0.25	0.33	0.5	0.33	0.33	0.5	0.5
P_3	0.33	0.33	0.25	0.5	0.5	0.5	0.33	0.33
P_4	0.33	0.5	0.5	0.25	1	1	1	0.33
P_5	0.5	0.33	0.5	1	0.25	0.5	1	1
P_6	0.5	0.33	0.5	1	0.5	0.25	1	1
P_7	0.5	0.5	0.33	1	1	1	0.25	0.5
P_8	0.5	0.5	0.33	0.33	1	1	0.5	0.25

Corresponding membership values of processors

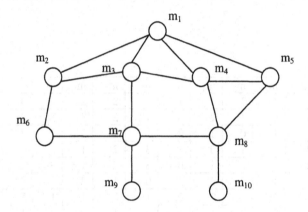

Fig. 8.7. Task graph with corresponding modules

According to the algorithm (section 8.2.5), the following module clusters of the

task have been formed as shown in Fig. 8.8.

T_m_cluster_1 : m_1, m_2, m_3, m_4, m_5

T_m_cluster_2: m_6, m_7

T_m_cluster_3: m_8, m_{10}

T_m_cluster_4: m_9

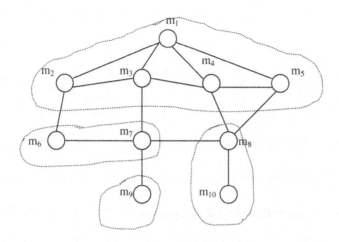

Fig. 8.8. Cluster formation of modules

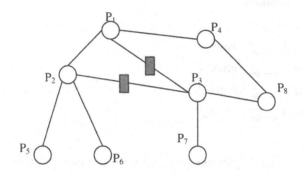

Fig. 8.9. Processor graph

According to the algorithm (section 8.2.5) the following processor clusters have been formed (Fig. 8.10).

P_cluster_1 : P_1, P_2, P_4

P_cluster_2 : P_5

P_cluster_3 : P_6

P_cluster_4 : P_3, P_7, P_8

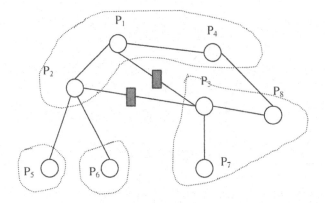

Fig. 8.10. Cluster formation of processors

As per the allocation algorithm, the module clusters are mapped onto the processor clusters as follows

T_m_cluster_1 $\longrightarrow$ P_cluster_1
T_m_cluster_2 $\longrightarrow$ P_cluster_4
T_m_cluster_3 $\longrightarrow$ P_cluster_2
T_m_cluster_4 $\longrightarrow$ P_cluster_3

Finally P_cluster_4 splits one processor from its cluster. P_cluster_1 merge with that processor and the other P_clusters remain as it is.

Cluster based load partitioning and assignment is used for real-time applications. The proposed approach has the potential for scalability and support for system heterogeneity. Scalability is achieved by Merge and Split cluster formation of the processors. The approach considers the communication aspect in the cluster formation as it incurs more overheads. This is also a realistic approach as the other algorithms, based on the same, uses the priori knowledge of the execution of the modules of the task on the processors of the DCS. The communication bandwidth is already known while designing the system, so it is not difficult to measure the IMC time for the modules of the task. A new fuzzy approach is applied to form the clusters. Examples illustrate the algorithm.

8.3 The LBTA Strategy for Multiple Tasks Using A*

In this section, an algorithm has been developed for the LBTA strategy for multiple tasks. A heuristic approach to solve LBTA problem for multiple tasks using A* technique has been presented. The load on a processing node for multiple tasks proposed in the chapter 6 has been used as a cost function for the algorithm in this chapter. An illustrative example has been worked out using the algorithm. Few examples have been worked out using the software implementation of the algorithm. Finally the GT shows the corresponding allocation of the tasks, which achieves balanced load among the processing nodes of a DCS.

A DCS is a network of workstations, personal computers and/or other computing systems. Such a system may be heterogeneous in the sense that the computing nodes may have different architectural capabilities as well as different speeds and memory capacities. A DCS accepts tasks from users and executes different modules of these tasks on various nodes of the system. Various modules of a task have a precedence relation depicted by its task graph and their communicational requirements are given by the IMC matrix. A good number of task allocation algorithms have been proposed in the literature. These algorithms allocate a given task on to the DCS nodes and aim to minimize the turn around time of the given task and do not consider the multiple task allocation in a DCS. Such algorithms do not consider (both) the number of modules that can be accepted by the individual computing nodes and the memory capacity of the nodes. Factually, in a DCS the nodes may share some specified load within their memory capacity constraints. Further, the above mentioned algorithms consider only one given task. In this work, we have considered the number of modules that can be accepted by individual nodes along with their memory capacities and arrival of multiple disjoint tasks (there are no inter task communication among tasks) to the DCS from time to time. The algorithm proposed here, attempts to allocate modules of a task on to such processing nodes that takes minimum possible time for execution of the concerned modules. It is only when such a processing node, that requires smaller time for the concerned module, will become overloaded because of this assignment; the concerned module is allocated to a processing node that may take more time to execute. Such an arrangement obtains the minimization of turn around time up to the possible extend for the concerned task. Finally the resultant possible minimum possible turn around times of all the tasks will ensure enhancement of throughput. It will not be out of place to mention that an allocation that overloads processors looking only at the execution time and IMC matrix of concerned task will certainly increase the turn around times of the task and result in a poor throughput.

To exploit effective parallelism on a DCS, tasks must be properly allocated to the processing nodes. The task assignment problem is well known to be NP-Hard.

A task allocation algorithm seeks an assignment that optimizes a certain cost-function, for example maximum throughput or minimum turnaround time. However, most of the reported algorithms yield sub-optimal solutions. In general, optimal solutions can be found through an exhaustive search, but as there is n^m ways in which m modules can be assigned to n processing nodes, an exhaustive search is often not possible. Thus, optimal solution algorithms exist only for restricted cases or very small problems. The other possibility is to use an informed search to reduce the state space [3].

Like other NP-hard problems, there are three common ways to get a solution of the problem [17]:

- Relaxation: some of the requirements can be relaxed or restrict the problem.
- Enumerative optimization: to compromise with the solution's optimality enumerative methods such as dynamic programming and branch-and-bound can be used.
- Approximate optimization: heuristics can be used to solve the problem while aiming for near optimal or good solution.

8.3.1 The Proposed Algorithm

Though a plethora of algorithms have been proposed, most of them have not taken the realistic view that only a finite number of modules can be allocated to a processor, depending upon the architectural capability of the processors. Secondly, earlier algorithms [3, 26] have continued to assume that all the modules will be eventually allocated without considering the status of the system in terms of remaining memory and the additional no. of modules that the individual processors can accept as per the allocations that have already been made for the previous tasks. These algorithms do not consider the requirement of allocation of modules of multiple tasks. All the algorithms give the solution to single task allocation case.

In the proposed algorithm, we have shed off these unrealistic assumptions and make use of a data structure STATUS associated with every processor, which has two fields showing:

a)   The maximum no. of modules that can be allocated to this processor and
b)   The memory capacity of the processor.

Whenever a module is chosen for allocation onto a processor, the STATUS is checked and it is ascertained whether the processor can accommodate the module at hand. If not, another processor is chosen if available. The consequence might be that a certain task is not allocated at all. STATUS is of the type

$$
\begin{aligned}
&Struct\{ \\
&\quad int\ no\_of\_modules; \\
&\quad int\ mem\_capacity; \\
&\} STATUS;
\end{aligned}
$$

A matrix L^i_{pq} which indicates whether two processors are directly connected or not (i.e. L^i is an adjacency matrix). Let us have a coefficient matrix C_f that has n entries. The ith entry corresponds to communication between two processors via i links. While calculating the load of a processor, as in section 6.5, when the 2nd expression in R.H.S. of equation 6.5 amounts to zero and p is not the same as q (i.e. Processors p and q are not directly connected), we find out L^2, multiply it by C_{f2} (2nd field of C_f), and check whether this comes out to be non-zero; if it does, we replace L^1 in equation 3.4 with this; if not we find out L^3 and multiply it with C_{f3} and check whether the product comes out to be non-zero. We continue like this until we find a non-zero value and then replace L^i in equation 3.4 with this (it should be noted that we'll find a non-zero value within n multiplications, where n is the no. of processing nodes). In section 8.3.5 (case 1), an illustrative example elaborates the use of L^i_{pq} and C_{fi}. Thus we modify equation 6.5 as following, which is 'load' in a processor p.

$$Load = \sum_{l=1}^{k}\sum_{i=1}^{m}X_{ilp}.M_{ilp} + \sum_{\substack{q=1\\q\ne p}}^{n}\sum_{l=1}^{k}\sum_{i=1}^{m}\sum_{\substack{j=1\\j\ne i}}^{m}(C_{ijl}+CC_{pq}).M_{ilp}.M_{jlq} \qquad (8.9)$$

Where, $CC_{pq} = C_{fi} . L^i_{pq}$

X_{ilp} = Execution cost of module i of task l on processor p

$$M_{ilp} = \begin{cases} 1 & \text{if module } m_i \text{ of task } l \text{ is assigned to processing node } p, \\ 0 & \text{otherwise} . \end{cases}$$

C_{ijl} = Communication cost between i^{th} and j^{th} module of task l

L^i_{pq} = Connection matrix of two processors p and q, describing the   links (direct/ one indirect/ two indirect etc.) of connection paths among the processing nodes in Processor Graph(PG).

Cf_i = Coefficient matrix which has n entries describing the IPC costs for the links of connection paths among the processing nodes.

For example, C_{f1}=5(for direct connection between the processors), C_{f2}=10 (for processors which are indirectly connected by one link), C_{f3}= 20(for processors which are indirectly connected by two links) etc.

$$M_{jlq} = \begin{cases} 1 & \text{if module } m_j \text{ of task } l \text{ is assigned to processing node } q, \\ 0 & \text{otherwise} . \end{cases}$$

The work assumes that task graphs and processor graph of a DCS are given. Communication matrices are given for IMC among modules of tasks. It is also assumed that the execution times of all the modules of the task are given in Execution Matrix.

A heuristic approach is applied to solve LBTA problem for multiple tasks. In the proposed algorithm, we have considered the above factors and have applied the well-known A* algorithm. A* is a best-first search heuristic technique for a larger search space [3].

8.3.2 The A*

In the A* algorithm [3], for a tree search, it starts from the root, called the start node (usually a null solution of the problem). Intermediate tree nodes represent the partial solutions, and leaf nodes represent the complete solution or goal. A cost function f computes each node's associated cost. The value of f for a node n, which is the estimated cost of the cheapest solution through n, is computed as

$$f(n) = g(n) + h(n) \qquad\qquad (8.10)$$

Where $g(n)$ is the search-path cost from the start node to the current node and $h(n)$ is a lower-bound estimate of the path cost from current node to the goal node(solution), using any heuristic information available. To expand a node means to generate all of its successors or children and to compute the f value for each of them. The nodes are ordered for search according to cost; that is, the algorithm first selects the node with the minimum expansion cost. The algorithm maintains a sorted list, called OPEN, of nodes (according to their f values) and always selects a node with the best expansion cost. Because the algorithm always selects the best-cost node, it guarantees an optimal solution.

For the task allocation problem under consideration:

- the search space is a tree,
- the initial node (the root) is a null-assignment node, that is no modules are assigned as yet,
- intermediate nodes are partial-assignment nodes, that is only some modules are assigned,
- a solution (goal) node is a complete-assignment node, that is all the modules of the tasks are assigned.

To compute the cost function, $g(n)$ is the cost of partial assignment at node n-the load on the heaviest loaded (p_i); this can be done using the equation 8.8. For the computation of $h(n)$, two sets A_p (the set of modules that are assigned to the heaviest loaded p) and U (the set of modules that are unassigned at this stage of the search and have one or more communication link with any module in set A_p) are defined. Each module m_i in U will be assigned either to p or any other processor q that has a direct or indirect communication link with p. So, two kinds of costs with each m_i's assignment can be associated: either X_{ilp} (the execution cost of m_i of task l on p) or with the sum of communication costs of all the modules in set A_p that have a link with m_i. This implies that to consider m_i's assignment, it is decided whether m_i should go to p or not (by taking the minimum of these two cases' cost).

8.3.3 Control Abstraction of the LBTA for Multiple Tasks

1. *Calculate the status of the global Table (GT) for each processor in terms of available memory (M) and the modules that are already assigned to it.*

2. *Maintain a list S of unallocated tasks with all modules (all tasks are in S at the beginning) and a list OPEN, empty at the beginning.*

3. *Take one Task t_a from S and put it in another list V and reset OPEN (i.e. OPEN is empty now).*

4. *If allocation of modules in V is possible using the A*(equation 8.9) algorithm and verifying STATUS, then allocate the modules; if allocation is not possible, de-allocate the allocated modules of the task and move onto the next task, modifying the STATUS in between and update the Global Table(GT).*
    /* The Pseudocode for step 4 is given below */

5. *If S is not empty yet, go to step 2.*

6. *Stop (end of allocation).*

Pseudocode for step 4

while(V!=NULL) {

$$m_a = V;$$

$m_a = V \rightarrow next;$

$if((STATUS[P].no\_of\_modules! = 0)$ &&

$(STATUS[P].mem\_capacity<$

$MEMORY[t_a][m_a]))$

{

$flag = 1;$

/* flag is supposed to have been initialized to zero.

*/

MODIFY_OPEN( );

/* This function includes the node under consideration

i.e. m_a in OPEN */

FIND_LOAD( );

/* This function finds out the Load [eqn. 8.8] at every

processor and stores them in an array

*/

FIND_COST( );

/* This function finds out the Cost f(n) for the processor

with   heaviest load [equation 8.8]   */

}

if (flag = = 0)

{

DE-ALLOCATE_TASK( );

/* This function de-allocates the partially allocated

modules under consideration and moves onto the

next task   */

MODIFY_STATUS( );

/* *This function modifies the STATUS of each proces-*

  sor to   which the modules of the task, most re-

  cently moved to V, had been allocated, by incre-

  menting the fields of STATUS corresponding to

  the particular module. Thus de-allocation is com-

  *pleted   */*

}

FIND_LEAST_COST();

/* *This function finds out the least value stored in the*

  array in

(i) *above.   */*

MODIFY_STATUS( );

/* This function modifies the status of each processing node

  according to the allocated modules and used mem-

  ory */

MODIFY_OPEN( );

/* *This function removes the least cost from OPEN   */*

}

The complexity of the algorithm is $O(p^2m^3)$ where p is the no. of processing nodes and m is the total no. of modules of all the tasks, although optimal task assignment, like many other graph matching problem, needs exponential time in worst case [3].   The complexity of the algorithm is calculated by analyzing the step counts in pseudo-code. The corresponding code of void *allocation( )* can be referred to for ascertaining the step counts [appendix-A]. The proof has been given in sec 8.3.7.

8.3.4 An Illustrated Example

The following example illustrate the operation of allocation of the algorithm using A* technique for the LBTA problem. A task with its modules $\{m_{11}, m_{21}, m_{31}, m_{41}, m_{51}\}$ and a set of three processing nodes in a DCS $\{P_0, P_1, P_2\}$ are given in fig. 8.11. The execution and IMC matrix are assumed to be given in units of time. The resulting search tree is shown in the Figure. 8.12.

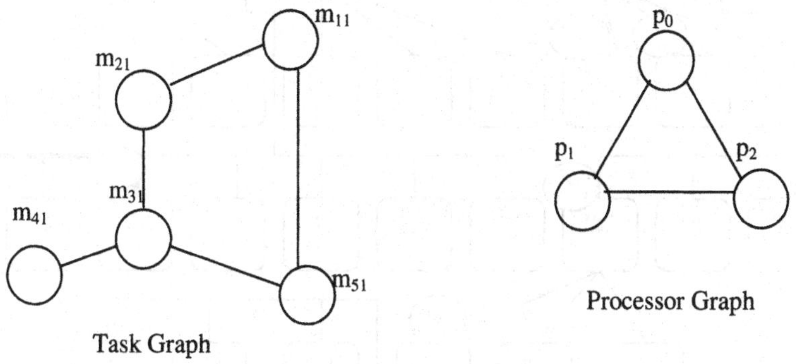

Fig. 8.11.Task graph and Processor graph

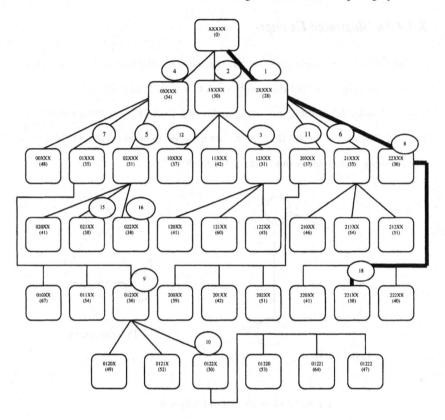

Fig. 8.12. Search tree for the example 8.3.4   (continued on next page)

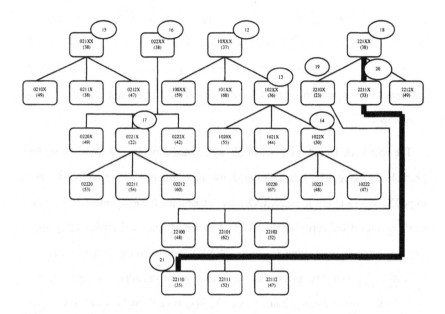

Fig. 8.12. Search tree for the example 8.3.4 (63 nodes generated, 21 nodes expanded)

	p_0	p_1	p_2
m_{11}	17	13	11
m_{21}	16	14	10
m_{31}	18	15	8
m_{41}	7	6	5
m_{51}	12	11	9

Execution Time Matrix of the modules

	m_{11}	m_{21}	m_{31}	m_{41}	m_{51}
m_{11}	0	9	0	0	8
m_{21}	9	0	7	0	0
m_{31}	0	7	0	6	5
m_{41}	0	0	6	0	0
m_{51}	8	0	5	0	0

IMC cost matrix

A search node includes partial allocation of modules of the task to processing nodes and the value of f, which is the cost of the partial assignment. A partial allocation means that some modules are unassigned. The value X indicates that i^{th} module has not been assigned yet. The allocation of the module to a processing node replaces an X value in the allocation string with some processing node's number. Node expansion means adding a new module assignment to the partial assignment.

The root node includes the set of all unassigned modules XXXXX. Next, for example, in figure 8.12, it is considered, the allocation of m_{11} to p_0(0XXXX), m_{11} to p_1(1XXXX) and m_{11} to p_2(2XXXX), by determining the assignment costs at the tree's first level and verifying the STATUS to see whether the corresponding allocation is possible. Allocating m_{11} to p_0 (0XXXX) results in the total cost $f(n)$ that is equal to 34. The $g(n)$, is this case, according to the equation 8.8, equals to 17, which is the cost of executing m_{11} on p_0. The $h(n)$ is equal to 17, which is the sum of the minimum execution or the communication costs of m_{21} and m_{51}(the modules communicating with m_{11}). Similarly, the costs of assigning m_{11} to p_1(30) and m_{11} to p_2(28) is calculated. The algorithm inserts these three nodes into the list OPEN. 28 is the minimum among the costs. So the algorithm selects the node 2XXXX for expansion. Further the algorithm expands node 2XXXX in the following manner.

Now the algorithm will consider m_{21} for assignment and 20XXX, 21XXX and 22XXX are three possible assignments after verifying STATUS. The value of $f(n)$ for 20XXX is 37 and it is computed as follows: first the processing node with heaviest load is selected, which is p_0 in this case. $g(n)$ is equal to 30, which is the cost of executing m_{21} on p_0(16) plus the cost of communication between m_{21} and m_{11}(14), because they are assigned to two different processing nodes, where the IMC is 9 and the minimum communication cost between the processing nodes by direct link (C_{f1}=5) is 5. $h(n)$ is equal to 7, which is the minimum execution or communication cost of m_{31} (the only unassigned module communicating with m_{21}).

Similarly the values of $f(n)$ for 21XXX(35) and 22XXX(36) are calculated. At this point, nodes 0XXXX(34), 1XXXX(30), 20XXX(37), 21XXX(35) and 22XXX(36) are in the OPEN list. The 1XXXX(30) has the minimum node cost, the algorithm expands it next.

Here, in the following order 10XXX, 11XXX and 12XXX, the nodes are expanded. The numbers in the circles attached to some of the nodes show the sequence in which nodes are selected for expansion. Bold lines shows the edges connecting the nodes that lead to an optimal assignment. Here, in the example, we assumed that the Inter processor Communication (IPC) cost for C_{f1} =5(for direct link), C_{f2} =10(for one indirect link) and C_{f3} =20 (for two indirect links) in units of time.

The descriptions of the OPEN are as follows:

OPEN_1 : 0XXXX(34), 1XXXX(30), **2XXXX(28)** .
                                                        1

2XXXX(28) is the minimum cost node. So, it is expanding. And it is removed from the OPEN. The underlined nodes with numbers show the order of expansion.

OPEN_2 : 0XXXX(34), **1XXXX(30)**, 20XXX(37), 21XXX(35), 22XXX(36) .
                              2

OPEN_3: 0XXXX(34), 20XXX(37), 21XXX(35), 22XXX(36), 10XXX(37), 11XXX(42), **12XXX(31)** .
                                                                            3

OPEN_4: **0XXXX(34)**, 20XXX(37), 21XXX(35), 22XXX(36), 10XXX(37),
            4
            11XXX(42), 120XX(41), 121XX(60), 122XX(43) .

OPEN_5 :   20XXX(37), 21XXX(35), 22XXX(36), 10XXX(37), 11XXX(42),
            120XX(41), 121XX(60), 122XX(43), 00XXX(41), 01XXX(35),
            02XXX(31) .
            5

OPEN_6 : 20XXX(37), **21XXX(35)**, 22XXX(36), 10XXX(37), 11XXX(42),
                    6
    120XX(41), 121XX(60), 122XX(43), 00XXX(41), 01XXX(35),
020XX(41), 021XX(38), 022XX(38) .

OPEN_7 : 20XXX(37), 22XXX(36), 10XXX(37), 11XXX(42), 120XX(41),
    121XX(60), 122XX(43), 00XXX(41), **01XXX(35)**, 020XX(41),
                                                    7
    021XX(38), 022XX(38) .

OPEN_8 : 20XXX(37), **22XXX(36)**, 10XXX(37), 11XXX(42), 120XX(41),
                    8
    121XX(60), 122XX(43), 00XXX(41), 020XX(41), 021XX(38),
022XX(38), 010XX(67), 011XX(54), 012XX(36) .

OPEN_9 : 20XXX(37), 10XXX(37), 11XXX(42), 120XX(41), 121XX(60),
    122XX(43), 00XXX(41), 020XX(41), 021XX(38), 022XX(38),
010XX(67), 011XX(54), **012XX(36)**, 220XX(41), 221XX(38),
                                    9
    222XX(40) .

OPEN_10 :   20XXX(37), 10XXX(37), 11XXX(42), 120XX(41), 121XX(60),
    122XX(43), 00XXX(41), 020XX(41), 021XX(38), 022XX(38),
010XX(67), 011XX(54), 220XX(41), 221XX(38), 222XX(40),
0120X(49), 0121X(52), **0122X(30)** .
                                    10

OPEN_11: **20XXX(37)**, 10XXX(37), 11XXX(42), 120XX(41), 121XX(60),
          11
    122XX(43),   00XXX(41),   020XX(41),   021XX(38),
022XX(38), 010XX(67), 011XX(54), 220XX(41), 221XX(38),
222XX(40),   0120X(49), 0121X(52), 01220(53), 01221(64),
01222(47) .

OPEN_12: **10XXX(37)**, 11XXX(42), 120XX(41), 121XX(60), 122XX(43),
          12

00XXX(41), 020XX(41), 021XX(38), 022XX(38), 010XX(67), 011XX(54), 220XX(41), 221XX(38), 222XX(40), 0120X(49), 0121X(52), 01220(53), 01221(64), 01222(47), 200XX(59), 201XX(42), 202XX(51) .

OPEN_13: 11XXX(42), 120XX(41), 121XX(60), 122XX(43), 00XXX(41),

020XX(41), 021XX(38), 022XX(38), 010XX(67), 011XX(54), 220XX(41), 221XX(38), 222XX(40), 0120X(49), 0121X(52), 01220(53), 01221(64), 01222(47), 200XX(59), 201XX(42), 202XX(51), 100XX(59), 101XX(60), **102XX(36)** .
13

OPEN_14 : 11XXX(42), 120XX(41), 121XX(60), 122XX(43), 00XXX(41), 020XX(41), 021XX(38), 022XX(38), 010XX(67), 011XX(54), 220XX(41), 221XX(38), 222XX(40), 0120X(49), 0121X(52), 01220(53), 01221(64), 01222(47), 200XX(59), 201XX(42), 202XX(51), 100XX(59), 101XX(60), 1020X(55), 1021X(44), **1022X(30)** .
14

OPEN_15 : 11XXX(42), 120XX(41), 121XX(60), 122XX(43), 00XXX(41),

020XX(41),   **021XX(38)**,   022XX(38),   010XX(67), 011XX(54),   **15**

220XX(41),   221XX(38),   222XX(40),   0120X(49), 0121X(52), 01220(53), 01221(64), 01222(47), 200XX(59), 201XX(42), 202XX(51), 100XX(59), 101XX(60), 1020X(55), 1021X(44), 10220(67), 10221(48), 10222(47) .

OPEN_16 : 11XXX(42), 120XX(41), 121XX(60), 122XX(43), 00XXX(41), 020XX(41),   **022XX(38)**,   010XX(67),   011XX(54), 220XX(41),   **16**

221XX(38), 222XX(40), 0120X(49), 0121X(52), 01220(53), 01221(64), 01222(47), 200XX(59), 201XX(42), 202XX(51), 100XX(59), 101XX(60), 1020X(55), 1021X(44), 10220(67), 10221(48), 10222(47), 0210X(49), 0211X(38), 0212X(47).

OPEN_17 : 11XXX(42), 120XX(41), 121XX(60), 122XX(43), 00XXX(41),
             020XX(41), 010XX(67), 011XX(54), 220XX(41), 221XX(38),
             222XX(40), 0120X(49), 0121X(52), 01220(53), 01221(64),
             01222(47), 200XX(59), 201XX(42), 202XX(51), 100XX(59),
             101XX(60), 1020X(55), 1021X(44), 10220(67), 10221(48),
             10222(47), 0210X(49), 0211X(38), 0212X(47), 0220X(49),
             0221X(22), 0222X(42) .
                 17

OPEN_18 : 11XXX(42), 120XX(41), 121XX(60), 122XX(43), 00XXX(41),
             020XX(41), 010XX(67), 011XX(54), 220XX(41), **221XX(38)**,
                                                                18
             222XX(40), 0120X(49), 0121X(52), 01220(53), 01221(64),
             01222(47), 200XX(59), 201XX(42), 202XX(51), 100XX(59),
             101XX(60), 1020X(55), 1021X(44), 10220(67), 10221(48),
             10222(47), 0210X(49), 0211X(38), 0212X(47), 0220X(49),
             0222X(42), 02210(53), 02211(54), 02212(60) .

OPEN_19 : 11XXX(42), 120XX(41), 121XX(60), 122XX(43), 00XXX(41),
             020XX(41), 010XX(67), 011XX(54), 220XX(41), 222XX(40),
             0120X(49), 0121X(52), 01220(53), 01221(64), 01222(47),
             200XX(59), 201XX(42), 202XX(51), 100XX(59), 101XX(60),
             1020X(55), 1021X(44), 10220(67), 10221(48), 10222(47),
             0210X(49), 0211X(38), 0212X(47), 0220X(49), 0222X(42),
             02210(53), 02211(54), 02212(60), **2210X(23)**, 2211X(33),
                                                       19
             2212X(45) .

OPEN_20 : 11XXX(42), 120XX(41), 121XX(60), 122XX(43), 00XXX(41),
             020XX(41), 010XX(67), 011XX(54), 220XX(41), 222XX(40),
             0120X(49), 0121X(52), 01220(53), 01221(64), 01222(47),
             200XX(59), 201XX(42), 202XX(51), 100XX(59), 101XX(60),
             1020X(55), 1021X(44), 10220(67), 10221(48), 10222(47),
             0210X(49), 0211X(38), 0212X(47), 0220X(49), 0222X(42),
             02210(53), 02211(54), 02212(60), **2211X(33)** , 2212X(45),
                                                        20

             22100(48), 22101(62), 22102(52).

OPEN_21 : 11XXX(42), 120XX(41), 121XX(60), 122XX(43), 00XXX(41),
             020XX(41), 010XX(67), 011XX(54), 012XX(36), 220XX(41),
             222XX(40), 0120X(49), 0121X(52), 01220(53), 01221(64),

01222(47), 200XX(59), 201XX(42), 202XX(51), 100XX(59),
101XX(60), 1020X(55), 1021X(44), 10220(67), 10221(48),
10222(47), 0210X(49), 0211X(38), 0212X(47), 0220X(49),
0222X(42), 02210(53), 02211(54), 02212(60), 2212X(45),
22100(48), 22101(62), 22102(52), **22110(35)**, 22111(52),
21
22112(47) .

The search continues and expands nodes until the node with the complete assignment (22110) is selected. This is the goal node because the node has a complete assignment (22110) i.e. all the modules of the task have been allocated according to the minimum costs. So, this is a goal node. Figure 8.12 shows the order
in which the algorithm considers the modules for assignment. During the search
for an optimal solution, 63 nodes are generated and 21 nodes are expanded.

8.3.5 Implementation

The software for the above algorithm is developed in C and the studies have
been carried out by using few examples cited below to judge the efficiency of the
algorithm. Here, we assume that the IMC matrices, the execution time matrices
and the adjacency matrices of processing nodes (connectivity of the processing
nodes) are given for every module of each task in units of time. Tasks with their
corresponding modules are presented as Task Graphs (TG) and processing nodes
of a DCS are presented as Processor Graph (PG).

The algorithm has been applied to work out allocation for the tasks and processors interconnection graph given below. Here, we have considered three different
cases. The first field of STATUS represents the maximum number of modules that
can be allocated to the processing node and the second field represents the mem-

ory capacity of the processing node. The Global Table (GT) shows the present status of the processing nodes of the DCS after allocating each task.

Case 1

Given a set of three tasks with their corresponding modules $T_1(m_{11}, m_{21}, m_{31}, m_{41})$, $T_2(m_{21}, m_{22}, m_{32})$, $T_3(m_{13}, m_{22}, m_{33})$ and a set of four processors $\{p_1, p_2, p_3, p_4\}$ (fig.8.13).

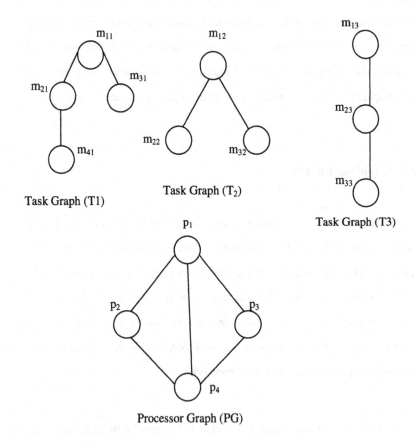

Task Graph (T1)

Task Graph (T$_2$)

Task Graph (T3)

Processor Graph (PG)

Fig. 8.13. Task Graphs and Processor Graph

	p_1	p_2	p_3	p_4
m_{11}	10	20	5	25
m_{21}	35	10	15	15
m_{31}	10	15	25	10
m_{41}	20	35	20	5

Execution Cost of Modules of the task T_1

	p_1	p_2	p_3	p_4
m_{12}	20	5	35	10
m_{22}	10	10	10	10
m_{32}	15	10	20	15

Execution Cost of Modules of the task T_2

	p_1	p_2	p_3	p_4
m_{13}	15	25	15	10
m_{23}	30	40	25	20
m_{33}	20	5	10	15

Execution Cost of Modules of the task T_3

	m_{11}	m_{21}	m_{31}	m_{41}
m_{11}	0	10	50	20
m_{21}	10	0	10	50
m_{31}	50	10	0	50
m_{41}	20	50	50	0

IMC Cost of Modules task T_1

	m_{12}	m_{22}	m_{32}
m_{12}	0	5	10
m_{22}	5	0	60
m_{32}	10	60	0

IMC Cost of Module of the task T_2

	m_{13}	m_{23}	m_{33}
m_{13}	0	5	40
m_{23}	5	0	10
m_{33}	40	10	0

IMC Cost of Modules of the task T_3

	p_1	p_2	p_3	p_4
p_1	0	1	1	1
p_2	1	0	0	1
p_3	1	0	0	1
p_4	1	1	1	0

Adjacency Matrix of Processors L^1_{pq}

	p_1	p_2	p_3	p_4
p_1	0	1	1	1
p_2	1	0	1	1
p_3	1	1	0	1
p_4	1	1	1	0

Adjacency Matrix of Processors L^2_{pq}

m_{11}	m_{21}	m_{31}	m_{41}	m_{12}	m_{22}	m_{32}	m_{13}	m_{23}	m_{33}
5	3	2	4	3	2	1	4	2	3

Memory Requirement of Modules in Units

STATUS[1] = [4, 10]

STATUS[2] = [3, 8]

STATUS[3] = [4, 9]

STATUS[4] = [5, 12]

The above STATUS indicates that the maximum number of modules that can be allocated to first processing node is 4 and the memory capacity of the first processing node is 10 in units. The other STATUS also indicates the present status of the second, third and fourth processing nodes respectively.

So, the present status of the Global Table is as follows:

I	II	III	IV	V	VI
Processor	Max. no. of Modules*	Memory Capacity	Modules Assigned	Remaining No. of Modules**	Remaining Memory
p_1	4	10		4	10
p_2	3	8		3	8
p_3	4	9		4	9
p_4	5	12		5	12

*The column III represents the maximum number of modules that can be allocated to a processing node.

**The column V represents the remaining number of modules that can be allocated to a processing node after some modules have been assigned to the processing node.

Now applying the software in Pentium 100 MHz, the following results have been obtained.

Here, in the results, "Task 1 has been allocated as : 4141" indicates that the four modules(m_{11}, m_{12}, m_{13}, m_{14}) of the task T_1 have been allocated onto the processing node p_4, p_1, p_4, p_1 respectively. "The cost of allocation for processing node no. 1 is 55" means the execution and communication costs of the modules of tasks by this allocation onto the processing node 1 by the allocation is 55 in units of time. "The status of the processing node 1 is 1" indicates that after allocation has been completed, the remaining number of modules that can be allocated to the processing node p_1 is 1 and remaining number of memory that is available in the processing node p_1 is 1 in units.

Results:

Task 1 has been allocated as: 4141

Task 2 has been allocated as: 212

Task 3 has been allocated as: 323

The cost of allocation for processing node no. 1 is 55

The status of the processing node 1 is 1   1

The cost of allocation for processing node no. 2 is 120

The status of the processing node 2 is 0   2

The cost of allocation for processing node no. 3 is 180

The status of the processing node 3 is 2   2

The cost of allocation for processing node no. 4 is 145

The status of the processing node 4 is 3   5

Total cost of allocation is 500

Time required by the algorithm was: 0.06 seconds

The modules of task T_1 has been allocated as

Processor	Max. no. of Modules	Memory Capacity	Modules Assigned	Remaining No. of Modules	Remaining Memory
p_1	4	10	m_{21} m_{41}	4	3
p_2	3	8		3	8
p_3	4	9		4	9
p_4	5	12	m_{11} m_{31}	3	5

The modules of task T_2 has been allocated as

Processor	Max. no. of Modules	Memory Capacity	Modules Assigned	Remaining No. of Modules	Remaining Memory
p_1	4	10	m_{21} m_{41} m_{22}	1	1
p_2	3	8	m_{12} m_{32}	1	4
p_3	4	9		4	9
p_4	5	12	m_{11} m_{31}	3	5

The modules of task T_3 has been allocated as

Table 8.2. Final status of the GT of all the tasks for case 1

Processor	Max. no. of Modules	Memory Capacity	Modules Assigned	Remaining No. of Modules	Remaining Memory
p_1	4	10	m_{21} m_{41} m_{22}	1	1
p_2	3	8	m_{12} m_{32} m_{23}	0	2
p_3	4	9	m_{13} m_{33}	2	2
p_4	5	12	m_{11} m_{31}	3	5

The above table (8.2) shows the final status of the Global Table. The table describes the status of allocation of every module of each task of DCS. It also shows
that a balanced load is obtained.

Case 2

Given a set of three tasks (fig. 8.14) with their corresponding modules $T_1(m_{11},$
$m_{21}, m_{31}, m_{41}, m_{51}), T_2(m_{12}, m_{22}, m_{32}, m_{42}), T_3(m_{13}, m_{23}, m_{33}, m_{43}), T_4(m_{14}, m_{24}, m_{34},$
$m_{44}, m_{54}, m_{64}, m_{74}), T_5(m_{15}, m_{25}, m_{35}, m_{45}, m_{55}, m_{65}, m_{75}, m_{85})$ and a set of five processing nodes $(p_1, p_2, p_3, p_4, p_5)$.

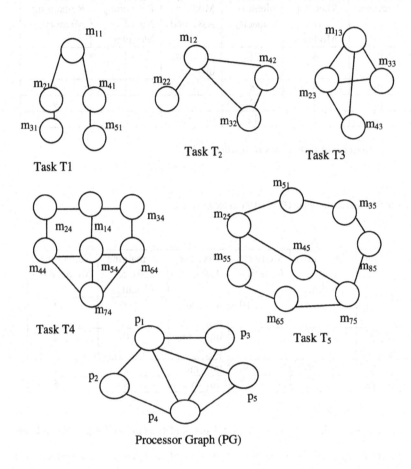

Task T1

Task T₂

Task T3

Task T4

Task T₅

Processor Graph (PG)

Fig. 8.14. Task graphs and Processor graph

	p_1	p_2	p_3	p_4	p_5
m_{11}	10	20	5	25	5
m_{21}	35	10	15	15	10
m_{31}	10	15	25	10	20
m_{41}	20	35	20	5	25
m_{51}	10	5	10	5	10

Execution Time Matrix of T_1

	p_1	p_2	p_3	p_4	p_5
m_{12}	20	5	35	10	5
m_{22}	10	10	10	10	10
m_{32}	15	10	20	15	15
m_{42}	10	15	20	15	30

Execution Time Matrix of T_2

	p_1	p_2	p_3	p_4	p_5
m_{13}	15	25	15	10	10
m_{23}	30	40	25	20	5
m_{33}	20	5	10	15	10
m_{43}	10	5	5	15	20

Execution Time Matrix of T_3

	P_1	p_2	p_3	p_4	p_5
m_{14}	5	10	25	20	30
m_{24}	10	25	5	5	5
m_{34}	25	10	5	10	25
m_{44}	5	10	15	25	25
m_{54}	10	15	20	25	30
m_{64}	5	10	10	10	10
m_{74}	5	10	10	20	20

Execution Time Matrix of T_4

	p_1	p_2	p_3	p_4	p_5
m_{15}	5	10	6	3	2
m_{25}	7	8	10	3	1
m_{35}	6	5	15	10	20
m_{45}	8	10	12	14	16
m_{55}	11	10	12	5	6
m_{65}	5	10	12	8	6
m_{75}	6	8	10	11	12
m_{85}	8	9	2	3	1

Execution Time Matrix of T_5

	m_{11}	m_{21}	m_{31}	m_{41}	m_{51}
m_{11}	0	10	20	20	5
m_{21}	10	0	10	50	20
m_{31}	20	10	0	50	10

m_{41}	20	50	50	0	20
m_{51}	5	20	10	20	0

IMC cost T_1

	m_{12}	m_{22}	m_{32}	m_{42}
m_{12}	0	5	10	10
m_{22}	5	0	60	60
m_{32}	10	60	0	5
m_{42}	10	60	5	0

IMC cost of T_2

	m_{13}	m_{23}	m_{33}	m_{43}
m_{13}	0	5	15	10
m_{23}	5	0	10	5
m_{33}	15	10	0	70
m_{43}	10	5	70	0

IMC cost of T_3

	m_{14}	m_{24}	m_{34}	m_{44}	m_{54}	m_{64}	m_{74}
m_{14}	0	5	10	15	15	15	20
m_{24}	5	0	80	10	80	80	15
m_{34}	10	80	0	80	80	5	10
m_{44}	15	10	80	0	10	15	5
m_{54}	15	80	80	10	0	5	5
m_{64}	15	80	5	15	5	0	5
m_{74}	20	15	10	5	5	5	0

IMC cost of T_4

	m_{15}	m_{25}	m_{35}	m_{45}	m_{55}	m_{65}	m_{75}	m_{85}
m_{15}	0	5	10	10	15	20	40	45
m_{25}	5	0	90	5	10	15	35	40
m_{35}	10	90	0	90	90	90	90	10
m_{45}	10	5	90	0	90	90	10	15
m_{55}	15	10	90	90	0	5	25	30
m_{65}	20	15	90	90	5	0	20	25
m_{75}	40	35	90	10	25	20	0	5
m_{85}	45	40	10	15	30	25	5	0

IMC cost of T_5

	p_1	p_2	p_3	p_4	p_5
p_1	0	1	1	1	1
p_2	1	0	0	1	0
p_3	1	0	0	1	0
p_4	1	1	1	0	1
p_5	1	0	0	1	0

Adjacency Matrix of Processors L^1_{pq}

	p_1	p_2	p_3	p_4	p_5
p_1	0	1	1	1	1
p_2	1	0	1	1	1
p_3	1	1	0	1	1
p_4	1	1	1	0	1
p_5	1	1	1	1	0

Adjacency Matrix of Processors L^2_{pq}

Memory requirement of the modules of the tasks (in units) are given.

m_{11}	m_{21}	m_{31}	m_{41}	m_{51}	m_{12}	m_{22}	m_{32}	m_{42}	m_{13}	m_{23}	m_{33}	m_{43}	m_{14}
6	3	5	2	4	1	6	3	5	2	4	1	4	5

m_{24}	m_{34}	m_{44}	m_{54}	m_{64}	m_{74}	m_{15}	m_{25}	m_{35}	m_{45}	m_{55}	m_{65}	m_{75}	m_{85}
6	3	2	1	2	3	4	2	3	1	2	4	3	1

STATUS[1] = [10, 50]

STATUS[2] = [9, 40]

STATUS[3] = [7, 35]

STATUS[4] = [6, 30]

STATUS[5] = [4, 10]

Results:

Task 1 has been allocated as : 41421

Task 2 has been allocated as : 1231

Task 3 has been allocated as : 2311

Task 4 has been allocated as : 1213411

Task 5 has been allocated as : 42535352

The cost of allocation for processing node no. 1 is 263

The status of the processing node 1 is 0 19

The cost of allocation for processing node no. 2 is 300

The status of the processing node 2 is 3   21

The cost of allocation for processing node no. 3 is 343

The status of the processing node 3 is 2   21

The cost of allocation for processing node no. 4 is 365

The status of the processing node 4 is 2   14

The cost of allocation for processing node no. 5 is 314

The status of the processing node 5 is 2   12

Total cost of allocation is 1585

Time required by the algorithm was: 0.17 seconds

The modules of task T_1 has been allocated as

Processor	Max. no. of Modules	Memory Capacity	Modules Assigned	Remaining No. of Modules	Remaining Memory
p_1	10	50	m_{21} m_{51}	8	43
p_2	9	40	m_{41}	8	38
p_3	7	35		7	35
p_4	6	30	m_{11} m_3	4	19
p_5	4	10		4	10

The modules of task T_2 has been allocated as

Processor	Max. no. of Modules	Memory Capacity	Modules Assigned	Remaining No. of Modules	Remaining Memory
p_1	10	50	m_{21} m_{51} m_{12} m_{42}	6	37
p_2	9	40	m_{41} m_{22}	7	32
p_3	7	35	m_{32}	6	32
p_4	6	30	m_{11} m_{31}	4	19
p_5	4	10		4	10

The modules of task T_3 has been allocated as

Processor	Max. no. of Modules	Memory Capacity	Modules Assigned	Remaining No. of Modules	Remaining Memory
p_1	10	50	m_{21} m_{51} m_{12} m_{42} m_{33} m_{43}	4	32
p_2	9	40	m_{41} m_{22} m_{13}	6	30
p_3	7	35	m_{32} m_{23}	5	28
p_4	6	30	m_{11} m_{31}	4	19
p_5	4	10		4	10

The modules of task T_4 has been allocated as

Processor	Max. no. of Modules	Memory Capacity	Modules Assigned	Remaining No. of Modules	Remaining Memory
p_1	10	50	m_{21} m_{51} m_{12} m_{42}	0	19
p_2	9	40	m_{41} m_{22}	5	24

p_3	7	35	m_{32}	4	26
p_4	6	30	m_{11} m_{31}	3	18
p_5	4	10		4	10

The modules of task T_5 has been allocated as

Table 8.3.Final status of the GT after allocation of all the tasks for case 2

Processor	Max. no. of Modules	Memory Capacity	Modules Assigned	Remaining No.of Modules	Remaining Memory
p_1	10	50	m_{21} m_{51} m_{12} m_{42} m_{33} m_{43} m_{14} m_{34} m_{64} m_{74}	0	19
p_2	9	40	m_{41} m_{22} m_{13} m_{24} m_{25} m_{85}	3	21
p_3	7	35	m_{32} m_{23} m_{44} m_{45} m_{65}	2	21
p_4	6	30	m_{11} m_{31} m_{54} m_{15}	2	14
p_5	4	10	m_{35} m_{55} m_{75}	1	2

The table shown above (Table 8.3) describes the status of allocation of every module of each task of DCS. It also shows that a balanced load is obtained.

8.3.6 Conclusive Observations

The TA algorithms that consider the only modules of a single task do not consider the limitation of the memory or the number of modules that can be assigned to a particular processor. This is so because these algorithms are not meant for assignment of modules belonging to multiple disjoint tasks. Such a single task assignment problem is easier to solve because of this reason.

Our algorithms consider the case of multiple tasks with the possibility of one or more tasks being submitted simultaneously. Apart from this, the memory capacity and the no. of modules that can be assigned to a particular processor as constraints are also considered on possible allocations.

Most of the algorithms, except few reported in [18, 27] have dealt with only a single task assignment over DCS. Therefore, no known algorithms to compare with the model discussed in this section.

We can execute the Single Task Allocation (STA)algorithm [3] multiple times ones for each task using the global table data structure to record the status of allocation and the system as done in our multiple task allocation algorithm. Now we may compare the execution time requirement of this method and our multiple task allocation algorithms.

The STA based on A* [3] referred to as EA* in the subsequent discussion has been executed multiple times and the run times have been obtained. The graphs in figures 8.15, 8.16, 8.17 shows the comparative results using our algorithm proposed in sec. 8.3 and earlier algorithm (EA*) proposed in [3].

So in the experiment, we have executed the tasks one by one for the cases 1, 2 and 3 without considering the processor connectivity (how the processor are connected i.e. with direct connection / indirect connection etc.) for the EA* as described in the algorithm of [3]. In the work [26], another modified version of EA* is proposed but it was also developed for single task allocation and their modules

by using the same idea of [3]. So, here we did not use the idea of [26] for our

comparison purpose.

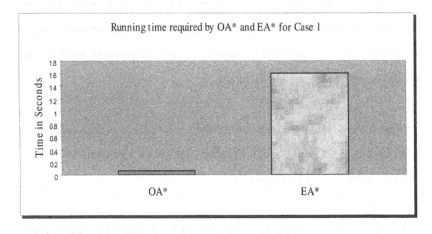

Fig. 8.15. Running time required by Our Algorithm using A* (OA*) and EA* for case 1

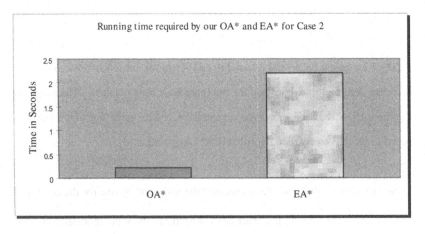

Fig. 8.16. Running time required by OA* and EA* for case 2

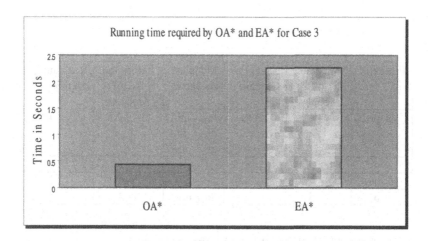

Fig. 8.17. Running time required by OA* and EA* for case 3

If we look at the results shown in the tables 8.4, 8.5, 8.6 for allocation of tasks using EA* for the cases 1, 2 and 3 respectively, it is observed that balanced load allocation can not be achieved. In all the cases presented below, some processing nodes are overloaded as per the Vth column of the GT considering their existing architectural capabilities. Thus it is justified that the EA*, in the form reported in [3, 26], can not be used for the allocation of the multiple tasks.

Table 8.4. The final status of the GT by using EA* for case 1

Processor	Max. no. of Modules	Memory Capacity	Modules Assigned	Remaining No. of Modules	Remaining Memory
p_1	4	10	m_{21} m_{41} m_{22} m_{32} m_{23} m_{33}	-2	1
p_2	3	8	m_{12} m_{13}	1	2
p_3	4	9		4	2
p_4	5	12	m_{11} m_{31}	3	5

Table 8.5. The final status of the GT by using EA* for case 2

Processor	Max. no. of Modules	Memory Capacity	Modules Assigned	Remaining No. of Modules	Remaining Memory
p_1	10	50	m_{21} m_{51} m_{12} m_{42} m_{23} m_{43} m_{14} m_{34} m_{25} m_{85} m_{74}	-1	19
p_2	9	40	m_{41} m_{22} m_{13} m_{24} m_{55}	4	21
p_3	7	35	m_{32} m_{33} m_{44} m_{45} m_{65}	2	21
p_4	6	30	m_{11} m_{31} m_{54}	2	14
p_5	4	10	m_{15} m_{64} m_{75}	1	2

Table 8.6. The final status of the GT by using EA* for case3

Processor	Max. no. of Modules	Memory Capacity	Modules Assigned	Remaining No. of Modules	Remaining Memory
p_1	10	70	m_{11} m_{21} m_{41} m_{52} m_{13} m_{33} m_{63} m_{14} m_{34} m_{44} m_{15} m_{55} m_{16} m_{46} m_{66} m_{17} m_{47} m_{18} m_{48} m_{58}	-10	35
p_2	8	50	m_{31} m_{23} m_{24} m_{35} m_{26} m_{27} m_{38}	1	23
p_3	6	40	m_{53} m_{36} m_{37} m_{38}	2	20
p_4	7	35	m_{43} m_{25} m_{45} m_{56}	3	16
p_5	6	40	m_{32}	2	22
p_6	6	33	m_{12} m_{22} m_{42}	3	8

8.3.7 Proof of the Algorithm

An algorithm consists of steps that are carried out one or more number of times depending on the loops that may enclose these steps. The following theorem describes the method [28].

Theorem : If $A(n) = a_m n^m + ... + a_1 n + a_0$ is a polynomial of degree m then $A(n) = O(n^m)$

Where, if some $a_i = 0$, then the corresponding term n^i does not appear in the step counts for any of the steps.

What this theorem says is the complexity of the algorithm is defined by the most expensive part of the algorithm. In our LBTA for multiple tasks, the allocation part is the most expensive one as it contains the maximum number of nested for loops. The skeleton structure of the allocation part of the algorithm can be depicted as follows:

```
void allocation( )
    {
        ---
1          for i= 1 to k tasks
            {
2              for j =1 to m_i modules of i-th task
                {
3                  for k = 1 to p processors
                    {
                        ---
                    // Calculate hp by using find_heaviest_load( )
                        {
                            ---
4                          for x= 1 to p processors

                                ---
                                {
                            // Calculate  load on processors using the load( )
5                              for y = 1 to k tasks
                                {
```

6 *for x= 1 to m$_i$ modules of i-th task*

{

}

}

7   *for e = 1 to k tasks*

{

8   *for f = 1 to m$_i$ modules of i-th task*

{

9   *for g = 1 to m$_j$ module of i-th task*

{

}

}

}

}

}

}

}

}

---

11   *for pl= 1 to p processors*

{

Call to load as in loop numbered 5

        }

    }

The skeleton shown above has three nested for loops numbered 1, 2 and 3 and the loop no. 3 has calls to the *find_heaviest_proc( )* and the *load( )*. The *load( )* contains two nested for loops numbered 5, 6 followed by another set of nested loops numbered 7, 8 and 9 .

For loop 5 and 6, there are to execute all the modules of the multiple tasks and hence the combined execution of the loops iterates m times. The execution of nested loops 7 and 8 similarly give *m* iterations and for every iteration out of *m*, the loop numbered 9 takes *m* iterations. And hence, the number of iterations for the function load is equal to m^2.

The call to *find_heaviest_proc( )* contains the for loop 4 in which call to the function *load( )* appears. The loop no. 4 will have *p* iterations and hence the complexity of the *find_heaviest_proc( )* becomes pm^2.

The similar arguments will give the complexity of the block of consisting of loops numbered 2 and 3 as $O(m.p.pm^2)$ *or* $O(p^2m^3)$.

The complexity of loop numbered 11 is pm^2.

The loop numbered 1 will have execution complexity as polynomial $((pm^2+p^2m^3) + pm^2)$ which is $O(p^2m^3)$ as per the theorem stated above.

So, the complexity of *allocation ( )* is $O(p^2m^3)$.

8.4 The LBTA Strategy for Multiple Tasks Using GA

For the LBTA problem with multiple tasks allocation, we define the following assumptions:

1) The proposed algorithm makes use of a data structure for "chromosome" to describe allocations. It is an array of positive integers showing the index of the processing node to which a particular module is assigned. It has as many elements as the total number of modules of all tasks.

2) Initially all the elements are zero indicating that none of the modules are allocated to any of the processing node.

3) A data structure STATUS associated with every processing node, which has two fields showing; the maximum no. of modules that can be allocated to the processing node and the maximum memory capacity of the processor.

Whenever a module is chosen for allocation onto a processing node, the STATUS is checked and it is ascertained whether the processing node can accommodate the module at hand. If not another processing node is chosen, if available.

8.4.1   The Fitness Function

The fitness function, in our problem, is the inverse of the load (the sum of loads on all the processors corresponding to a chromosome) described in the equation 8.8.

8.4.2   The Proposed Algorithm

1) *Randomly generate five chromosomes, verify STATUS and take one chromosome with maximum fitness value.*

   / This fitness value is our threshold limit. Any chromosome below the threshold will be rejected and not included in the population. */*

2) *Generate an initial population of 50 chromosomes above the threshold limit.*

3) *SELECT: probability of selection of parents is linearly dependent on the fitness value [37].   /* i.e. ax+b, where x is the fitness value, a and b are arbitrary.*/*

4) *Perform crossover with probability P_c at a randomly chosen point.*

5) *If*

   Total no. of Chromosome(generated) < 100

   goto

   SELECT

6) *Pick up ten chromosomes randomly, using the probability of selection as in SELECT.*

   Take out the one(chromosome) with maximum fitness.

/* This represents the allocation. */

Here, the complexity of the algorithm is $O(pm^2)$ where p is the no. of processing nodes and m is the total no. of modules of all the tasks . The complexity is derived in the same manner as described in sec 8.3.7 and obtained from the most expensive *gen50( )*[appendix B] and *threshold( )* code [appendix-B]. This simple GA based model uses crossover without mutation and the population size of 50 to provide good results for the allocation.

8.4.3   Description of SELECT

To effectuate the probability of selection, we would produce several copies of the same chromosome. The idea is to take out chromosomes with their best fitness values randomly from all the chromosomes (included copies).

Let there be P_a copies of chromosome a, where $a=1...n$ and P_b copies of chromosome b, where, $b=1...m$.

Generate a random number (chromosome) r and find out, to which chromosome (a or b) this chromosome belongs. This can be done by the following expression i.e.

$$if, \quad \sum_{a=1}^{n} P_a < \sum_{b=1}^{m} P_b$$

then the r belongs to chromosome b i.e. chromosome r is a copy of chromosome b.

However, this method would require memory for each copy of every chromo-some. To save memory we could instead attach a field with each new chromosome generated. In this field, we store an 'integer number' directly proportional to the fitness value of chromosome. Thus the chromosome represents 'X_i' copies of the chromosome, where 'X_i' is the number in its field and $i=1,2,...n$.

When a chromosome is to be randomly selected, a random number is generated in the range of 1 to $\sum(X_1+X_2+...+X_n)$, where X_i is the number in the field associated with the ith chromosome. Let us say, the number generated is Y and $X_1+X_2+...+X_k < Y < X_1+X_2+...+X_{k+1}$.

Thus the chromosome selected is X_{k+1}^{th} chromosome. This can be explained elaborately by the following example.

For example, let the following chromosome have the corresponding fitness values as follows:

Chromosome 1 : fitness value = 10
Chromosome 2 :   "   "   = 12
Chromosome 3 :   "   "   = 15
Chromosome 4 :   "   "   = 8

Let the probability of selection be $(a * (fitness\ value) + b)$, where a & b are arbitrary. Here, $a=10$, $b=0$ and $X_1=10$.

Let us generate 100 copies of chromosome 1($X_1=100$), 120 copies of chromosome 2 (i.e. $X_2=120$).... and so on.

Thus total number of chromosome $(X_1+X_2+X_3+X_4) = 100+120+150+80 = 450$.

We generate a random number = 230

Now, $100 + 120 < 230 < 100 + 120 + 150$

$\quad\quad X_1 \quad X_2 \quad\quad\quad X_1 \quad X_2 \quad X_3$

Hence, the 230th chromosome will be a copy of chromosome 3 i.e. X_3. It is easy to see that the probability of selection in this case is proportional to the fitness value.

8.4.4   An Illustrative Example

Given a set of three tasks with their corresponding modules $T_1(m_{11},\ m_{21},\ m_{31},\ m_{41})$, $T_2(m_{21},\ m_{22},\ m_{32})$, $T_3(m_{13},\ m_{22},\ m_{33})$ and a set of 3 processors $\{\ p_1,\ p_2,\ p_3\ \}$.

So, the total number of modules of all tasks is 10.

The initial status of each processing node is as follows:

STATUS [1] = [4, 40]

STATUS [2] = [4, 50]

STATUS [3] = [3, 30]

The first field of STATUS represents the maximum number of modules that can be allocated onto the processing node and the second field represents the memory capacity of the processing node.

The Threshold Value and the Initial Population:

Step 1: randomly generate 5 chromosomes and check whether they satisfy status of each processing node. Let us assume that memory required by each module, satisfies the existing memory of each processing node.

Let the chromosome generated be

1) 1132311231: status of processing node 1 is not satisfied, because processing node 1 can only take 4 modules. So, it is discarded. (Here, each number in the chromosome represents the number of processing node).

2) 2113221231: status of every processing node is satisfied, so it is accepted.

3) 1323213312: status of processing node 3 is not satisfied, so it is not accepted.

4) 3123132123: status of processing node 4 is not satisfied, so it is not accepted.

5) 1123311232: status of every processing node is satisfied, so it is accepted.

Then fitness of all the chromosomes is found out by the equation described in 8.3.1 and the maximum of these fitness values is taken as the threshold value. Any chromosome above the threshold will be accepted and included in the population.

Crossover:

Let us assume that 50 chromosomes have been generated as the initial population. Each chromosome is associated with a field that gives the frequency of selection as discussed in section 8.4.3.

Label: Let, two chromosomes are selected for reproduction. They be

2113221231 and 1323321121

Then crossover takes place as follows:

First a random point of crossover is found; say it comes out to be 4. Thus crossover will take place after 4th bit i.e. the offspring are

2113---321121 and   1323---221231

It is now verified whether the offspring are

  a) satisfying the status and
  b) identical to an existing chromosome of the population.

If none of the above is true, crossover is completed and the chromosomes are included in the population and their fitness values being calculated.

In the above example, the first offspring is invalid (it does not satisfy the status of processing node 1; hence crossover begins all over from label. Let the new chromosomes selected be

2113122133   and   1132113222

Let the point of crossover be 5.

Thus the offspring are 21131---13222 and 11321---22133
Both of these satisfy the status of all three processors, hence are acceptable, if they do not already have an identical copy in the population.

If total no. of crossovers performed is less than 100, again a new crossover occurs (step **label**). Then pick up ten chromosomes randomly from the new population, find out the fitness value of each and take out one (chromosome) with maximum fitness value which represents the allocation

8.4.5   Implementation

The software for the above algorithm is developed in C. Applying the software in a Pentium 100 MHz machine, the following studies have been carried out by using the given task graphs, processor graphs, IMC matrices, execution matrices etc. for case 1, case 2, and case 3 of sec 8.3.5 to judge the efficiency of the algorithm.

Case 1

Given a set of three tasks with their corresponding modules $T_1(m_{11}, m_{21}, m_{31}, m_{41})$, $T_2(m_{21}, m_{22}, m_{32})$, $T_3(m_{13}, m_{22}, m_{33})$ and a set of four processors $\{p_1, p_2, p_3, p_4\}$ fig. 8.13. Further, the inputs are provided from case 1 of sec 8.3.5 and the following results are obtained.

Here, in the results, "Selected Chromosome is 3234241134" represents the total number of modules of all the tasks that have been allocated onto the corresponding processing node. "Task 1 has been allocated as : 3234" indicates that the four modules$(m_{11}, m_{12}, m_{13}, m_{14})$ of the task T_1 have been allocated onto the processing node p_3, p_2, p_3, p_4 respectively. *"The cost at the processing node no. 1 is 20 " means the execution and communication costs of the modules of tasks on the processing node 1 by the allocation is 55 in time units.* " The status of the processing node 1 is 2   5" indicates that after allocation has been completed the remaining number of modules that can be allocated to the processing node p_1 is 2 and remaining number of memory that is available in the processing node p_l is 5 in units.

Results for Case 1

Selected Chromosome is 3234241134

Task 1 has been allocated as: 3234

Task 2 has been allocated as: 241

Task 3 has been allocated as: 134
The cost at the processing node no. 1 is 20
The status of the processing node 1 is 2   5

The cost at the processing node no. 2 is 25
The status of the processing node 2 is 1   2

The cost at the processing node no. 3 is 50
The status of the processing node 3 is 1   0

The cost at the processing node no. 4 is 25
The status of the processing node 4 is 2   3

Total cost at all the processing nodes is 120

Time required by the algorithm was: 18 seconds

The modules of task T_1 have been allocated as

I	II	III	IV	V	VI
Processor	Max. no. of Modules[*]	Memory Capacity	Modules Assigned	Remaining No. of Modules[**]	Remaining Memory
p_1	4	10		4	10
p_2	3	8	m_{21}	2	5
p_3	4	9	$m_{11}\ m_{31}$	2	2
p_4	5	12	m_{41}	4	8

[*]The column III represents the maximum number of modules that can be allocated

to a processing node.

[**]The column V represents the remaining number of modules that can be allocated to   a processing node after some modules have been assigned to the processing node.

The modules of task T_2 have been allocated as

Processor	Max. no. of Modules	Memory Capacity	Modules Assigned	Remaining No. of Modules	Remaining Memory
p_1	4	10	m_{32}	3	9
p_2	3	8	$m_{21}\ m_{12}$	1	2
p_3	4	9	$m_{11}\ m_{31}$	2	2
p_4	5	12	$m_{41}\ m_{22}$	3	6

The modules of task T_3 have been allocated as

Table 8.7. Final status of the GT after the allocation of all tasks for case 1

Processor	Max. no. of Modules	Memory Capacity	Modules Assigned	Remaining No. of Modules	Remaining Memory
p_1	4	10	$m_{32}\ m_{13}$	2	5
p_2	3	8	$m_{21}\ m_{12}$	1	2
p_3	4	9	$m_{11}\ m_{31}$ m_{23}	1	0
p_4	5	12	$m_{41}\ m_{22}$ m_{33}	2	3

The table 8.7 describes the status of allocation of every module of each task of

DCS. It also shows that a balanced load is obtained.

Case 2

Given, a set of five tasks with their corresponding modules $T_1(m_{11}, m_{21}, m_{31}, m_{41}, m_{51})$, $T_2(m_{12}, m_{22}, m_{32}, m_{42})$, $T_3(m_{13}, m_{23}, m_{33}, m_{43})$, $T_4(m_{14}, m_{24}, m_{34}, m_{44}, m_{54}, m_{64}, m_{47})$, $T_5(m_{15}, m_{25}, m_{35}, m_{45}, m_{55}, m_{65}, m_{75}, m_{85})$ and a set of five processors $(p_1, p_2, p_3, p_4, p_5)$ (fig.8.14). Further, the following inputs are provided from case 2 of sec 8.3.5 and the following results are obtained.

Results for Case 2

Selected Chromosome is 1244223231523134113142134125

The chromosome represents the total number of modules of all the tasks that have been allocated on to the corresponding processing node i.e.

Task 1 has been allocated as: 12442

Task 2 has been allocated as: 2323

Task 3 has been allocated as: 1523

Task 4 has been allocated as: 1341131

Task 5 has been allocated as: 42134125

The cost at the processing node no. 1 is 61
The status of the processing node 1 is 2   24

The cost at the processing node no. 2 is 51

The status of the processing node 2 is 2   23

The cost at the processing node no. 3 is 62

The status of the processing node 3 is 1   11

The cost at the processing node no. 4 is 33

The status of the processing node 4 is 1   14

The cost at the processing node no. 5 is 6

The status of the processing node 5 is 2   5

Total cost at all the processing nodes is 213

Time required by the algorithm was: 167 seconds

The modules of task T_1 have been allocated as

Processor	Max. no. of Modules*	Memory Capacity	Modules Assigned	Remaining No. of Modules**	Remaining Memory
p_1	10	50	m_{11}	9	44
p_2	9	40	$m_{21}\ m_{51}$	7	33
p_3	7	35		7	35
p_4	6	30	$m_{31}\ m_{41}$	4	23
p_5	4	10		4	10

The modules of task T_2 have been allocated as

Processor	Max. no. of Modules	Memory Capacity	Modules Assigned	Remaining No. of Modules	Remaining Memory
p_1	10	50	m_{11}	9	44
p_2	9	40	$m_{21}\quad m_{51}$ $m_{12}\ m_{32}$	5	29
p_3	7	35	$m_{22}\ m_{42}$	5	24
p_4	6	30	$m_{31}\ m_{41}$	4	23
p_5	4	10		4	10

The modules of task T_3 have been allocated as

Processor	Max. no. of Modules	Memory Capacity	Modules Assigned	Remaining No. of Modules	Remaining Memory
p_1	10	50	m_{11} m_{13}	8	42
p_2	9	40	m_{21} m_{51} m_{12} m_{32} m_{33}	4	28
p_3	7	35	m_{22} m_{42} m_{43}	4	20
p_4	6	30	m_{31} m_{41}	4	23
p_5	4	10	m_{23}	3	6

The modules of task T_4 have been allocated as

Processor	Max. no. of Modules	Memory Capacity	Modules Assigned	Remaining No. of Modules	Remaining Memory
p_1	10	50	m_{11} m_{13} m_{14} m_{44} m_{54} m_{74}	4	31
p_2	9	40	m_{21} m_{51} m_{12} m_{32} m_{33}	4	28
p_3	7	35	m_{22} m_{42} m_{43} m_{64} m_{24}	2	12
p_4	6	30	m_{31} m_{41} m_{34}	3	20
p_5	4	10	m_{23}	3	6

The modules of task T_5 have been allocated as

Table 8.8. Final status of GT after the allocation of all the tasks for case 2

Processor	Max. no. of Modules	Memory Capacity	Modules Assigned	Remaining No. of Modules	Remaining Memory
p_1	10	50	$m_{11}\, m_{13}$ $m_{14}\, m_{44}$ $m_{54}\ m_{74}$ $m_{35}\, m_{65}$	2	24
p_2	9	40	$m_{21}\, m_{51}$ $m_{12}\, m_{32}$ $m_{33}\, m_{25}$ m_{75}	2	23
p_3	7	35	$m_{22}\, m_{42}$ $m_{43}\, m_{64}$ $m_{24}\, m_{45}$	1	11
p_4	6	30	$m_{31}\, m_{41}$ $m_{34}\, m_{15}$ m_{55}	1	14
p_5	4	10	$m_{23}\, m_{85}$	2	5

The table describes the status of allocation of every module of each task of DCS. It also shows that a balanced load is obtained.

This chapter proposes four realistic allocation models. In one (sec. 8.1) a uniform cost search and A* techniques are applied for multiple tasks allocation in a DCS. All the previous models consider only a single task, though the DCS is meant for execution of multiple tasks dynamically arriving and leaving the system.

In second (sec. 8.2), a cluster-based approach is proposed. This has the greatest advantage of avoiding the priori requirement of execution time of modules on

PEs, as required in other models. This algorithm can be tested on a real DCS platform and will be of great help in implementation of the scheduler of the DCS.

Section 8.3 and 8.4 proposes the LBTA strategy for multiple tasks based on A* and GA.

BIBLIOGRAPHY

[1]Pereng-yi RICHARD MA, Edward Y.S.LEE, Masahiro TSUCHIYA, "A Task Allocation Model for Distributed Computing Systems", *IEEE Trans. on Computers*, Vol.C-31, No. 1, January 1982, pp. 41-47.

[2]D.P.Vidyarthi, A.K.Tripathi, "Precedence Constrained Task Allocation in Distributed Computing System", *Int. J. of High Speed Computing*, Vol. 8, No. 1, 1996, pp. 47-55.

[3]Chien-Chung Shen, Wen-Hsiang Tsai, "A Graph Matching Approach to Optimal Task Assignment in Distributed Computing Systems using a Minimax Criterion", *IEEE Trans. on Computers*, Vol. C-34, No.3, March 1985, pp. 197-203.

[4]Sol. M. Shatz, Jia-Ping Wang, "Models & Algorithm for Reliability-Oriented Task allocation in Redundant Distributed Computer Systems", *IEEE Trans. on Parallel and Distributed Systems*, Vol.38, No. 1, April 1989, pp. 16-27.

[5]Wesley W Chu, Lance M.T.Lan, "Task Allocation and Precedence Relations for Distributed Real Time Systems", *IEEE Trans. on Computers*, Vol. C-36, No.6, June 1987, pp. 667-679.

[6]C. Siva Ram Murthy, K.N.Balsubramaniya Murthy, A.Sreenivas, "Scheduling of Precedence-Constrained Parallel Program Tasks on Multiprocessors", *Microprocessing and Microprogramming*, Vol. 36, 1992/93, pp. 93-104.

[7]Edwin S.H.Hou, Nirwan Ansari, Hong Ren, "A Genetic Algorithm for Multiprocessor Scheduling", *IEEE Trans. on Parallel and Distributed Systems*, Vol. 5, No. 2, Feb 1994, pp. 113-120.

[8]D.P.Vidyarthi, A.K.Tripathi, "Exploiting Parallelism in Genetic Task Allocation Algorithm", *Int. J. of Information and Computing Science*, Vol. 4 No. 1, June 2002, pp. 22-26

[9]S.Kartik, C.S.Ram Murthy, "Task Allocation Algorithms for Maximizing Reliability of Distributed Computing Systems", *IEEE Trans. on Computers*, Vol.46, No.6, June1997, pp. 719-724.

[10]Sol.M.Shatz, Wang Goto, "Task Allocation for Maximizing Reliability of Distributed Computing Systems", *IEEE Trans. on Computers*, Vol.41, No.9, September 1992, pp. 1156-1168.

[11]S. Karthik, C. Siva Ram Murthy, " Improved Task Allocation Algorithms to Maximize Reliability of Redundant Distributed Systems", *IEEE Trans. on Reliability*, Vol. 44, No. 4, Dec. 1995, pp. 575-586.

[12]A.K.Tripathi, D.P.Vidyarthi, A.N.Mantri, "A Genetic Task Allocation Algorithm for Distributed Computing System Incorporating Problem Specific Knowledge", *International J. of High Speed Computing*, Vol.8, No.4, 1996, pp. 363-370.

[13]D.P.Vidyarthi, A.K.Tripathi, "Maximizing Reliability of Distributed Computing Systems with Task Allocation using Simple Genetic Algorithm", *J. of Systems Architecture*, Vol. 47, 2001, pp. 549-554.

[13]C.Siva Ram Murthy, V. Rajaraman, "Task Assignment in Multiprocessor Systems", *Microprocessing and Microprogramming,* Vol.26, 1989, pp. 63-71.

[15]D.P.Vidyarthi, A.K.Tripathi, B.K.Sarker, "Allocation Aspects in Distributed Computing System", *IETE Technical Review,* Vol. 18, No. 6, Nov.-Dec. 2001, pp.279-285.

[16]N.J.Nilson, *Problem Solving Methods in Artificial Intelligence,* McGraw Hill International Edition, New York, 1971.

[17]M.Kafil, I.Ahmed, "Optimal Task Assignment in Heterogeneous Distributed Computing System", *IEEE Concurrency,* July - September 1998, pp. 42-51.

[18]D.P.Vidyarthi, A.K.Tripathi, B.K.Sarker, "Multiple Task Management in Distributed Computing Systems", The *Journal of the CSI,* Vol. 31, No. 1 Sep. 2000, pp. 19-25.

[19]C.J.Hou, K.G.Shin, "Replication and Allocation of Task Modules in Distributed   Real Time Systems", *Proc. 24th IEEE Symp. Fault Tolerant Computing Systems,* June 1994, pp. 26-35.

[20]S.B.Shukla, D.P.Agrawal, "A Framework for Mapping Periodic Real Time Applications on Multicomputers", *IEEE Transaction on Parallel and Distributed Systems,* Vol.5, No.7, July 1994, pp. 778-784.

[21]Y.Oh, S.H.Son, "Scheduling Hard Real-Time Tasks with Tolerance to Multiple Processor Failures", *Multiprocessing and Multiprogramming,* Vol. 40, 1995, pp.193-206.

[22]T.S.Tia, J.W.S. Liu, "Assigning Real Time Tasks and Resources to Distributed Systems", *International Journal of Mini and Microcomputer,* Vol. 17, No. 1, 1995, pp.18-25.

[23]S.S.Wu, D.Sweeping, "Heuristic Algorithms for Task Assignment and Scheduling in a Processor Network", *Parallel Computing,* Vol.20, 1994, pp. 1-14.

[24]T.F.Abdelzaher, K.G.Shin, "Period–Based Load Partitioning and Assignment for Large Real-Time Applications", *IEEE Transaction on Computers,* Vol. 49, No.1, January 2000, pp. 81-87.

[25]D.P.Vidyarthi, A.K.Tripathi, " A Fuzzy IMC Cost Reduction Model for Task Allocation in Distributed Computing Systems", *Proceedings of the Fifth International Symposium on Methods and Models in Automation and Robotics,* Vol. 2, Szczecin, Poland, August 1998, pp. 719-721.

[26]A.B.Tucker, Jr., *The Computer Science and Engineering Handbook,* CRC Press, 1997.

[27]A.K.Tripathi, B.K.Sarker, N.Kumar and D.P.Vidyarthi, "Multiple Task Allocation with Load Considerations," *International Journal of Information and Computing Science,* vol.3, no.1, June 2000, pp. 36-44.

[28]E. Horowitz, S. Sahni and S. Rajasekaran, *Computer Algorithms,* W.H.Freeman and Company, 1997.

CHAPTER 9

Other Approaches for Task Allocation

This book is aimed to consider applicability of load balancing and task alloca-tion strategies aimed at proper distribution of computational loads in a DCS. A good deal of research work on both a) load balancing [1-6] and b) task allocation [7-12] in DCS is available in the literature. The purpose of task allocation in a DCS is to reduce turnaround time of a task. This is done by maximizing the utili-zation of resources while minimizing the communication among processing nodes. While minimizing IPC tends to assign the whole task to a single processing node, load balancing tries to distribute the program modules of a task almost evenly among the processing nodes. So, the idea was to consider whether a combined ap-proach (load balancing task allocation) can promise a better performance charac-teristic of a DCS such as throughput, compared to separate applications of "Load Balancing" and "Task Allocation" strategies. In our proposed LBTA strategy we tried to make compromise between these two criterions.

The work was started with consideration of existing load balancing techniques (strategies) and identification of other possible and promising strategies for the purpose. It has been identified that the task migration, because of its significant overhead, can be one of the major factors in decreasing the throughput of a DCS. The most of the existing algorithms described in chapter 5 consider allocation of the modules of only a single task to various processing nodes whereas the number of tasks, for execution, is usually substantive. So, the idea of multiple tasks have been proposed in the work and incorporated in the proposed LBTA strategy, which is described in chapter 8.

Nodes of the heterogeneous DCS may be lightly loaded or heavily loaded because of incoming various tasks from time to time to it and due to various architectural capabilities of the nodes. So, it has been tried to combine load balancing while tasks are allocated to the DCS. For this purpose, a concept of Global Table (GT) has been introduced in chapter III that keeps track of each and every module of different tasks. The table shows the possibility of allocation or assignment of incoming modules of different tasks according to the memory constraints and modules (Max. no. of modules a processing node can accommodate) constraints. From this table, the present status of the DCS is easily informed, such as presently allocated modules of different tasks, the load of every processing nodes etc. so that the DCS further does not attempt to allocate any module of tasks to the processing nodes which are already heavily loaded or to the processing nodes those are not able to accept more modules for executing according to its architectural capabilities.

Further The LBTA strategy has been implemented using well-known A* algorithm and Genetic Algorithm (GA). The load of multiple tasks has been used as a cost function for the purpose. An algorithm has been developed using A* technique in chapter 8. A heuristic search space technique is employed to find an optimal solution path in the state space after expanding fewer nodes during the search. Such a heuristic search algorithm can speed up the search of an optimal solution, which is usually, time consuming for graphs with large numbers of vertices and edges. It minimizes IPC and optimizes load balancing by minimizing the task turn around time. Comparative results with the earlier work are shown for the purpose which justifies that our algorithm performs better.

Another approach of LBTA strategy for multiple tasks using Genetic Algorithm has been proposed in the thesis in chapter 8. An algorithm has been developed using the GA technique. Genetic Algorithm can run in parallel on several processing nodes at a time. For this nature, GA technique has been considered in our LBTA strategy for multiple tasks for a DCS. GA has been successfully used to solve various task allocation problems. These earlier works have mainly concentrated on single task allocation using GA. In this case inverse of load on a processor (equation 8.8) is the fitness function for the GA. Illustrated examples also show a good balanced load situation in the results (sec. 8.4). Comparative results with A* algorithm (sec 8.2) using A* have been presented in the present chapter. The results show that the GA based algorithm performs better than A* in terms of allocation and total cost (execution and communication) of allocation.

9.1 Comparative Analysis of TA Models

The following figures (9.1, 9.2 and 9.3) shows the time required by the algorithms using A* and GA technique for all the cases (1, 2 and 3) respectively.

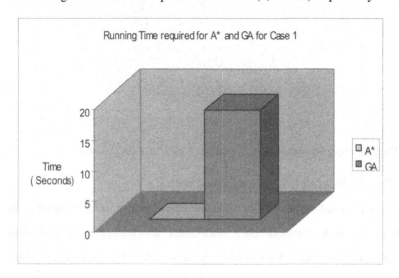

Fig. 9.1. Running time required by the algorithms using A* and GA for case 1

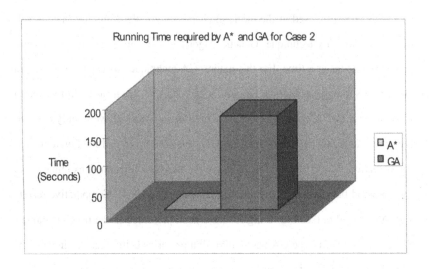

Fig. 9.2. Running time required by the algorithms using A* and GA for case 2

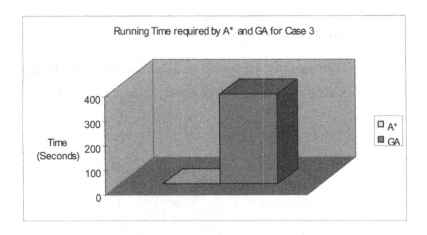

Fig. 9.3. Running time required by the algorithms using A* and GA for case 3

From the figures 9.1, 9.2, 9.3, it is found that:

The running time taken by A* technique (our algorithm) for implementing the algorithm with the given example is much smaller than the time taken by the algorithm using GA. This is because GA is using several hundred invocations of the 'random' function, which has a constant complexity. This increases the run time of GA.

The following figure 9.4 shows the comparisons among the results of the earlier algorithm (EA*) used in [8] and our algorithms using A*(OA*) presented in sec. 8.3 and the algorithm using GA technique (sec. 8.4).

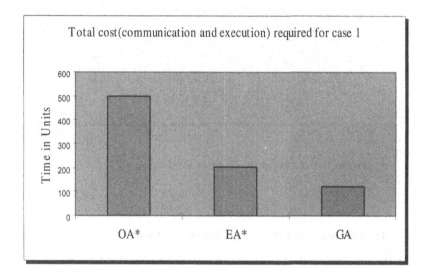

Fig. 9.4.Total cost required by OA*, EA* and GA for case 1

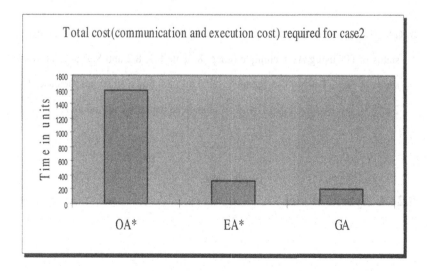

Fig. 9.5.Total cost required by OA*, EA* and GA for case 2

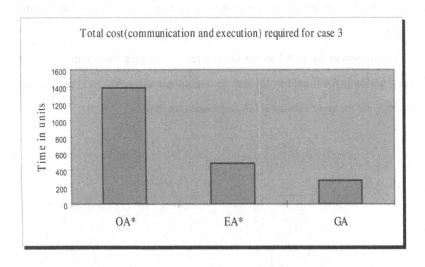

Fig. 9.6. Total cost required by OA*, EA* and GA for case 3

From the figures 9.4, 9.5 and 9.6, it is observed that

a) The cost (communication and execution) by the allocation for tasks using GA technique is less than the cost using OA* technique (our algorithm) and EA*(earlier algorithm proposed in [8]) .

b) GA gives a better allocation than A*. According to the Vth column of the final status of GT using A* technique (chap. 8, table 8.1, 8.2 and 8.3) and the final status of the GT using GA (chap. 8, table 8.7, 8.8 and 8.9) for all the cases (1, 2 and 3), it is observed that GA shows balanced load allocation than A*.

9.2   A Hybrid Model

The A* algorithm, an informed search algorithm guarantees an optimal solution but does not work for large problems because of its high time and space complexities [13]. One can obtain awareness of high time and space requirements of the A* algorithm by making use of some initial solution to prune a good number of nodes from a state space tree [13]. By making use of this idea and keeping in mind to reduce the search space we have proposed another algorithm in this chapter. This idea can be implemented to improve the performance of our proposed algorithm using A*(sec. 8.3) as it shows inferior results compared with the results of GA. The algorithm proposed below, first generates a random solution, and prunes all the nodes with higher than this solution during the optimal solution search. This is because the optimal solution cost will never be higher than this random-solution cost. By pruning unnecessary nodes not only saves memory, but also saves the time required by reducing the search space [13].

9.2.1 The Proposed Algorithm

1)   *Calculate the status of the global Table (GT) for each processing node in terms of available memory (M) and the modules that are assigned to it.*

2)   *Generate a random solution. Let R_{sol} be the cost of the solution.*

3)   *Maintain a list S of unallocated tasks with all modules (all tasks are in S at the beginning) and a list OPEN, empty at the beginning.*

4)   *Take one task ta from S and put it in another list V and reset OPEN as empty state.*

5) *If allocation of the modules in V is possible using the f(n)=g(n)+h(n) of A**
    algorithm(sec.4.1.1) then check whether f(n) ≤ R$_{sol}$.

6) *If f(n) ≤ R$_{sol}$*
        then goto step 7
            else discard the node from OPEN.

7) *Verify the STATUS and allocate the modules; if allocation is not possible, de-*
    allocate the allocated modules of the task and move onto the next task, modi-
    fying the STATUS in between and update the Global Table.

8) *If S is not empty yet, go to step 2.*

9) *Stop (end of allocation).*

9.2.2 An Illustrated Example

As per the algorithm in sec. 9.2.1, the given example in sec. 4.2 has been worked out in the following. In our example, the cost of random solution is 38. Therefore, all nodes with a cost greater than 38 are discarded. Fig. 9.7 shows the search tree.

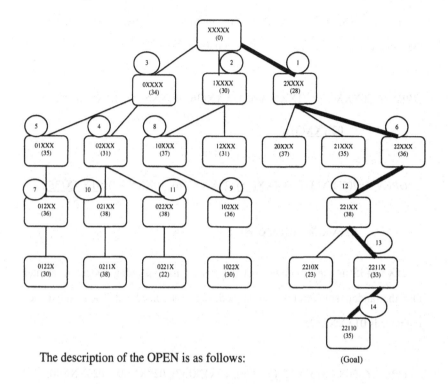

The description of the OPEN is as follows: (Goal)

Fig. 9.7. Search tree for the example 9.2.2 using Random Solution (22 nodes generated, 14 nodes expanded)

2XXXX(28) is the minimum cost. So, it is expanded.

$$OPEN\_2: \underline{\mathbf{1XXXX(30)}}, 0XXXX(34), 20XXX(37), 21XXX(35), 22XXX(36).$$
$$2$$

$$OPEN\_3: \underline{\mathbf{0XXXX(34)}}, 20XXX(37), 21XXX(35), 22XXX(36), 10XXX(37),$$
$$3$$

$$\underline{12XXX(31)}$$
$$\mathbf{X}$$

12XXX(31) is the minimum, but the cost of its expanding nodes are greater than the random solution (38), so the nodes are not considered. The next expanding node is 0 XXXX (34) according to the minimum cost. Here, "X" indicates that the node will not be considered further in the OPEN.

OPEN_4: 20XXX(37), 21XXX(35), 22XXX(36), 10XXX(37), 01XXX(35),

        02XXX(31).
        4

OPEN_5: 20XXX(37), 21XXX(35), 22XXX(36), 10XXX(37), **01XXX(35)**,
                      X   5

    021XX(38), 022XX(38).

21XXX(35) is the minimum, but the cost of its expanding nodes are greater than the random solution (38), so the nodes are not considered. The next expanding node is 01XXXX(35).

OPEN_6: 20XXX(37), **22XXX(36)**, 10XXX(37), 021XX(38), 022XX(38),
                      6
    012XX(36).

OPEN_7: 20XXX(37), 10XXX(37), 021XX(38), 022XX(38), **012XX(36)**,
                                              7
    221XX(38).

OPEN_8: 20XXX(37), **10XXX(37)**, 021XX(38), 022XX(38), 221XX(38),
        X   8

      0122X(30) .
      X

0122X(30) is the minimum, but the cost of expanding nodes are greater than the random solution (38), so the nodes are not considered. 20XXX(37) is next minimum cost node, but it is not also considered for the same reason. Then, the next expanding node is 10XXX(37).

OPEN_9: 021XX(38), 022XX(38), 221XX(38), **102XX(36)**.
                                                              9

OPEN_10: **021XX(38)**, 022XX(38), 221XX(38), 1022X(30) .
                 10   X

1022X(30) is the minimum cost, but the costs of expanding nodes are greater than the random solution (38). Then, the next expanding node is 021XX(38).

OPEN_11: **022XX(38)**, 221XX(38), 0211X(38).
                 11

OPEN_12: **221XX(38)**, 0211X(38), 0221X(22).
                 12   X

0221X(22) is the minimum cost, but the costs of expanding nodes are greater than the random solution (38). Then, the next expanding node is 221XX(38).

OPEN_13: 0211X(38), 2210X(23), **2211X(33)**.
                              X   13
2210X(33) is the minimum cost, but the costs of expanding nodes are greater than the random solution (38). Then, the next expanding node is 2211X(33).

OPEN_14: 0211X(38), **22110(35)** .
                            14

22110(35) is the minimum cost node. But there is node to expand. So, this is the Goal State.

The algorithm described above, generates a random solution, and prunes all the nodes with costs higher than this solution during the optimal solution search. This is because the optimal solution cost will never be higher than this random solution cost [13]. Pruning unnecessary nodes not only save memory but also save the time required to insert the nodes into OPEN.

The idea of generation of initial population in GA can be used to find a random solution [sec. 5.3]. In our example, the cost of random solution was 38. Therefore, all nodes with a cost greater than 38 are discarded. As a result, in fig. 9.7, only 22 nodes are generated and 14 nodes are expanded while the earlier solution reported in sec. 8.3.4 (in fig. 8.12) produced 63 generated nodes and 21 expanded nodes for the same optimal solution 22110 which shows a balanced load is obtained among the processing nodes. It is to mention that this algorithm's efficiency depends on the initial solution's quality   [13]. It may incur more cost for generating the good quality of the initial solution. This cost is to be added with the total cost of the allocation.

The results demonstrates that the random solution approach can also be a meaningful approach to improve the performance of the algorithm using A* (sec. 8.3) with the LBTA strategy for multiple tasks.

As the existing task Allocation algorithms consider only single task, the complexity and performance of these algorithms are not comparable with that of algorithms, proposed in this thesis, based on LBTA strategy for multiple tasks. As the algorithms proposed in chapters IV, V, VI of this thesis do balance the load also during the allocation process, the complexity of these algorithms involves cubic term for the no. of modules (m^3) as opposed to square term (m^2) in the case of single task allocation algorithms reported in the literature[14].

It is assumed that the allocator will come to know when the modules of the tasks leave the system. The allocator maintains information regarding which modules are present in the system including the new arrivals and the departures of modules in the system and updates the GT accordingly. These algorithms have been proposed considering LBTA strategy for multiple task allocation in a DCS. It is observed that the tasks arrive, for the execution, in a dynamic fashion. An incoming task will be invoking the algorithms. The status of Global Table is dynamic and the algorithm in its execution for a particular task will incorporate the modification in the table (GT) with reference to that particular task.

9.3 Object Allocation in Distributed Computing Systems

Object Oriented Programming, in recent, has become exceedingly popular. It is realized that the problem of real world can exactly map the object and thus object-oriented view came into existence. Software engineering stream is now completely moved towards object and most of the software is now being developed using the features of object-oriented technology. Compiler writers also rushed and many object oriented programming languages came into existence (e.g. Object Pascal, C++, JAVA etc.). Object oriented languages have many features. Method and data hiding, Inheritance, Polymorphism is to name a few [14].

Distributed Computing Systems (DCS) is characterized by the distribution of memory and clock to all the processing elements of the system. It has the possibility of keeping the processing sites at a large geographical distance. The processing site of the system is also known as the node. One of the very useful features of the DCS is scalability. This type of system is well suited for the present environment of computing.

Object based distributed computing is a technique for constructing large heterogeneous computing and communication system based on the concept of objects. Object based allocation, in DCS, brings new challenges and opportunities for the use and development of formal methods.

9.3.1 The Object Model

Previous allocation strategies, proposes the allocation of computing task to optimize one or more characteristic parameters [7-9, 12, 15, 16-19]. The allocation model, presented in this section, is based on the objects. Each object is characterized by the typical structure formed by the state and the operations, and also embodies independent execution facilities [20]. This facility is useful for dynamically adopting the allocation of a parallel application. In order to affect the state or even determine the state of an object, one must perform an appropriate operation on it. The identity of the objects is derived from the set of operations for that object. The combination of the operations with their internally defined data structures and computations represents an object instantiations [21].

Objects in a DCS

The objects in a DCS (hardware, programs or data) are generalizations of abstract data types. This refers to the objects' representation. They are, first, data structures and, second, operations on the data structures. The data structures represent executable modules, interprocess communications, and hardware resources etc., which are viewed as an object, with a fixed set of operations that defines its context within the system.

The objects are represented as singular entities. Objects may be active (process object) or passive (data object). The structure of objects differs from system to system, but they are all exhibiting the same basic components; an external part and an internal part. The external part provides the operations allowable. The internal part is comprised of the internal specification (data types etc.)

In a DCS, objects operating on one host may require to invoke an operation in an object on another host. The object model requires constructing a communication object to control and carry out Inter Object Communications (IOC).

9.3.2 The Allocation Problem

The allocation of a task deals with the assignment of its parallel components to the resources of the DCS. The allocation is static if it is decided before execution. It is dynamic if it is decided during execution [22]. Parallel objects of an application are created dynamically and thus allocation is to be decided at run time. The application needs of execution and communication resources are decided statically at the beginning and dynamic allocation takes place during execution.

There are two main requirements of the allocation problem of DCS, both in static and dynamic case:

1.   the user should be unaware of the allocation for a given architecture, and
2.   the allocation must tend to optimize the characteristic parameters.

The parallel object environment assumes parallel objects and exploits this parallelism in two forms. Inter object parallelism is based on the execution of independent parallel objects. Intra object parallelism permits multiple execution thread within the same object. Communication, among the objects, is carried through message passing. Thus inter object parallelism is achieved among the independent objects by allowing the communication among them as and when required. Intra object parallelism is achieved by the introduction of the multiple threads within the same object. In this, an object can serve more than one request in parallel by allowing each thread to serve one.

9.3.3 Capabilities in the Object

Controlled use of objects is essential to provide logical, efficient and accurate use of the system. To guarantee this, objects are allowed access only for those objects that are authorized to access that.

The external part is the part accessible to the outside world; the internal part is protected one. Users can request services but cannot actively process the object's internals. However, only the structure of an object does not guarantee the integrity of an object. A concept "protection domain" is introduced to make this control. An object operates within a protection domain, which specifies what resources and rights to it an object may access. Each domain defines a set of objects and the operations on it that can be invoked. These rights associated with an object provide its protection from unwanted objects. All objects, within that domain, have the rights to objects controlled by it. The matrix showing the access right is known as Access matrix.

The structure of the access matrix is shown below.

Object Domain	File1	File2	Port1
D1	READ	EXECUTE	READ/WRITE
D2	-	READ/WRITE	-
D3	READ/EXECUTE	-	WRITE

Typically in these systems access list is used, as access matrix is sparse.

Access list

File /list
    Domain 1; Read
    Domain N; Write
End list

Quite often an alternative is used in object based system design. Instead of as-
sociating columns of the access matrix with the objects as an access list, we asso-
ciate each row with its domain. This provides to the domain the list of objects it
can access and the operations it can perform on them. This new association is
called a capability list. An object is represented by a physical address called the
capability. The user must acquire capability in order to use it.

9.3.4. Object Allocator

Object allocator deals with the creation, execution, and destruction of objects in
the object based DCS. The nodes of the DCS must posses a capability manager for
object creation, operation, destruction, synchronization, communication etc. All
the nodes have a capability manager that maintains the capabilities for the objects
that exist on it. Only the Capability Manager (CM) has the rights to change the
state of capabilities of its objects.

Creation of objects implies bringing them into the system and making their
existence known to all who requires it. The object creation may be local or remote.
The object scheduled to execute on the node is given control of the node. After
completion it leaves its control.

Allocation manager is responsible for object allocation in its node. It can direct
the creation manager for object creation locally. It may contact another allocation
manager on other node for remote object creation. It can also decide the allocation
of components of distributed objects.

Monitoring manager monitors the application i.e. no. of objects allocated in the node, no. of threads in object etc (Fig. 9.8).

The allocator provides some synchronization primitives for the synchronization of objects. Signal/wait primitive or mailbox does this. The communication between distributed objects is in the form of shared data objects, message objects or control interactions. Communication may be synchronous or asynchronous.

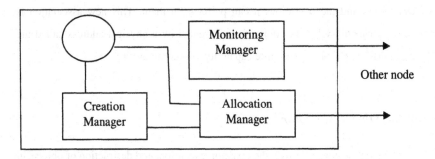

Fig. 9.8. Interaction of managers for object allocation

Thus the object allocation is comprised of the following jobs.

- Creation of objects
- Operations on objects
- Scheduling of objects
- Deletion of objects
- Communication among objects

The allocation manager receives the request such as

Run A;

Create A;
Abort A;
Send A, B;
Receive A, B;
Fork;
Join;

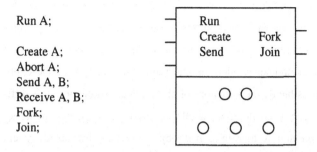

Fig. 9.9.Object interface

9.3.5 Communication Manager

A communication manager object provides communication facility among communicating objects, as shown in figure 9.8. An object can invoke any other object on the system by sending it a request message. Only the name of the object is enough to route any message as the rest is taken care by the communication manager. Generally the following operations are included.

SEND(OBJ,OPR,MSG)

RECEIVE(OBJ,OPR,MSG)

Sometime a request primitive is used for a particular service.

REQUEST(OBJ,OPR,MSG)

A typical use of communication is shown (fig. 9.10) in which communication is being done through port object A.

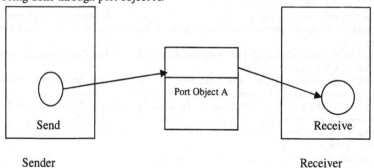

Fig. 9.10.Communication in Objects

Objects are created and destroyed dynamically in the system. Every newly created object may create another object in turn and may send request to it. Moreover the presence of multiple execution activities i.e. threads designed to support concurrency, imposes another problem in object allocation. In view of these, object allocation is possible by the variations of abovementioned method. It is difficult to measure the characteristic of object allocator as it is possible only by its actual implementation and testing in a real object oriented distributed system environment. The prototype for object oriented distributed systems are being developed by the researchers of the discipline [23].

BIBLIOGRAPHY

[1]A.B.Tucker, Jr., *The Computer Science and Engineering Handbook*, CRC Press, 1997.

[2]Edwind S.H. Hou, N. Ansari and H.Ren, "A Genetic Algorithm for Multiprocessor Scheduling " *IEEE Trans. Parallel and Distributed Systems*, Vol.5,1994, pp.113.

[3]F.C.Lin and R.M.Keller, "The Gradient Model Load Balancing Method", *IEEE Trans. Software Engg.* Vol. SE-13, No.1, Jan., 1988, pp.32-38.

[4]L.M.Ni, C.W.Xu and T.B.Gendreau, "A Distributed Drafting Algorithm for Load Balancing" *IEEE Trans. , Software Engg.*, Vol.SE-13, No.10, October1985, pp.1153-1161.

[5]P.K.Sinha, *Distributed Operating Systems, Concepts and Design*, Printice-Hall of India, 1997.

[6]T.C.K. Chou and J.A.Abraham, "Load Balancing in Distributed Systems", *IEEE Trans. Software Eng.*, Vol. SE-8, No.4, July 1982, pp.401-412.

[7]A.K.Tripathi, D.P.Vidyarthi and A.N.Mantri, "A Genetic Task Allocation Algorithm for Distributed Computing Systems Incorporating Problem Specific Knowledge", *International Journal of High Speed Computing*, Vol.8, No.4,1996, p.363-370.

[8]C.C.Shen and W.H.Tsai, "A Graph Matching Approach to Optimal Task Assignment in Distributed Computing System Using a Minimax Criterion", *IEEE Trans. Computers*, Vol. c-34, No.3, March, 1985. pp. 197-203.

[9]D.P.Vidyarthi and A.K.Tripathi, "Precedence Constrained Task Allocation in Distributed Computer Systems", *International Journal of High Speed Computing*, Vol.8, No.1,1996, pp.47-55.

[10]K.Efe, "Heuristic Models of Task Assignment Scheduling in Distributed Systems", *IEEE Computer*, Vol.15,1982, p.50-56.

[11]P.Y.R.Richard Ma, E.Y.S.Lee and J. Tsuchiya, "A Task Allocation Model for Distributed Computing Systems", *IEEE Trans. Computer*, Vol. C-31, No.1, pp. 41-47, Jan.1982.

[12]W.W.Chu, M.T.Lan, "Task Allocation and Precedence Relations for Distributed Real-Time Systems" *IEEE Trans. Computer*, Vol.c-36, No.6, June 1987, pp. 667-679.

[13]M.Mitchell, *An Introduction to Genetic Algorithms*, Prentice-Hall of India Private Limited, India, 1998.

[14]Timothy Budd, *An Introduction to Object Oriented Programming*, Addison-Wesley, 1991, pp 1-15.

[15]Sol. M. Shatz, Jia-Ping Wang, "Models & Algorithm for Reliability-Oriented Task allocation in Redundant Distributed Computer Systems", *IEEE Trans. on Parallel and Distributed
Systems*, Vol.38, No. 1, April 1989, pp. 16-27.

[16]C. Siva Ram Murthy, K.N.Balsubramaniya Murthy, A.Sreenivas, "Scheduling of Precedence-Constrained Parallel Program Tasks on Multiprocessors", *Microprocessing and
Microprogramming*, Vol. 36, 1992/93, pp. 93-104.

[17]Sol.M.Shatz, Wang Goto, "Task Allocation for Maximizing Reliability of Distributed Computing Systems", *IEEE Trans. on Computers*, Vol.41, No.9, September 1992, pp. 1156-1168.

[18]S. Karthik, C. Siva Ram Murthy, " Improved Task Allocation Algorithms to Maximize Reliability of Redundant Distributed Systems", *IEEE Trans. on Reliability*, Vol. 44, No. 4, Dec.
1995, pp. 575-586.

[19]D.P.Vidyarthi, A.K.Tripathi, "Maximizing Reliability of Distributed Computing Systems
with Task Allocation using Simple Genetic Algorithm", *J. of Systems Architecture*, Vol. 47,
2001, pp. 549-554.

[20]Antonio Corradi, Letizia Leonardi, Franco Zambonelli, "Parallel Object Migration: A Fine
Grained Approach to Load Distribution", *Journal of Parallel & Distributed Computing*, Vol.
60, 2000, pp 48-71.

[21]Paul J. Fortier, *Design of Distributed Operating System*, Mc-Graw Hill International Editions, 1988, pp 154-191.

[22]Antonio Corradi, Letizia Leonardi, Franco Zambonelli, "High Level Management of Allocation in a Parallel Objects Environment", Vol. 45, 1998, pp 47-63.

[23]Didier Buchs and Nicolas Guelfi, "A Formal Specification Framework for Object-Oriented
Distributed System", *IEEE Trans. on Software Engineering*, Vol. 26, No. 7, July 2000, pp.
635-652.

CHAPTER 10

Scheduling in Computational Grid

During the past few years grid computing has emerged as an effective computing environment for data and compute intensive operations. There are issues and challenges in grid computing discipline and are to be addressed by the research community before the environment is in widespread use. In this chapter, an overview is sought over the grid computing with the benefits and challenges of the grid architecture from scheduling point of view.

Future of computer system design lies in High Performance Computing (HPC) systems. In various applications, demand for increasing performance is persuasive argument. Besides other benefits (e.g. resource sharing, scalability etc.) compute intense jobs demand parallel execution by exploiting parallelism in the jobs.

"As computer networks become cheaper and more powerful, a new computing paradigm is poised to transform the practice of science and engineering"- Ian Foster

Grid is a type of parallel and distributed system that enables the sharing, selection, and aggregation of geographically distributed "autonomous" resources dynamically at runtime depending on their availability, capability, performance, cost, and user's quality-of-service requirements [1]. Grid aims at exploiting synergies that result from cooperation--ability to share and aggregate distributed computational capabilities and deliver them as service. The autonomous resources in the Grid can span across a single or multiple organizations. The key distinction between clusters and grids mainly lie in the way resources are managed. In case of clusters, a centralized resource manager performs the resource allocation and all the nodes cooperatively work together as a single unified resource. In case of a Grid, each node has its own resource manager and do not aims for providing a single system view [1, 12].

Grid technology takes Cluster computing to the next level by providing a distributed architecture that delivers compute and data resources over the web in much the same manner the electricity is delivered over the power grid - making resources available to users when and where they are needed. Grid computing is one of the fastest-growing trends in high-end scientific and engineering computing. By utilizing a flexible computing architecture based on clusters, organizations can develop and tailor grids to continually match changing requirements. Grids can be designed in any shape and size and deliver the flexibility to harness the power of any available resource, regardless of whether it is a desktop machine or a campus supercomputer [2].

10.1 Need for Grid Computing

Grid Computing delivers the potential in the growth and abundance of network connected systems and bandwidth: computation, collaboration and communication over the advanced web. At the heart of Grid computing is an infrastructure that provides dependable, consistent, pervasive and inexpensive access to computational capabilities. By pooling federated assets into a virtual system, a grid provides a single point of access to powerful distributed resources.

Researchers working to solve many of the most difficult scientific problems have long understood the potential of such shared distributed computing systems. Development teams focused on technical products, e.g. semiconductors, are using Grid computing to achieve higher throughput. Likewise, the business community is beginning to recognize the importance of distributed systems in applications such as data mining and economic modeling.

With a grid, networked resources - desktops, servers, storage, databases, even scientific instruments - can be combined to deploy massive computing power wherever and whenever it is needed most. Users can find resources quickly, use them efficiently, and scale them seamlessly.

10.2 Scalability for Global Computing

No two grids are alike, and no size fits all. Organizations can create and recreate grids to exactly match changing requirements by utilizing a flexible computing architecture based on clusters systems and software that manage the work on the distributed systems. Grids can scale from single systems to supercomputer-class clusters by utilizing thousands of processors. Grids can be classified based on the scalability as below.

Cluster Grids

Cluster grids are the most popular and simplest form of a grid. Cluster grid consists of one or more systems, working together, to provide a single point of access to users. Cluster grid meets the need of most of the organizations. Typically used by a team of users such as a single project or a department, a cluster grid supports both high throughput and better performance for the jobs.

Campus Grids

Campus grids enable multiple projects or departments to share computing resources in a cooperative way. It is also referred as the cooperative grid. Campus grids may consist of dispersed workstations and servers, as well as centralized resources located in multiple administrative domains, in departments, or across the enterprise.

Global Grids

When application needs exceed the capacity of a campus grid, organizations can tap partner resources through a global grid. Designed to support and address the needs of multiple sites and organizations, global grids provide the power of distributed resources to users anywhere in the world for computing and collaboration. Individuals or organizations sending overflow work to a grid provider or by multiple companies working together and sharing data - crossing organizational boundaries with ease can use the global grid.

10.3 Data and Computational Grids

The Grid infrastructure in which the emphasis is given on the computation is refereed as computational grid. In this, the large computing problem is divided into sub-problems and then solved over the nodes of the grid independently. Large scale problems in Science and Engineering are being solved on the computational grid. This not only allows the sharing of the resources but also reduces the execution time. The computing power need is analogous to the electrical power need of the early 90s making the electrical power grid a reality. The computing environment of a computational grid provides a demand driven, reliable, powerful and yet an inexpensive power for its customers [10]. Thus a computational grid environment consist of one or more hardware and software enabled environments that provide dependable, consistent, pervasive and inexpensive access to high end computational capabilities [9].

In data grid, the emphasis is over the management of the data that is being held in a variety of data storage facilities in geographically dispersed locations. The data sources may be databases, file systems and storage devices. The grid must also provide data virtualization services to satisfy various transparency issues e.g. transparency for data access, integration, and processing. Security and privacy is very important requirements of data in grid system and is very complex [10].

10.4 Scheduling in Computational Grid

Being able to submit a job from a networked client to a job submission service requires that the placement of such jobs can be optimized over available grid resources. This takes place through a 'super-scheduler' that matches the job to the resource's capabilities and constraints. Such a scheduling framework is being addressed by the research community and under development with many grid centers as middleware. Problems of scheduling in the distributed computing system persist in grid computing also and are to be resolved. The author had worked over the problem of scheduling in the distributed computing systems and is now extending the same for the computational grids [3-8].

The requirement of most of the compute intense jobs is parallel/concurrent execution of their subjobs (modules) on the nodes of the computing system so that the overall time for execution is minimized. Besides, the system offers other advantages in terms of resource sharing, fault tolerant execution, high throughput, scalability, use of commodity systems, better price performance ratio etc. We discuss the distribution of compute intense jobs onto a grid system.

Most important consideration of compute intense jobs is to how to distribute the computational loads amongst the nodes of the system. This distribution has different characteristic requirement in different systems. In distributed computing system, the objective is how quickly the submitted job completes the execution by exploiting both the available hardware and software. In cluster, the objective is enhanced availability besides the performance. In grid it is often desired to utilize the available resources, available anywhere but connected by the commodity network, whenever more computing power is required.

In a distributed computing system, all the computing nodes do participate in computation as per their capabilities. Number of nodes in a DCS interacts with the user and the user can submit his job at any node. Submitted job is partitioned in modules and as per the policy of the load distribution these modules are allocated onto the computing nodes of a DCS. Once a load is distributed, more or less it is fixed. Some DCS allows the user of the system to specify the load distribution, but mostly the allocator of the DCS with some predefined policy decides it.

User's job can be exploited for the existence of parallel/concurrent modules and these modules are allocated onto the computing nodes of the grid. The objective of this allocation can be the decrease in completion time of the job, increase in fault tolerant execution or some other characteristic. The distribution of the compute job will often be on the neighbor nodes so that the result obtained from allocated modules can be reproduced quickly. The distribution will usually consider just one aspect; what nodes in the neighbor are free or relatively less loaded. Optimization of any other characteristic, as considered in the distributed computing system, is absent in the grid and this will make the allocation relatively easy. It is assumed that all the processing nodes are capable enough to execute computational jobs. So the computing grids are utilized as and when there is the requirement of computing. Load distribution in case of the grid is never fixed.

Job super scheduler architecture has been proposed by Shan et. al.[11]. In this the job scheduling is conducted via autonomous local schedulers that cooperate through a superscheduler using grid middleware. The superscheduler is responsible for discovering grid resources, monitoring system utilization, and migrating load to the local queues of the distributed resource centre.

10.5 Challenges in Grid Computing

Increased network bandwidth, more powerful computers, and the acceptance of the internet have driven the ongoing demand for new and better ways to compute.

Commercial enterprises, academic institutions, and research organizations alike continue to take advantage of these advancements, and constantly seek new technologies and practices that enable them to reinvent the way they conduct business. However, many challenges still remain and are to be resolved. Increasing pressure on development and research costs, faster time-to-market, greater throughput, and improved quality and innovation are always foremost in the minds of administrators - while computational needs are outpacing the ability of organizations to deploy sufficient resources to meet growing workload demands.

On top of these challenges is the need to handle dynamically changing workloads. Flexibility is the most desired criterion and is the key. In a world with rapidly changing markets, both research institutions and enterprises need to quickly provide compute power where it is needed most. Indeed, if systems could be dynamically created when they are needed, teams could harness these resources to increase innovation and better achieve their objectives. Few pertinent questions are:

- How hard is it to build a grid?

  Sony Devices Europe created a Sun grid in just two days.

- How capable are grids?

  The Durham University Cosmology Engine performs 465 billion arithmetic operations per second on a Sun Cluster Grid.

- Is Grid computing real?

  Sun has a grid of over 7,500 total CPUs across three U.S sites; with over 98 percent CPU utilization executing over 50,000 EDA jobs a day [2].

10.6 Research Issues in Grid Scheduling

Schedulers are responsible for management of jobs amongst the nodes of the grid, such as allocation of resources needed for any specific application, job partitioning to allow parallel execution, event correlation, and service level management. The jobs submitted to a grid for the execution are evaluated based on their requirements and allocated to the node accordingly. So the services provided by the scheduler for the computational grid must include:

- Resource determination (reservation)
- Task and resource policy management for better turnaround or any other characteristics
- Monitoring the status of the task execution
- Rescheduling for load balancing
- Task migration
- Security and authentication on the grid nodes for scheduling

All the above points are very important for a computational grid scheduler and require the attention of research communities specially working for grid scheduler. Given a job for the execution over the grid, how to determine the resources becomes the first and foremost activity. Problem, being the NP-Hard, perpetuate various possibilities for the resource determination. How to achieve better turnaround is one of the objectives of the grid systems. Proper resource utilization for better turnaround is a key research problem of computational grid. Status monitoring of the job execution, so that the migration may take place, as and when required, is also very important. Load balancing, as has been discussed in chapter 4, finds place in the grid scheduler also and is very important research issue. Task migration is the repercussion of the load balancing. Security for scheduling is exclusively most important research issue and requires a great attention of the research community. As the task execution activity is transparent, how to allow only an authentic job becomes very important aspect of the secure scheduling.

All these research issues are being addressed by the researchers of this discipline.

BIBLIOGRAPHY

[1]http://www.gridcomputing.com
[2]http://www.sun.com
[3]D.P.Vidyarthi, A.K.Tripathi, "Precedence Constrained Task Allocation in Distributed Computing System", *Int. J. of High Speed Computing*, Vol. 8, No. 1, 1996, pp. 47-55.
[4]A.K.Tripathi, D.P.Vidyarthi, A.N.Mantri, "A Genetic Task Allocation Algorithm for Distributed Computing System Incorporating Problem Specific Knowledge", *International J. of High Speed Computing*, Vol.8, No.4, 1996, pp. 363-370.
[5]D.P.Vidyarthi, A.K.Tripathi, "Maximizing Reliability of Distributed Computing Systems with Task Allocation using Simple Genetic Algorithm", *J. of Systems Architecture*, Vol. 47, 2001, pp. 549-554.
[6]D.P.Vidyarthi, A.K.Tripathi, "Studies on Reliability with Task Allocation of Redundant Distributed Systems", *IETE J. of Research*, Vol. 44, No. 6, Nov-Dec. 1998, pp. 279-285.
[7]D.P.Vidyarthi, A.K.Tripathi, B.K.Sarker, "Multiple Task Management in Distributed Computing Systems", *The Journal of the CSI*, Vol. 31, No. 1 Sep. 2000, pp. 19-25.
[8]D.P.Vidyarthi, A.K.Tripathi, B.K.Sarker, "Allocation Aspects in Distributed Computing System", *IETE Technical Review*, Vol. 18, No. 6, Nov.-Dec. 2001, pp.279-285.
[9]Ian Foster, Carl Kesselman, *The Grid: Blueprint for a New Computing Infrastructure*, Morgan Kaufmann, 2004.
[10]Joseph J., Fellenstein C., *Grid Computing*, Pearson Education, 2004.
[11]Shan H., Oliker L., Biswas R., "Job Superscheduler Architecture and Performance in Computational Grid Environments", *Proceedings of the ACM/IEEE SC2003 Conference*.

[12]D.P.Vidyarthi, "Some observations on HPC Capabilities of Grid, Cluster and Distributed Computing Systems", *COMSOMATH, Magazine on Computing, Social Science and Mathematics, Special Issue, May 2005.*

CHAPTER 11

Concluding Remarks

This book aims at consideration of existing task allocation models with their simplifying assumptions for proposing better TA algorithms that consider the realistic situations of a task and DCS i.e. the precedence of the execution among the modules of the task, consideration of more than one tasks for execution, functional limitations of processing elements of DCS etc. The work is being summarized in the next section. In section 11.2, we have briefed the structure and place of scheduler in distributed operating system. Future possibilities have been explored and pointed out in section 11.3.

11.1 Summary of Findings

Distributed Computing System is emerging as a future computing system because of its certain useful characteristics. Reliability, throughput, scalability are to name a few. DCS has taken a lead as a future computing system in comparison to Tightly Coupled Multiprocessor.

Task scheduling (allocation) is very important phase in the development of operating system of a DCS and this work deals mainly with the task allocation problem of the DCS. A task, consisting of the modules, is given to the DCS for execution. The execution of this task takes place under various constraints imposed by the task and the system as well. The execution has to satisfy certain characteristic parameters to prove it to be a good allocation. Before allocation, the task is to be divided in modules (subtasks). Thus the task execution requires two steps: partitioning and allocation.

Partitioning exploits the parallelism present in the task to its maximum possible extent and based on that, modules are created. There are many techniques for task partitioning. Our proposal of task partitioning using Genetic Algorithm appears in [1], though this book does not address the task partitioning problem and it requires an exclusive discussion in its entirety.

The problem of allocation of tasks in a DCS has been thoroughly discussed in this book by identifying various relative factors: (i) precedence amongst the modules of a task (ii) reliability with task allocation of a DCS (iii) completion time (iv) limitations and capabilities of the processing nodes (v) multiplicity of tasks (vi) balanced load and (vii) migration. Factors (i), (ii), (iii) & (iv) are related to "Single Task Allocation" models whereas all the factors (i to vii) have been dealt with keeping in mind the relative situation that the number of tasks in DCS is usually substantive (not one as considered in previous models reported in the literature).

After a brief discussion over the distributed computing system and the scheduling problem in distributed computing system in beginning chapters, the Load Balancing aspect has been thoroughly discussed in chapter 4. The chapter 4 also briefs the various other issues related with the task scheduling, in general and load balancing in particular. It discusses the task migration and threads. It also explores the conflicts that may occur for the allocation of a task due to load balancing or imbalancing.

The precedence relation, amongst the modules of the task, can be analyzed to identify such modules that may coexist on one and the same node, as the sequential execution of concurrent modules sets may allow this. A precedence constrained task allocation is proposed in chapter 5; section 5.3, in which the emphasis is on the precedence of the modules [2]. This model minimizes the turn-around time of the given tasks, but at the same time considers the precedence constraint of the modules of the task. The earlier models discussed in section 5.1 do not consider the precedence of the modules of a task. Moreover the effect of already allocated modules of other tasks on processing elements comprising the system is considered (assuming round robin scheduling). This consideration has not been there in earlier models. As models proposed by us make considerations that are essential, the other models discussed herein, sec 5.1, (without these aforesaid consideration) are not comparable.

Communication among the modules, adds the cost of allocation if these communicating modules are executing on distant processing nodes of the DCS. This problem has been considered and IMC cost reduction model using fuzzy logic is proposed in the same chapter 5, section 5.4, of the book [3]. This IMC cost reduction model can be introduced in any task allocation algorithms at minimum cost.

Load Balancing Task Allocation (LBTA) has been discussed in chapter 6. This chapter not only discusses the LBTA strategy and issues, it also proposes LBTA solution. This also proposes a load measure for a single task as well multiple tasks.

Genetic Algorithms (GA), based on the Darwin's theory "Survival of the fittest", is emerging as a successful tool for the optimization problem [4]. As the task allocation problem is an NP-Hard problem, GA is found to be quite suitable to solve task allocation problem. GA is parallel in nature so it is well suited to TA problem of DCS. The various activities of GA based task allocation can be performed in parallel on various processing nodes of DCS [19]. We applied GA for task allocation with many variations. In one, a problem specific knowledge is incorporated in GA. The TA model proposed in section 7.1 is based on a finding that the incorporation of some problem specific knowledge in construction of GA improves its performance and solution converges quickly [5]. GA is also used to maximize reliability of DCS with task allocation in section 7.2. The algorithm not only gets the advantage of GA for quick convergence but also produces better solutions in terms of allocation with improved reliability [6]. The result is compared with that of Shatz and it shows better one. Many more inferences are drawn.

So far, most of the literature shows an allocation policy for a single task. We have proposed multiple task allocation in DCS, which considers the allocation based on the dynamic nature of task arrival and departure in the DCS. To achieve

this, the concept of Global Table is introduced [7]. A heuristic task allocation al-

gorithm for multiple task allocation appears in chapter 8, section 8.1 of the thesis.

The result shows that all the processors are being utilized for the purpose of exe-

cution. The resultant allocation infers that the modules of a particular task are also

distributed among the processing nodes of the DCS. The implementation of global

table will incur an overhead but this is inevitable for the management of the multi-

ple tasks execution. In this chapter, allocation algorithms that consider multiple

tasks and status of PEs due to previous allocations are given and hence these are

not comparable with other models proposed in the literature.

A cluster based load partitioning and allocation in DCS is discussed in chapter

8, section 8.2. Cluster is formed of the modules of the task and processing nodes

as well. Allocation is decided from task cluster to processor cluster. Cluster based

load partitioning and assignment is used for real-time applications. The proposed

approach has the potential for scalability and support for system heterogeneity.

Scalability is achieved by Merge and Split cluster formation of the processors. The

approach considers the communication aspect in the cluster formation as it in-

volves more overheads. This is also a realistic approach as the other algorithms,

based on the same, uses the priori knowledge of the execution of the modules of

the task on the processors of the DCS. The communication bandwidth is already

known while designing the system, so it is not difficult to measure the IMC time

for the modules of the task. A new fuzzy approach is applied to form the clusters.

Examples illustrate the algorithm.

The idea of multiple tasks and global table caters to the needs of all types of DCS and tasks. It may accommodate single task situation as well. The problem is NP-Hard as such. The algorithms (and models), proposed, have similar complexities. These methodologies promise to be candidates for implementation.

Various task allocation models & algorithms are proposed in this book. These models use a number of search techniques e.g. list schedule, A*, GA etc. Obviously the model that uses GA or A* will have better execution efficiency than that of list schedule. GA based TA algorithms has the potential of parallel execution on DCS [8]. The models discussed in chapter 8 and 9, which considers multiple tasks execution, are more realistic than the models discussed in previous chapters. Depending on the DCS architecture and other requirements (minimization of turnaround time, improvement in reliability etc.) the model can be chosen for its implementation in distributed operating system.

11.2 Structures and Place of Scheduler in DOS

Any Operating System for a Distributed Computing System consists of elements to manage network communications, process operations, device management, I/O management, and memory management as shown in the figure below.

The scheduler comes under the process management part of the Distributed Operating System.

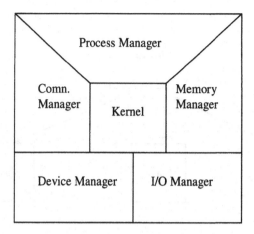

Fig. 11.1. Structure of Distributed Operating System

In a single local computer, all these managers reside on the same system, as there is no other choice [9]. The place of the scheduler in DOS is little difficult to decide as it leaves many possibilities with its advantages and disadvantages. The effective place to decide the place of scheduler is an open research problem.

The simplest choice is that of Master/Slave in which the scheduler resides on one of the nodes, called master, and sticks to that node till its lifetime. In this or-ganization the task submitted for execution goes to the master first and it decides how the modules are given to the other nodes for execution. The result produced by the individual nodes is given back to the master, which after reassembling pro-duces it to the users [10].

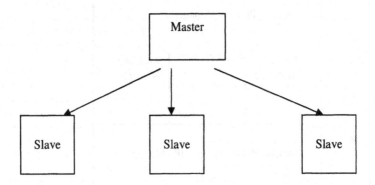

Fig. 11.2. Master-Slave design of DOS

This type of scheme is simple but inefficient as the master node may be a bot-tleneck in case of failure.

Another scheme proposes to allow the scheduler to float from one node to the other from time to time. Whenever the scheduler process is to be migrated, all the relevant data are also to be moved. Thus the movement of scheduler process in-curs an overhead if the size of the scheduler is big enough. This overhead is added if the relevant data are large [11].

The third and efficient scheme is to divide the scheduler process in modules and allocate these modules onto the different available nodes of the DCS. In this case, the scheduler process will be treated as other users' process with more prior-ity. The various modules of the scheduler often have to cooperate on various is-sues. This type of scheme is better but poses extra burden, as every module of the scheduler must know the whereabouts of the other modules.

Scheduler (Task Allocator) can be structured according to any of the scheme discussed above and can be incorporated in the operating system of the DCS.

11.3 Future Possibilities

The problem of task scheduling i.e. allocation has been considered in this book and various models for the same are proposed. As the technology in software and hardware is growing fast, it is necessary that all the functionalities of the operating system also adapt to the new technology. So the work that remains from this book have been pointed out in this section.

Most of the algorithms, proposed in the literature and discussed in the book as well, are based on some priori knowledge (execution time, communication time etc.). In practice it is very difficult to estimate these times (at least execution time). So a good piece of research work is to how estimate these times with some other available information. Specifically, how much time a particular module takes on a particular computing node is to be determined. Speed of the processing node and size of the modules are generally available and the execution time is to be determined from this information. Similarly communication among modules is also to be determined by tracing the program. Precedence among modules is another research issue that is to be taken further.

With the introduction of the new hardware technology a new multicontext CPUs are being developed in which there may be more than one program counter for multiple independent executions. This type of CPUs supports the threading in the hardware. This amounts to having more than one processor on a single chip with a shared set of registers. Similarly with new software technology concept of multithreading is being introduced. Thus another dimension for future research is that how these task allocation models can adapt to the DCS consisting of multi-context computing nodes and how the thread allocation can be made. Threads are the finer execution entities. Obviously the thread allocation will improve the execution characteristics of the task for execution.

Prototype for the object oriented distributed computing systems are also being introduced [17] and future computing systems are to be object based. Of course the execution entity on such systems will be objects not processes (tasks) as considered in conventional distributed computing systems. How the object allocation on object oriented distributed computing systems will be done, is another research work for the future [12-18].

BIBLIOGRAPHY

[1] D.P.Vidyarthi, A.K.Tripathi, A.N.Mantri, "Task Partitioning using Genetic Algorithm", *Proceedings of International Conference on Cognitive Systems*, Vol. 1, Dec. 1997, New Delhi, pp. 248-254.
[2] D.P.Vidyarthi, A.K.Tripathi, "Precedence Constrained Task Allocation in Distributed Computing System", *Int. J. of High Speed Computing*, Vol. 8, No. 1, 1996, pp. 47-55.
[3] D.P.Vidyarthi, A.K.Tripathi, " A Fuzzy IMC Cost Reduction Model for Task Allocation in Distributed Computing Systems", *Proceedings of the Fifth International Symposium on Methods and Models in Automation and Robotics*, Vol. 2, Szczecin, Poland, August 1998, pp. 719-721.

[4]J.L.R.Filho, P.C.Treleaven, C.Alippi, "Genetic Algorithm Programming Environments", *IEEE Computer*, June 1994, pp. 29-42.

[5]John J. Grefenstelle, "Incorporating Problem Specific Knowledge into Genetic Algorithm", *Genetic Algorithm and Simulated Annealing*, Morgan Kaufman Publisher, California, 1987.

[6]D.P.Vidyarthi, A.K.Tripathi, "Maximizing Reliability of Distributed Computing Systems with Task Allocation using Simple Genetic Algorithm", *J. of Systems Architecture*, Vol. 47, 2001, pp. 549-554.

[7]D.P.Vidyarthi, A.K.Tripathi, B.K.Sarker, "Multiple Task Management in Distributed Computing Systems", The *Journal of the CSI*, Vol. 31, No. 1 Sep. 2000, pp. 19-25.

[8]D.P.Vidyarthi, A.K.Tripathi, "Exploiting Parallelism in Genetic Task Allocation Algorithm", *Int. J. of Information and Computing Science*, Vol. 4 No. 1, June 2002, pp. 22-26

[9]A.Silberschatz, P.B. Galvin, *Operating Systems Concepts*, Addison-Wesley, 1998.

[10]Kai Hwang, F.A.Briggs, *Computer Architecture and Parallel Processing*, McGraw Hill International Edition, 1995.

[11]Kai Hwang, *Parallel Computer Architecture*, Mc-Graw Hill International Edition,1995.

[12]Timothy Budd, *An Introduction to Object Oriented Programming*, Addison-Wesley, 1991.

[13]Antonio Corradi, Letizia Leonardi, Franco Zambonelli, "Parallel Object Migration: A Fine Grained Approach to Load Distribution", *Journal of Parallel & Distributed Computing*, Vol. 60, 2000, pp. 48-71.

[14]Paul J. Fortier, *Design of Distributed Operating System*, Mc-Graw Hill International Editions, 1988.

[14]Antonio Corradi, Letizia Leonardi, Franco Zambonelli, "High Level Management of Allocation in a Parallel Objects Environment", *Journal of Systems Architecture*, Vol. 45, 1998, pp. 47-63.

[15]D.T.Peng, K.G.Shin, "Static Allocation of Periodic Task with Precedence", *Proceedings of the Int'l Conf. Distributed Computing Systems*, June 1989, pp.190-198.

[16]Didier Buchs, Nicolas Guelfi, "A Formal Specification Framework for Object-Oriented Distributed System", *IEEE Trans. on Software Engineering*, Vol. 26, No. 7, July 2000, pp. 635-652.

[17]K.Mani Chandy, Adam Rifkin, "Systematic Composition of Distributed Objects: Processes and Sessions", *The Computer Journal*, Vol. 40, No. 8, 1997, pp. 465-478.

[18]D.P.Vidyarthi, A.K.Tripathi, "Exploiting Parallelism in Genetic Task Allocation Algorithm", *Int. J. of Information and Computing Science*, Vol. 4 No. 1, June 2002, pp. 22-26

ABBREVIATIONS

DCS	Distributed Computing System
CPU	Central Processing Unit
PE	Processing Element
RDS	Redundant Distributed System
TA	Task Allocation
IPC	Inter Process Communication
IMC	Inter Module Communication
AET	Accumulative Execution Time
GA	Genetic Algorithm
TG	Task Graph
PG	Processor Graph
TIG	Task Interaction Graph
TPG	Task Precedence Graph
DOS	Distributed Operating System
TSP	Traveling Salesperson Problem
MTA	Multiple Task Allocation
LAN	Local Area Networks
CP	Communication Penalty
OS	Operating System
VLSI	Very Large Scale Integration
WAN	Wide Area Network
ATM	Asynchronous Transfer Mode
NOS	Network Operating System
ISO	International Standard Organization
LS	Load Sharing
LB	Load Balancing
LBTA	Load Balancing Task Allocation
TM	Task Migration
GT	Global Table

Appendix A

This appendix has a listing of a program using the algorithm in sec.8.3. The program has been written in C language under Windows 98 operating system in Turbo C++ environment.

ASTAR.C

```c
#include<stdio.h>
#include<stdlib.h>
#include<conio.h>
#include<iostream.h>
#include<dos.h>
#include<string.h>
#define max_proc 10
#define max_task 10
#define max_mod 10
struct st{

                int mod_cap_present;


                int mem_cap;
        }status[max_proc];/* Status of processing nodes*/

struct open{
                        int fx;
                        char string[max_proc];
                        open()
                        {
                        strcpy(string,"XXXXXXXXX");
                        }/*structure for OPEN list as in sec.4.2 */


                        struct open *next;
                }*open_list;
        int load(int);
        /* To find the load on each processing node according to equation 4.1 */

        int check_status(int,int,int);
        /* It checks STATUS of processors according to the available no. of modules
and available memory */
```

```
int find_heaviest_proc();
/* To find the heaviest loaded processor using equ. 4.1*/
int heur_cost(int);
/* To find the cost h(n) according to equ.4.2 */

int min_cost_IPC(int,int,int);
int min(int,int);
/*Minimum between the two costs*/

void insert_open(int,int,int,charstr[max_proc]);
/* This function insert the cost into OPEN as explained in sec. 4.2 */

void modify_mod_at_proc(int,int,char*);
/* This function insets 'X' for no allocation as in sec 4.2 */

void allocation();
/* This function allocates the modules onto the processors according to mini-
mum cost using the algorithm (sec.4.1.2)*/

void modify_status(int,int);
/* This function modifies the STATUS of each processor*/

char * remove_min_from_open();
/* This function selects the minimum cost node from OPEN, expand it and re-
move it after expanding nodes */

int no_of_proc,no_of_modules[max_task],no_of_tasks;

int X[max_mod][max_task][max_proc];
/* Execution cost of the modules of tasks onto a processing node */

int M[max_mod][max_task][max_proc];
/*Assignment of the modules to a processor*/

int C[max_mod][max_task][max_proc];
/* Communication cost between the two modules of the task */

int CC[max_proc][max_proc];
/*IPC cost among between the processing nodes */

int mod_at_proc[max_mod][max_task];
/* The module of a task */

int L[max_proc][max_proc];
/* Connection matrix of two processing nodes direct link*/
```

```
int L1[max_proc][max_proc];
/* Connection matrix of two processing nodes by one indirect link */

int L2[max_proc][max_proc];
/* Connection matrix of two processing nodes by two indirect link */

int mem_req[max_task][max_mod];
/* Memory required by each module */

int cf0,cf1,cf2;
/* Cost for the link matrix L */

int load(int proc)
{

    int p,n,k,i,j,ex_cost,q,comm_cost;
    p=proc;
    ex_cost=0;
    comm_cost=0;
    n=no_of_proc;
    for(k=1;k<=no_of_tasks;k++){
        for (i=1;i<=no_of_modules[k];i++){
            if(mod_at_proc[k][i]==p)M[i][k][p]=1;
            ex_cost+=X[i][k][p] * M[i][k][p];
        }
    }
    for (k=1;k<=no_of_tasks;k++){
        for(i=1;i<=no_of_modules[k];i++){
            /* q is the proc on which j is executing*/
            for(j=1,q=1;j<=no_of_modules[k] && q<n;j++,q++){
                if(i!=j && p!=q){
                    comm_cost=  M[i][k][p] * M[j][k][q]
                    * (   C[i][k][j] + CC[p][q]);
                }
            }
        }
    }
    return(ex_cost + comm_cost);
}
void allocation()
{
    int k,i,j,p,hp,gx,hx,fx,l,xx,xxx,i1,p1;
    char *str,*str1;
    for(k=1;k<=no_of_tasks;k++){
        open_list=NULL;
```

```
            strcpy(str,"XXXXXXXXX");
            i1=0;
            for(i=1;i<=no_of_modules[k];i++){
                    for(p=1;p<=no_of_proc;p++){
                            if(check_status(p,i,k)==1){
                                    mod_at_proc[i][k]=p;
                                    hp=find_heaviest_proc();
                                    gx=load(hp);
                                    hx=heur_cost(p);
                                    fx= gx + hx;
                                    insert_open(i,p,fx,str);
                            }
                    }
//                  find_min_fx_open();
                    strcpy(str1,str);
                    str=remove_min_from_open();
                    xx=0;

                    while(str[xx+1]<60)xx++;


//                  if(i<i1){
                            for(xxx=1;xxx<=i;xxx++){

    status[str1[xxx]].mod_cap_present+=1;

    status[str1[xxx]].mem_cap+=mem_req[k][xxx];

                            }
//                  }
                    i=xx;
                    for(i1=1;i1<=xx;i1++){
                    modify_mod_at_proc(i1,k,str);
                    modify_status(i1,k);
                    }
            }
            printf("\n\n Task %d has been allocated as : ",k);
            for(l=1;l<=no_of_modules[k];l++)printf("%d",str[l]);
    }
    int m,m1;
    m=0;
    for (p1=1;p1<=no_of_proc;p1++){
            m1=load(p1);
            printf("\nThe cost at the processing node %d is %d",p1,m1);
```

```
        printf("\nThe status of processing node %d is %d      %d",p1,
    status[p1].mod_cap_present,status[p1].mem_cap);
            m+=m1;
            }
        printf("\n\nTotal cost at all the processing nodes is %d",m);
}


int heur_cost(int p)
{
    int k,i,j,local_var,heur;
    heur=0;
    for(k=1;k<=no_of_tasks;k++){
            for(i=1;i<=no_of_modules[k];i++){
                    if(mod_at_proc[i][k]==p){
    /*ith module of kth task is on proc p then we are proceeding*/
                            for(j=1;j<=no_of_modules[k];j++){
                            /*checking if jth module communicates with ith
mod. */
                            if(C[i][j]>0){
    /* if ith mod is the same as jth, then C[i][j]==0, if no comm is there, C[i][j]==-
1*/
                                    if(mod_at_proc[j][k]==0){
    /* we have checked that if jth module has yet been allocated, 0 shows it hasn't
*/
                                                        lo-
cal_var=min_cost_IPC(j,k,p);//local_var gives the processor onto which j can be
allocated &CC[p][loc..] is min

        heur+=min(X[j][k][p],(C[i][k][j]+local_var));
                                                        }
                                            }
                                    }
                            }
                    }
            }
        return(heur);
}
int min_cost_IPC(int mod,int task ,int proc)
{
    int i,aa,flag;
    for(i=1;i<no_of_proc;i++){
            if(i!=proc){
                    aa=check_status(mod,task,i);
```

```
            if(aa==1 && CC[proc][i]==cf0)return(cf0);   //IPC is min. possible
                        else if(aa==1 && CC[proc][i]==cf1)flag+=0;
                        else flag+=0;
            }
            if (flag>0)return(cf1);
            else return(cf2);
        }
    }
    int min(int value1, int value2)
    {
      return ( (value1 < value2) ? value1 : value2);
    }

    int check_status(int proc,int module,int task)
    {
        if(status[proc].mod_cap_present>0    &&     status[proc].mem_cap    >
mem_req[task][module])return(1);
        else return(0);
    }
    void modify_status(int module,int task)
    {
        int proc;
        proc=mod_at_proc[module][task];
        status[proc].mod_cap_present-=1;
        status[proc].mem_cap-=mem_req[task][module];
    }
    int find_heaviest_proc()
    {
        int p,max,return_value;
        for(p=1;p<=no_of_proc;p++){
                if(p==1){
                        max=load(p);
                        return_value=p;
                }
                else
                if(max<load(p)){
                        max=load(p);
                        return_value=p;
                }
        }
        return(return_value);
    }
    void insert_open(int module_no, int proc, int fx,char str[max_proc])
    {
```

```
            struct open *temp, *temp1;
            temp= open_list;
            temp1=new open;
            strcpy(temp1->string,str);
            temp1->string[module_no]=proc;  /*remember to reset open after each
task*/
            temp1->fx=fx;
            if(open_list==NULL){
                    open_list=temp1;
                    open_list->next=NULL;
            }
            else{
                    temp= open_list;
                    while(temp->next!=NULL)temp=temp->next;
                    temp->next=temp1;
                    temp->next->next=NULL;
            }

    }
    char * remove_min_from_open()
    //remember to remove from open that node which lies latest in the list if two or
more fx's are equal
    {
            struct open *temp, *temp1;
            int  mini,flag=0;
            temp=open_list;
            if(temp==NULL)return("empty_lst");
            mini=temp->fx;
    //finding the minimum fx
            while(temp->next!=NULL){
                    temp=temp->next;
                    if(mini>= temp->fx)mini=temp->fx;
            }
    //removing the corresponding node
            temp=open_list;
            while(temp->fx != mini){
                    flag=1;
                    temp1=temp;
                    temp = temp->next;
            }
            if(flag==0){
                    open_list=temp->next;
                    return(temp->string);
            }
            else{
```

```
                    temp1->next=temp->next;
                    return(temp->string);
        }
//modifying mod_at_proc
/*      for(i=0;i<no_of_proc;i++){
                    if(temp->string!='X')
    */


}
void modify_mod_at_proc(int module,int task, char* str)
{
        int i;
        for(i=1;i<=no_of_modules[task];i++){
                    if(str[i]!='X')
                            mod_at_proc[i][task]=str[i];
//                  else mod_at_proc[module][task]=0;
        }
}
void input(void)
{
        int i,j,k,j1,c,p1,p,q,x;
        clrscr();
        printf("INPUT THE NO OF PROCESSORS\n");
        scanf("%d",&no_of_proc);
        printf("INPUT THE NO OF TASKS \n");
        scanf("%d",&no_of_tasks);
        for(k=1;k<=no_of_tasks;k++){
                    printf("ENTER THE NO OF MODULES OF TASK %d\t",k);
                    scanf("%d",& no_of_modules[k]);
        }
        clrscr();
        for(k=1;k<=no_of_tasks;k++){
                    clrscr();
                    printf("INPUT   THE   EXECUTION   MATRIX   FOR   TASK
%d\n",k);
                    for(p=1;p<=no_of_proc;p++){
                          gotoxy(8*(p),5);
                          printf("P%d",p);
                    }


                    for(j=1;j<=no_of_modules[k];j++){
                          gotoxy(2,5+j);
                          printf("m%d%d\t",k,j);
                          for(p=1;p<=no_of_proc;p++){
```

```
                                    gotoxy(8*p,5+j);
                                    scanf("%d",&X[j][k][p]);
                            }
                    }
            }
    //INTER MOD COMM COST
            for(k=1;k<=no_of_tasks;k++){
                    clrscr();
                    printf("INPUT THE INTER-MODULE COMMUNICATION
    MATRIX FOR TASK %d\n",k);
                    for(j1=1;j1<=no_of_modules[k];j1++){
                            gotoxy(8*(j1),5);
                            printf("m%d%d",k,j1);
                    }


                    for(j=1;j<=no_of_modules[k];j++){
                            gotoxy(2,5+j);
                            printf("m%d%d\t",k,j);
                            for(j1=1;j1<=no_of_modules[k];j1++){
                                    gotoxy(8*j1,5+j);
                                    if(j==j1)printf("0");
                                    else scanf("%d",&C[j][k][j1]);
                            }
                    }
            }
            clrscr();
            printf("INPUT THE ADJACENCY MATRIX FOR THE
    PROCESSORS\n");
            for(p=1;p<=no_of_proc;p++){
                    gotoxy(8*(p),5);
                    printf("P%d",p);
            }
            for(p=1;p<=no_of_proc;p++){
                    gotoxy(2,5+p);
                    printf("P%d\t",p);
                    for(p1=1;p1<=no_of_proc;p1++){
                            gotoxy(8*p1,5+p);
                            if(p!=p1){ while(1){
                                            c=getch();
                                            if(c==48 ||c==49)break;
                                    }
                                    if(c=='1'){
                                            L[p][p1]=1;
                                            printf("1");
```

```
                                          }
                                          else{
                                                    L[p][p1]=0;
                                                    printf("0");

                                          }
                        }
                        else{
                                printf("0");
                                L[p][p1]=0;
                        }
              }
      }
```

//MAKING THE SQUARE AND CUBE OF ADJACENCY MATRIX
/*FUNCTION TO MULTIPLY TO MATRICES*/

```
             for(x=1;x<=no_of_proc;x++){
                     for(p=1;p<=no_of_proc;p++){
                             L1[x][p]=0;
                     }
             }
      for(x=1;x<=no_of_proc;x++){
             for(p=1;p<=no_of_proc;p++){
                     for(q=1;q<=no_of_proc;q++){
                             L1[x][p]=L1[x][p]+L[x][q]*L[q][p];
                     }
                     if(L1[x][p]!=0)L1[x][p]=1;
             }
      }
      for(x=1;x<=no_of_proc;x++){
             for(p=1;p<=no_of_proc;p++){
                     L2[x][p]=0;
             }
      }
      for(x=1;x<=no_of_proc;x++){
             for(p=1;p<=no_of_proc;p++){
                     for(q=1;q<=no_of_proc;q++){
                             L2[x][p]=L2[x][p]+L1[x][q]*L[q][p];
                     }
                     if(L2[x][p]!=0)L2[x][p]=1;
             }
      }
```

//INPUTTING STATUS
        printf("\n\nINPUT THE STATUS OF PROCESSORS : MODULE
CAPACITY & MEMORY CAPACITY\n");

```
        for(p=1;p<=no_of_proc;p++){
                printf("STATUS[%d] = ",p);
                scanf("%d                    %d",&status[p].mod_cap_present,
&status[p].mem_cap);
        }
    // INPUTTING THE COEFF. FOR INTER PROCESSOR COMM.
        printf("\nenter the adjacency coeff. for direct link between proc : ");
        scanf("%d",&cf0);
        printf("\nenter the adjacency coeff. for one indirect link between proc :
");
        scanf("%d",&cf1);
        printf("\nenter the adjacency coeff. for two indirect links between proc :
");
        scanf("%d",&cf2);
        printf("\n\nENTER    THE    MEMORY    REQUIREMENTS    OF
MODULES\n");
        for(k=1;k<=no_of_tasks;k++){
                for(j=1;j<=no_of_modules[k];j++){
                        printf("\tm%d%d : ",k,j);
                        scanf("%d",&mem_req[k][j]);
                }
        }

        for(x=1;x<=no_of_proc;x++){
                for(p=1;p<=no_of_proc;p++){
                        if(x!=p){
                                if(L[x][p]==1)CC[x][p]=cf0;
                                else if(L1[x][p]==1)CC[x][p]=cf1;
                                else if(L2[x][p]==1)CC[x][p]=cf2;
                        }
                }
        }
    }

    void main()
    {

    struct time *time;
    unsigned long time1,time2;
    input();
    gettime(time);
        time1  =  time->ti_hour*60*60*100  +  time->ti_min*60*100  +  time-
>ti_sec*100 + time->ti_hund;
    allocation();
```

```
  gettime(time);
    time2 = time->ti_hour*60*60*100 + time->ti_min*60*100 + time-
>ti_sec*100+ time->ti_hund;
    printf("\nTime Reqd. was :0.%2d seconds\n" , time2 - time1);
    //  cout << endl << "Time Reqd. was : " << time2 - time1;

//getch();
    }
```

Appendix B

This appendix has a listing of a program using the algorithm in sec.5.3. The program has been written in C language under Windows 98 operating system in Turbo C++ environment. There are some common functions, which are used in both the ASTAR.CPP (appendix A) and the GA.CPP. So, Descriptions are not given here for those functions.

GA.CPP

```c
#include<iostream.h>
#include<stdio.h>
#include<stdlib.h>
#include<math.h>
#include<conio.h>
#include<string.h>
#include<dos.h>

#define max_proc 10
#define max_task 10
#define max_mod 10
#define MFACTOR 1000
/* It's a multiplicative factor */
#define NULL 0
#define NO_OF_GEN 50
/* Generate initial population 50*/
#define NO_OF_CROSSOVER 100


    struct st
    {
        int mod_cap_present;
        int mem_cap;
    }status[max_proc],resetstate[max_proc];
    struct String
    {
        float fx;
        char str;
        struct String *next;
        int freq;
    };
```

```
int load(int);
   /* This function calculates the load according to equ. 5.1 */
int check_status();
   /* It checks STATUS of processors according to the available no. of modules
and available memory */
int find_heaviest_proc();
int heur_cost(int);
int min_cost_IPC(int,int,int);
int min(int,int);
void crossover(float thresh);
   /* This function do crossover as described in
sec.5.3.2 */
void insert_open(int,int,int,char str[max_proc]);
void modify_mod_at_proc(char *);
   /* This function just sees which processor has been
mapped with which module of which task. */
int allocation();
void modify_status(int,int);
char *remove_min_from_open();
struct String * open_list_50;
void gen50chrom(float bstfx);
/* This function generates 50 chromosomes as initial
population */
   void crossover(int bst );
   /* This function do crossover as described in
sec.5.3.2 */
struct String * open_list;
float minimum;
int no_of_proc;
int no_of_modules[max_task];
int no_of_tasks;
int chrom_size;
int X[max_mod][max_task][max_proc];
int M[max_mod][max_task][max_proc];
int C[max_mod][max_task][max_proc];
int CC[max_proc][max_proc];
int mod_at_proc[max_mod][max_task];
int L[max_proc][max_proc];
int L1[max_proc][max_proc];
int L2[max_proc][max_proc];
int mem_req[max_task][max_mod];
int cf0,cf1,cf2;
   unsigned long no_of_chrom;

   void input(void)
```

```
{
    int i,j,k,j1,c,p1,p,q,x;
    clrscr();
    printf("INPUT THE NO OF PROCESSORS\n");
    scanf("%d",&no_of_proc);
    printf("INPUT THE NO OF TASKS \n");
    scanf("%d",&no_of_tasks);
    for(k=1;k<=no_of_tasks;k++)
    {
        printf("ENTER THE NO OF MODULES OF TASK
%d\t",k);
        scanf("%d",& no_of_modules[k]);
    }

    for(j=1;j<=no_of_tasks;j++)
    {
        chrom_size+=no_of_modules[j];
    }
    clrscr();
    for(k=1;k<=no_of_tasks;k++)
    {
        clrscr();
        printf("INPUT THE EXECUTION MATRIX FOR TASK
%d\n",k);
        for(p=1;p<=no_of_proc;p++)
        {
            gotoxy(8*(p),5);
            printf("P%d",p);
        }
        for(j=1;j<=no_of_modules[k];j++)
        {
            gotoxy(2,5+j);
            printf("m%d%d\t",k,j);
            for(p=1;p<=no_of_proc;p++)
            {
            gotoxy(8*p,5+j);
            scanf("%d",&X[j][k][p]);
//          X[j][k][p] = pow(-1,j)*10 + 10*j;
            }
        }
        }
//INTER MOD COMM COST
    for(k=1;k<=no_of_tasks;k++)
    {
        clrscr();
```

```
        printf("INPUT THE INTER-MODULE COMMUNICATION
MATRIX FOR TASK %d\n",k);
        for(j1=1;j1<=no_of_modules[k];j1++)
        {
         gotoxy(8*(j1),5);
         printf("m%d%d",k,j1);
        }

        for(j=1;j<=no_of_modules[k];j++)
        {
         gotoxy(2,5+j);
         printf("m%d%d\t",k,j);
         for(j1=1;j1<=no_of_modules[k];j1++)
         {
             gotoxy(8*j1,5+j);
             if(j==j1)printf("0");
             else
             scanf("%d",&C[j][k][j1]);
//           C[j][k][j1] = pow(-2,j*j1)*5 + 15*j1;
         }
        }
     }
     clrscr();
     printf("INPUT   THE   ADJACENCY   MATRIX   FOR   THE
PROCESSORS\n");
     for(p=1;p<=no_of_proc;p++)
     {
         gotoxy(8*(p),5);
         printf("P%d",p);
     }
     for(p=1;p<=no_of_proc;p++)
     {
       gotoxy(2,5+p);
       printf("P%d\t",p);
       for(p1=1;p1<=no_of_proc;p1++)
       {
           gotoxy(8*p1,5+p);
           if(p!=p1)
           {
                 while(1)
                 {
                  c=getch();
//                c = '1';
                  if(c==48 ||c==49)break;
                 }
```

```
                    if(c=='1')
                    {
                     L[p][p1]=1;
                     printf("1");
                    }
                    else
                    {
                     L[p][p1]=0;
                     printf("0");
                    }        .
            }
            else
            {
                    printf("0");
                    L[p][p1]=0;
            }
        }
    }
//MAKING THE SQUARE AND CUBE OF ADJACENCY MATRIX
    /*FUNCTION TO MULTIPLY TO MATRICES*/

        for(x=1;x<=no_of_proc;x++){
                for(p=1;p<=no_of_proc;p++){
                        L1[x][p]=0;
                }
        }
    for(x=1;x<=no_of_proc;x++){
        for(p=1;p<=no_of_proc;p++){
                for(q=1;q<=no_of_proc;q++){

    L1[x][p]=L1[x][p]+L[x][q]*L[q][p];
                }
                if(L1[x][p]!=0)L1[x][p]=1;
        }
    }
    for(x=1;x<=no_of_proc;x++){
        for(p=1;p<=no_of_proc;p++){
                L2[x][p]=0;
        }
    }
    for(x=1;x<=no_of_proc;x++){
        for(p=1;p<=no_of_proc;p++){
                for(q=1;q<=no_of_proc;q++){

    L2[x][p]=L2[x][p]+L1[x][q]*L[q][p];
```

```
                }
                if(L2[x][p]!=0)L2[x][p]=1;
            }
        }

//INPUTTING STATUS
    printf("\n\nINPUT  THE  STATUS  OF  PROCESSORS  :
MODULE CAPACITY & MEMORY CAPACITY\n");
    for(p=1;p<=no_of_proc;p++)
    {
        printf("STATUS[%d] = ",p);
        scanf("%d      %d",&status[p].mod_cap_present,
&status[p].mem_cap);
    //      status[p].mod_cap_present = 2*p;
    //      status[p].mem_cap = 50*p;
        resetstate[p].mod_cap_present              =
status[p].mod_cap_present;
        resetstate[p].mem_cap =  status[p].mem_cap;
    }
  // INPUTTING THE COEFF. FOR INTER PROCESSOR COMM.
    printf("\nenter the adjacency coeff. for direct
link between proc : ");
    scanf("%d",&cf0);
  //  cf0 = 1;
    printf("\nenter the adjacency coeff. for one in-
direct link between proc : ");
    scanf("%d",&cf1);
  //  cf1 = 2;
    printf("\nenter the adjacency coeff. for two in-
direct links between proc : ");
    scanf("%d",&cf2);
  //  cf2 = 3;
    printf("\n\nENTER  THE  MEMORY  REQUIREMENTS  OF
MODULES\n");
    for(k=1;k<=no_of_tasks;k++)
    {
        for(j=1;j<=no_of_modules[k];j++)
        {
            printf("\tm%d%d : ",k,j);
            scanf("%d",&mem_req[k][j]);
    //          mem_req[k][j] = 10*(j+k-1);
        }
    }

    for(x=1;x<=no_of_proc;x++){
```

```
                  for(p=1;p<=no_of_proc;p++){
                      if(x!=p){
                              if(L[x][p]==1)  CC[x][p]=cf0;
                              else
if(L1[x][p]==1)CC[x][p]=cf1;
                              else
if(L2[x][p]==1)CC[x][p]=cf2;
                          }
                  }
          }
    }

    void init(char * str, int no)
    {
        while(no)
             {
             *(str+no) = '\0';
             no--;
        }
    }

    char * Random(void)
    {
        char *str;
        int i,j = 0;
        int gen = 0;
        int state = 0;
        str = (char *)malloc(chrom_size + 1);
        if(str == '\0')
        {
         //    cout << "Error";
             exit(0);
        }
        init(str,chrom_size+1);
        while(j < chrom_size)
        {
        for( i = 0;   i < random(100); i = i + random(10)
+ 1)
        {
             gen += random(i);
        }
        state = abs(gen % (no_of_proc+1));
        if(state == 0 )
            continue;
        str[j] = char(state + '0');
```

```
        j++;
      }
      return str;
  }

  void modify_mod_at_proc(char* str)
  {
      int i,j,k=0;
      for(j=1;j<=no_of_tasks;j++)
          for(i=1;i<=no_of_modules[j];i++)
          {
            mod_at_proc[i][j] = str[k] - '0';
            k++;
          }
  }

int check_status()
  {
      int i,j;
      for(i=1;i<=no_of_proc;i++){
            status[i].mod_cap_present      =      reset-
state[i].mod_cap_present;
            status[i].mem_cap = resetstate[i].mem_cap ;
      }
      for(i=1;i <= no_of_tasks;i++)
            for(j=1;j<=no_of_modules[i];j++)
            {
                  if((--
status[mod_at_proc[j][i]].mod_cap_present  ) < 0 )
                        return 0;
                  if((status[mod_at_proc[j][i]].mem_cap
-= mem_req[i][j]) < 0)
                        return 0;
            }
      return(1);
  }

int load(int proc)
  {
      int p,n,k,i,j,ex_cost,q,comm_cost;
      p=proc;
      ex_cost=0;
      comm_cost=0;
      n=no_of_proc;
```

```
    for(k=1;k<=no_of_tasks;k++)
      for (i=1;i<=no_of_modules[k];i++)
          M[i][k][p]=0;

    for(k=1;k<=no_of_tasks;k++)
    {
        for (i=1;i<=no_of_modules[k];i++)
        {
            if(mod_at_proc[i][k]==p) M[i][k][p]=1;
            ex_cost+=X[i][k][p] * M[i][k][p];
        }
    }
    for (k=1;k<=no_of_tasks;k++)
    {
        for(i=1;i<=no_of_modules[k];i++)
        {
                /* q is the proc on which j is exe-
cuting*/
            for(j=1,q=1;j<=no_of_modules[k]                &&
q<n;j++,q++)
            {
                if(i!=j && p!=q)
                {
                        comm_cost=        M[i][k][p]        *
M[j][k][q] * ( C[i][k][j] + CC[p][q]);
                }
            }
        }
    }
    return(ex_cost + comm_cost);
}

float threshold()
/* To find a suitable threshold value, so that only
chromosomes having fitness value above that threshold
are included in the population. */
{
  char *str;
    float max=0;
    int i=5,j;
    int totload=0;
    float fx;
    minimum=32768.00;
    while(i)
    {
```

```
        str=Random();
        modify_mod_at_proc(str);
        if ( check_status() == 0)
    continue;
        for(j=1;j<=no_of_proc;j++)
         totload+=load(j);
        fx = (float)(1/(totload+0.1)*100*MFACTOR);
        if(max < fx )
    max=fx;
      // if(minimum > fx)
      //  minimum=fx;
        free(str);
        i--;
      }
  // cout << "minimum value is :" << minimum;
     return max;
  }
int identical(char *str ,struct String * list)
  {
       while(list)
       {
     if ( strcmp(str,list->str) == 0 )
         return 1;
     list=list->next;
       }
       return 0;
  }

  void gen50(float thresh)
  {
      struct String * temp;
      int i= NO_OF_GEN,j;
      int totload=0;
      open_list=NULL;

      while(i)
      {
      temp=(struct            String*)malloc(sizeof(struct
String));
      temp->next=NULL;
      temp->str=Random();
      modify_mod_at_proc(temp->str);
      if(check_status()    ==0    ||     identical(temp-
>str,open_list)==1)
        {
```

```
        free(temp->str);
        free(temp);
        continue;
    }
    totload=0;
    for(j=1;j<=no_of_proc;j++)
      totload+=load(j);
    temp->fx=float(1/(totload+0.1)*100*MFACTOR);
    temp->freq=int(temp->fx) - thresh;

    if(temp->fx < thresh )
    {
        free(temp->str);
        free(temp);
        continue;
    }
    no_of_chrom+=temp->freq;
    temp->next=open_list;
    //cout << endl<< temp->str << "\t" << temp->fx <<
"frequency is" << temp->freq;
    open_list=temp;
    i--;
    }
  }
  void main()
  {
      struct time *time;
      unsigned long time1,time2;
      float thresh;
      input();
      gettime(time);
      time1 = time->ti_hour*60*60 + time->ti_min*60 +
time->ti_sec;
      thresh=threshold();
      gen50(thresh);
      crossover(thresh);
      gettime(time);
      time2 = time->ti_hour*60*60 + time->ti_min*60 +
time->ti_sec;
     printf("\nTime Required by the algorithm was :0.%2d
seconds\n" , time2 - time1);
      int m,m1,p1;
      m=0;
      for (p1=1;p1<=no_of_proc;p1++){
            m1=load(p1);
```

```
            printf("\nThe cost at the processing node
%d is %d",p1,m1);
            printf("\nThe status of proc %d is %d
%d",p1, status[p1].mod_cap_present,status[p1].mem_cap);
            m+=m1;
            }
        printf("\n\nTotal cost at all the processing
nodes is %d",m);

    }
    void crossover(float thresh)
    {
        struct String *parent1 ,*parent2,*temp;
        int p1;
        int p2;
        int state1;
        int state2;
        int crosspoint;
        int i=NO_OF_CROSSOVER,j;
        char temp1;
        int totload;
        int number,k;
        long int max_iter = 300000;
        long int select;
        float max;
        //cout << " crossover begins";

        while(i)
        {
            p1=random(no_of_chrom);
            p2=random(no_of_chrom);
            if(p1 == p2)
             continue;
            max_iter --;
            state1=state2=0;
            temp=open_list;
            parent1=(struct     String*)malloc(sizeof(struct
String));
            if ( parent1 == NULL)
            {
        cout << " unable to allocate memory";
        return;
            }
            parent1->str= (char *)malloc(chrom_size +1);
            if ( parent1->str == NULL)
```

```
      {
cout << " unable to allocate memory";
return;
      }

    parent1->next=NULL;
    parent2=(struct        String*)malloc(sizeof(struct
String));
      if ( parent2 == NULL)
      {
cout << " unable to allocate memory";
return;
      }

    parent2->str= (char *)malloc(chrom_size +1);
    if ( parent2->str == NULL)
      {
cout << " unable to allocate memory";
return;
      }

    parent2->next=NULL;

    while(temp)
    {
      if(p1 > temp->freq)
        p1 -= temp->freq;
      else
      {
         strcpy(parent1->str,temp->str);
         p1 += no_of_chrom;
         state1=1;
      }
      if(p2>temp->freq)
         p2-=temp->freq;
      else
      {
        strcpy(parent2->str,temp->str);
         p2+=no_of_chrom;
         state2=1;
      }
      temp=temp->next;
      if((state1==1) && (state2==1))
         break;
    } //end while(temp)
```

```
      crosspoint=random(chrom_size);
      for(j=0;j<crosspoint;j++)
      {
       temp1=parent1->str[j];
       parent1->str[j]=parent2->str[j];
       parent2->str[j]=temp1;
      }
      modify_mod_at_proc(parent1->str);
      state1=0;
      totload=0;
      if(check_status()==1    &&    !identical(parent1-
>str,open_list))
       {
        for(j=1;j<=no_of_proc;j++)
          totload+=load(j);
        parent1-
>fx=float(1/(totload+0.1)*100*MFACTOR);
        parent1->freq=int(parent1->fx)-thresh;
        if ( parent1 -> fx < thresh )
        {
            free(parent1->str);
            free(parent1);
        }
        else
        {
            state1=1;
            no_of_chrom+=parent1->freq;
        }
       }
       else
       {
      free(parent1->str);
      free(parent1);
       }
       if(state1==1)
       {
      parent1->next=open_list;
      open_list=parent1;
        // cout << endl <<" fitness is " << parent1-
>fx << " frequency is "<< parent1->freq;
          }
      modify_mod_at_proc(parent2->str);
      state2=0;
      totload=0;
```

```
         if(check_status()==1   &&       !identical(parent2-
>str,open_list) )
         {
          for(j=1;j<=no_of_proc;j++)
               totload+=load(j);
          parent2->fx=float(1/(totload+0.1)*100*MFACTOR);
          parent2->freq=int(parent2->fx) - thresh;
          if ( parent2 -> fx < thresh )
          {
               free(parent2->str);
               free(parent2);
          }
          else
          {
               state2=1;
               no_of_chrom+=parent2->freq;
          }
          }
          else
          {
          free(parent2->str);
          free(parent2);
          }
          if(state2==1)
          {
       parent2->next=open_list;
       open_list=parent2;
           //  cout << endl << " fitness is " << parent2-
>fx << " frequency is " << parent2->freq;
             }

          if(state1==1 || state2==1)
      //    {
       i--;
       //    if(state1==1)
         //  {
       //          parent1->next=open_list;
       //          open_list=parent1;
       //          cout << endl << "chromosome fr parent1
is " << parent1->str << " fitness is " << parent1->fx;
       //    }
       //    if(state2==1)
         //  {
         //      parent2->next=open_list;
          //      open_list=parent2;
```

```
       //     cout << endl << "chromosome  fr  parent2
is " << parent2->str << " fitness is " << parent2->fx;
       //  }
     //  }
      if(max_iter < 0)
      {
     cout << endl << "Unable to find in 300000 itera-
tion";
      break;
       }
    }//end while
    k=10;
    max=0;
    number=0;
    char chromosome[25];
    while(k)
    {
        select = random(no_of_chrom);
   //      cout << endl << "select = " << select;
         temp=open_list;
        while(temp)
        {
        if(select > number)
        {
            number+=temp->freq;
            temp=temp->next;
        }
        else
        {
      //      cout << endl << "temp -> fx = " << temp ->
fx;
            if(max < temp->fx)
            {
              max=temp->fx;
              strcpy(chromosome,temp -> str);
            }
            break;
        }
        }
        k--;
    }
    cout<<"Best fitness value is " << max;
    cout << endl << "Chromosom : " << chromosome;
    cout << endl << "no_of_chrom = " << no_of_chrom;
   }//end crossover;
```

Index